EDWARD ELGAR AND THE
NOSTALGIC IMAGINATION

D1392560

During his lifetime, and in the course of the twentieth century, Edward Elgar and his music became sites for a remarkable variety of nostalgic impulses. These are manifested in his personal life, in the content of his works, in his critical and biographical reception, and in numerous artistic ventures based on his character and music (plays, poems, films, paintings and novels). Today Elgar enjoys renewed popularity in Britain, and nostalgia of various forms continues to shape our responses to his music. From one viewpoint, Elgarian nostalgia might be dismissed as escapist, regressive and reactionary, and the revival in Elgar's fortunes regarded as the symptom of a pernicious 'heritage industry' in post-colonial, post-industrial Britain. While there is undeniably a grain of truth to that view, Matthew Riley reveals a more complex picture of nostalgia, and sheds new light on Elgar and his cultural significance in the twentieth and twenty-first centuries.

MATTHEW RILEY is Lecturer in Music at the University of Birmingham. In 2005 he led the Music Department's celebration of the centenary of Elgar's appointment as the University's first Professor of Music. He is the author of *Musical Listening in the German Enlightenment: Attention, Wonder and Astonishment* (2004).

EDWARD ELGAR AND THE NOSTALGIC IMAGINATION

MATTHEW RILEY

University of Birmingham

CAMBRIDGE
UNIVERSITY PRESS

CAMBRIDGE UNIVERSITY PRESS
Cambridge, New York, Melbourne, Madrid, Cape Town, Singapore,
São Paulo, Delhi, Dubai, Tokyo

Cambridge University Press
The Edinburgh Building, Cambridge CB2 8RU, UK

Published in the United States of America by Cambridge University Press, New York

www.cambridge.org
Information on this title: www.cambridge.org/9780521121835

First published 2007
This digitally printed version 2009

A catalogue record for this publication is available from the British Library

ISBN 978-0-521-86361-2 Hardback
ISBN 978-0-521-12183-5 Paperback

Contents

Illustrations

Music examples

Most examples are reductions of orchestral and/or choral music onto two or three staves.

Acknowledgements

Chapter 3 is based on my article 'Rustling Reeds and Lofty Pines: Elgar and the Music of Nature', *19th-Century Music* 26/2 (2002), 155–77. Copyright © 2002 by the Regents of the University of California. Brief sections of Chapters 3 and 5 have appeared as part of the following publications: Review of Edward Elgar, *Dream Children* and *The Wand of Youth* (Suites Nos. 1 and 2): *Elgar Complete Edition*, vol. 25, *Nineteenth-Century Music Review* 2/1 (2005), 214–20; and 'Heroic Melancholy: Elgar's Inflected Diatonicism', in *Elgar Studies*, ed. J. P. E. Harper-Scott and Julian Rushton (Cambridge: Cambridge University Press, forthcoming). I am grateful for permission to use revised versions of these texts. I would like to thank the individuals and the staff of the institutions listed there for their assistance. The poems 'The Elgar Violin Concerto' by Siegfried Sassoon and 'Edward Elgar 1857–1934' by C. Day Lewis are reproduced by permission of the copyright holders. I am grateful to the Barbara Levy Literary Agency for the former, Jill Balcon and the PFD agency for the latter.

The two referees for Cambridge University Press provided helpful comments on drafts of various chapters. When an earlier version of Chapter 4 was in preparation as an article, James Hepokoski made stimulating suggestions. He, J. P. E. Harper-Scott and Aidan Thomson allowed me to read unpublished drafts of their respective writings on Elgar. I am grateful to various colleagues and friends for more informal reaction to my research at conferences, seminars and the like. My main intellectual debts, however, are recorded in the bibliography and in the footnotes. Of course, the text presented here remains my responsibility.

My work on Elgar has been aired at invited research seminar presentations at the University of Surrey (17 February 2004), Anglia Polytechnic University (28 February 2005) and the University of Birmingham (22 November 2005). I am grateful for the invitations to speak on those occasions. I would like to thank the staff of the following institutions: the Barber Music Library at the University of Birmingham, the Elgar Birthplace

Museum, the British Film Institute, the Bridgeman Art Library, BBC Research Central, BBC Motion Gallery and the National Meteorological Archive. The editorial team at Cambridge University Press, including my Commissioning Editor, Victoria Cooper, and Assistant Editor Rebecca Jones, provided invaluable assistance. Finally I am extremely grateful to my Head of Department, John Whenham, for supporting my research in many ways.

CHAPTER I

Nostalgia

There is a curious moment near the end of the cadenza in the finale of Elgar's Violin Concerto (Ex. 1.1). After a lengthy passage of double stopping for the unaccompanied solo violin (the orchestra accompanies much of the rest of the cadenza), there is a pause and a rest (fig. 105: 9). The violin then softly plays the head-motif of a lyrical theme from the first movement which has already been extensively quoted earlier in the cadenza (fig. 105: 9). It rises to a trill on a high A, the dominant note of the local tonic, D major. The orchestra now re-enters softly with a theme familiar from the concerto's slow movement. The violin's trill rises stepwise to the tonic where it pauses again. The orchestra falls silent once more, as though its attempt to break a spell had failed. Now comes the curious moment: the violin simply repeats its statement of the lyrical theme (fig. 106: 4–5). It is played an octave lower than before, but the key, harmonies (pre-dominant chord involving a G♯–D tritone followed by dominant $^6_4$), and preparation (the solo violin alone, pausing on D) are the same, and even the dynamic markings and double-stopped patterns are similar. The sense of apparent redundancy is exacerbated by the intensity of feeling with which the phrase has to be played on each occasion – it seems odd that such a poignant moment should be so easily recaptured. Most notably of all, the passage conspicuously invokes and then contradicts Classical/Romantic syntax. The first statement of the lyrical theme, by ending with the dominant $^6_4$ chord in D major and the trill, strongly implies a perfect cadence in D major. Such a combination is a well-established sign of a cadenza's imminent end, and a threshold. The trill may be greatly elaborated (through transposition, harmony and figuration) but in eighteenth- and much nineteenth-century practice it remains a 'penultimate thing'; it must lead to the resolution of the dominant harmony to the tonic and the onset of the movement's coda. It makes no sense to follow the portentous preparation of the $^6_4$ chord with another such preparation in quick succession. There can be no going back.

Ex. 1.1 Violin Concerto, III, fig. 105: 7–fig. 108: 1

To be sure, the second allusion to the first-movement theme does not long delay the coda. There is no trill on the A, which swiftly falls through G to F♯, the dominant of the concerto's home key, B minor. The orchestra now breaks in more decisively with the weighty opening theme of the first movement, observing its original pitch and key, the first bar marked *molto stringendo* and rising quickly from *piano* to *fortissimo* (fig. 107: 1–2). As this impulsive gesture dies away, the violin takes up a continuation which is again familiar from the first movement, but which now carries urgent expression markings (*lento, espress. nobilmente*) and pause marks above the highest and lowest notes of the phrase. The cadenza ends with a perfect cadence in the concerto's tonic, B minor, and music from the opening of the finale returns, leading to a high-spirited coda. The orchestra's second interjection, then, accomplishes what the first singularly failed to bring about, wrenching the violin out of its reverie, asserting the correct tonic, and drawing the cadenza to a close. Conventional order is restored: the coda can unfold and the concerto can end.

Thus the violin's thematic reiteration at fig. 106: 4–5 stands out as an anomaly, disrupting but not destroying concerto convention. Unsympathetic critics would doubtless dismiss it as a compositional misjudgement, or, still worse, a failure of taste – a willingness to linger self-indulgently in a melancholy mood when a swift resolution to the cadenza would have been more effective. On the other hand, to a well-disposed listener, a good performance of this passage may seem strangely moving. The gentleness of the first orchestral entrance, the solo violin's reluctance to relinquish the lyrical theme, the sterner utterance from the orchestra and the violin's answering phrase and perfect cadence in the minor hint at a miniature drama of loss, mourning and acceptance. Might it be feasible to regard the violin's seemingly unwarranted repetition as a deliberate redundancy – a gesture that ignores received wisdom about economy and propriety of expression and contradicts conventional cadential syntax in order to achieve some specific aesthetic effect?

This possibility invites a more global view of the passage. The allusions to themes from earlier movements fit into a wider pattern established in the later stages of the concerto's finale. The cadenza has already dwelt at length on two first-movement themes, the lyrical theme discussed above having been played in a variety of guises. In this regard, its appearance at the very end is a kind of formal reprise within the cadenza after the long passage of unaccompanied double-stopping. The two orchestral interjections likewise employ material from earlier movements. The content of the second interjection – the opening theme of the first movement – has already been invoked at the beginning of the cadenza with special instrumental effects (fig. 101), conveying an air of mystery. Both statements are in the tonic, B minor, with the melody at the same pitch level. The theme thus serves to mark out the boundaries of the cadenza – the area within which inter-movement reminiscence by the soloist may occur. Meanwhile, the first of the orchestra's two interjections similarly employs a phrase which has already been used as a 'frame-breaking' agent in the finale. Belonging originally to the second movement, it nevertheless furnishes the material for a long crescendo which occurs between the rounding-off of the reca-pitulation (in the movement's sonata-like form) and the transition to the cadenza (fig. 94 to fig. 96: 7). So there is a precedent for using it to herald an imminent, but not immediate, switch between musical worlds. The identity and order of the thematic allusions that occur at the end of the cadenza are thus far from gratuitous; each component already possesses certain associations with cyclic reminiscence and frame-breaking, which help to identify the passage as a 'liminal' zone – an area where boundaries and borders are traversed.

To the listener with a little specialist Elgarian knowledge, the violin's insistence on the lyrical theme suggests an even broader context – that of a semi-secret programme. The mysterious epigraph to the concerto – 'Aquí está encerrada el alma de . . . . .' ('Herein is enshrined the soul of . . . . .') – together with Elgar's admission that the soul was feminine and his use of the epithet 'Windflower' for two first-movement themes carry overtones of chivalry. 'Windflower' was his pet name for his friend Alice Stuart-Wortley, and her two themes are precisely those recalled tenderly in the course of the cadenza.[1] Yet during the closing moments of the cadenza the scenario suggested by this discreet gendering works not so much in a personal as in a mythic mode. It is akin to a final bidding of farewell to a 'female' memory which must be left behind in a lower region of conscious-ness while the 'male' violin returns to the musical present of the finale proper. At the critical moment of transition (after the trill but before the perfect cadence), when the violin is, as it were, traversing the liminal space between the two worlds, 'he' turns back to gaze just once more on the object of his longing. In the concerto, though, unlike the Greek myth, it is not the gaze itself that condemns 'her'. The final adherence to the conven-tions of concerto genre is enough to seal her fate – to guarantee her future confinement within the underworld of memory. Whatever musical powers of enchantment the violin might possess are devoted only to the staging of this drama. The violin's final repetition of the 'Windflower' theme captures a moment of alienated consciousness, for the protagonist must return to the upper world of the finale in order to round off the concerto, but cannot renounce his emotional home without a wrenching pain.

The return home – *nostos*; pain – *algos*: nostalgia. This Greek neologism was coined as late as 1688 in a dissertation by the Swiss physician Johannes Hofer. In so doing he co-opted into the scientific discourse of the early Enlightenment the humble complaint previously known simply as 'home-sickness', 'Heimweh' or 'maladie du pays'. Having identified this new 'disease', Hofer set about providing it with an aetiology and with symptoms and remedies. He had observed alarming symptoms among Swiss mercenaries sent abroad to fight far from their homeland. All too often the soldiers fell into despondency, refused food and languished in melancholy. They held fast to a single idea: the desire to go home. Adopting the vocabulary of seventeenth-century physiology, Hofer explained that, during their displacement, the men suffered from the continuous vibration of the 'animal spirits' through the fibres of the middle brain where traces of the Fatherland still clung. Repatriation was the only cure. Nostalgia, according to Hofer, was not to be taken lightly, for, if untreated, it could easily lead to death. Soon the military authorities forbade their Swiss troops from singing or whistling tunes that reminded them of home in case a contagion of nostalgia spread through the ranks.

The ailments that prompted these confident diagnoses of 'nostalgia' would doubtless appear to modern medicine in other, varied, guises. Indeed, some cases may have been feigned in the hope of discharge. But for the most part, the reports that late seventeenth-century patients expressed an overwhelming desire to return home are credible. Hofer invented his disease at a time when transport links were improving and cities expanding. The large-scale displacement of persons, whether for purposes of employment or military service, was becoming common. Localities had not yet lost their pronounced individuality in character and customs as they largely have today. At this moment it made sense to long for 'home' as a literal, geographical place. Later, however, doctors discovered that the symptoms of nostalgia were not always cured by repatriation. By the nineteenth century the condition began to be understood as psychological, and the object of desire a time rather than a place. It is not the location of childhood that the adult desires, but youth itself. And that is forever out of reach: upon returning home one is still unhappy, because things are different – at least through adult eyes.[2]

Today the term 'nostalgia' has been absorbed into everyday speech and has shed its pathological connotations of depression and obsessive disorder. Nostalgia can mean a passing mood, and one which may be partly pleasurable: a feeling of wistful reminiscence or the bittersweet recollection of episodes of personal history. In this sense, the nostalgic person may be open to accusations of sentimentality or self-indulgence ('wallowing in nostalgia'), but is hardly suffering from an affliction. On the other hand, nostalgia sometimes signifies something more permanent than a mood, but still less than a disorder: something more like a lifestyle choice. A liking for retro fashions, themed 1970s or 1980s evenings, or 'period' domestic items purchased from shops such as *Past Times* might make others want to groan or scoff, but not to call for a doctor.

These examples may suggest a trivialisation of the concept, but the significance of nostalgic impulses in contemporary Western culture is undeniable. Indeed the loosening and expanding of the term's meaning is a sign of the persistence and diversity of retrospective longing. In late twentieth-century Britain, evidence of homesickness could be detected amongst all sectors of society: immigrants and indigenous peoples alike, the rich as well as the poor, dispossessed aristocrats along with redundant former mineworkers. There are relatively few people today who are wholly untouched by nostalgia, for whom the siren call of 'home' does not find its way to some corner of their consciousness.

From a historical perspective, the thread of nostalgia appears to be woven deep into our society and collective memory, for as a broad cultural phenomenon (as opposed to a medical diagnosis) it is coeval with post-Enlightenment modernity. Nostalgia in this sense emerges from the shadow of the ideal of progress.[3] In the second half of the eighteenth century it appeared in literature and philosophy as a protest against the rationalism of the Enlightenment, the expansion of state bureaucracy, the early stages of the division of labour and the society of the modern metropolis. It came of age in the turbulent early decades of the nineteenth century following the French Revolution and, in England, the Industrial Revolution. The most eloquent nostalgist of the eighteenth century was Jean-Jacques Rousseau, who called into question the very premises of the Enlightenment, insisting that advances in science, technology and the arts had corrupted rather than improved human behaviour. Rousseau lamented the passing of earlier societies in which (so he maintained) people's desires were simpler, their compassion more sincere and their relationships more transparent. In the wake of the Terror unleashed by the French Revolution, Friedrich Schiller voiced a similar critique of modernity in his writings on aesthetics, arguing that modern human beings were fatefully divided, not just within themselves, but also from one another and from nature. The modern poet could not portray nature simply and directly, but perceived it as something distant, alien, or seemingly irrecoverable – something to long for rather than to enjoy. Schiller pointed to the distant, alluring example of ancient Greece for a model of the integrated individual. These classic accounts of modernity and its ills set the coordinates for many of the arguments pursued by its future discontents.

Romantic literature soon became saturated with modes of longing and dissatisfaction, as poets and writers sought a resolution to the perceived modern split between subject and object, mind and nature. Often these impulses had a pronounced atavistic component, such as the idealisation of childhood and of simple people, or a longing for the life and art of distant times such as antiquity or the middle ages. Philosophy grappled with dichotomies such as the rigorous dualism of Kant, which separated subject and object, inclination and duty, the world as we can know it from the world as it is. The Romantic poet Novalis ventured that 'philosophy is really nostalgia – the urge to be at home everywhere'.[4] Nostalgia was now fast becoming respectable. In some quarters, the yearning for a homeland or for the distant past, far from being an illness in need of cure, was seen as fashionable or even progressive. The English middle classes sought out picturesque ruins or admired Strawberry Hill, Horace Walpole's mock-medieval gothic mansion. Under the influence of the ideas of Johann Gottfried Herder, early nineteenth-century nationalists aimed to preserve local languages and cultures and to memorialise the history of individual nations, however small. These were thought to be the foundations of human identity. Localism – the very sentiment that military commanders had tried to stamp out – could now be held up as a patriotic virtue.

The rapid developments in society that began at the turn of the nineteenth century provided yet more fertile ground where nostalgia could flourish. In this period, for the first time, radical changes in society could take place within the span of a single lifetime. In Britain, the Industrial Revolution, and the consequent consolidation of urban centres and depopulation of the countryside, meant that the rate and scope of social dislocation were unprecedented. Later, the Victorians came to accept the rapid and fundamental changes wrought by new science and technology as natural and inevitable. Unsurprisingly, then, the nineteenth century cultivated a new sense of time, which was unknown to feudal and even to early capitalist societies. Time was viewed in predominantly linear rather than cyclical terms, and could be recorded, monitored and standardised through the use of precise instruments. If the future was now a source of unprecedented excitement, then the past, by the same token, could be said to be out of reach in a stronger sense than ever before.[5]

Of course, versions of nostalgia have been experienced at other times and places, long before the post-Enlightenment age or even the devising of a medical name. From the psalmist at the waters of Babylon to Odysseus sailing the Aegean and the pastoral poetry of ancient Greece and Rome, human beings have told stories of displacement and homesickness and have lamented the passing of better worlds. A nostalgic impulse is embedded in the religious consciousness of the three great Abrahamic faiths, for their doctrines all draw on stories of disinheritance, exile and the search for rehabilitation. The lost garden of Paradise and its Classical equivalent, the Golden Age, were standard points of literary reference long before Hofer's day in the seventeenth century. Furthermore, nostalgia's basic concern with the recovery of simplicity is articulated by Neoplatonic metaphysics. According to this doctrine, the first principle is the One or the Good, while the evil and multiplicity that are so evident in the world are a belated 'emanation' from unity. We naturally long to return to that unity. Today, nostalgia often draws on these ancient sources for its modes of expression, imagery or literary 'plot', and they can provide it with rich historical resonance. Nevertheless, an awareness of their existence should not blind us to the particularity of the modern version of the feeling. In the last two centuries nostalgia has expanded beyond its literary origins (which confined its expression to an educated elite) and its medical origins (which tied it to a single nationality). As the historian of twentieth-century nostalgia Svetlana Boym puts it, 'a provincial ailment, *maladie du pays*, became a disease of the modern age, *mal du siècle*'.[6]

In Britain, one of the most destabilising periods of the entire modern era was the four decades between 1873 and 1914. These years have often been perceived retrospectively as a lost golden age, especially the reign of Edward VII from 1901 to 1910. From a twentieth-century perspective, and in the light of two world wars, it is easy to understand why people might envy that time its apparent security, unhurried ease and leisure, when the empire was at its zenith and human beings less cynical. And in some respects this picture is accurate, especially as regards the affluent classes. But beneath the idyll, a collection of heterogeneous factors challenged the established order and spread unease about the future. Britain's place as the world's leading political and economic power began to seem distinctly vulnerable, while mid-Victorian convictions about the stability of society, the laws of laissez-faire economics and the inevitability of steady progress were called into question. There was a series of severe economic depressions, resulting in mass unemployment; Britain's trade figures showed a worrying decline in exports; Germany and the United States negated Britain's early lead in manufacturing and then overtook her. The British army's difficulties in suppressing a small but determined force of Boer fighters in South Africa in the war of 1899–1902 boded ill for her military prowess in the new century. The existence of a new German navy threatened the foundation of Britain's power, her command of the seas. At home, careful studies of urban poverty overturned complacent assumptions and struck at the heart of Victorian economic theory. There was concern bordering on panic over the nation's health, living conditions in the large cities, and the possibility of 'racial degeneration' which threatened to sap Britain's vitality. In the arts, late nineteenth-century developments showed tendencies towards 'decadence', and the conviction of Oscar Wilde in 1895 for gross indecency seemed to confirm the undesirability of this trend. Meanwhile the political sands were shifting. During the 1880s the hitherto entrenched power of the aristocracy was undermined by a collapse in agricultural prices and land value and by the Third Reform Act – the beginning of a long process of decline for that class. Radical political movements such as socialism, trade unionism, Irish nationalism and women's suffrage posed serious challenges to the two-party system that had dominated Victorian politics.[7]

Almost predictably, then, this period witnessed a renewed upsurge of interest in the past – both personal and collective, real and imaginary. Societies devoted to the preservation of ancient buildings and the country-side were established; literature and art that celebrated rural life became immensely popular, from Thomas Hardy, Samuel Palmer and Richard Jeffries to the 'Georgian' poets; enduring classics of children's literature were composed by Robert Louis Stevenson, James Barrie and Kenneth Grahame, and were read by adults as much as by their offspring; searching autobiographies such as those of John Ruskin and Edmund Gosse delved into the personal experience of childhood for an explanation of adult identity; artists such as William Morris and Edward Burne-Jones turned to medieval myth and fantasy in deliberate revolt against the present. The 'invention of tradition' became a flourishing practice, on both official and unofficial levels, bestowing a dubious sense of antiquity on royal ceremonial and other public events.[8] So although this was undoubtedly an age of relative peace and of continuing progress in technology, it was also a time of sustained and sometimes gloomy reflection on the relationship between past, present and future, with confidence dwindling that the latter would be an improvement.

It was in this world that Edward Elgar, born in 1857 and brought up in provincial Worcester, spent most of his adult life, and practically all his creative life. During those years and later, in the course of the twentieth century, Elgar and his music became sites for an almost unrivalled variety of nostalgias. The most obvious of these belong to the composer himself and the themes of his works. First there is his well-documented attachment to certain people, places and times from his past: the Worcester of his youth, the surrounding countryside, the cottage where he was born and, by the 1920s, what may have seemed to him a prelapsarian world before the cataclysm of the Great War. In his music there are moments such as that in the Violin Concerto finale when a theme from one movement breaks through the 'frame' set up by a later movement, sounding like a recollection, a haunting memory, or a fixation induced by bereavement. There are consciously archaic gestures and episodes which draw a line between a specifically musical 'past' and 'present'. On a more invigorating note, at certain moments of magical transformation the music seems to pass across a threshold from a mundane sphere to a yearned-for world of enchantment somewhere 'beyond'. Such episodes are usually transient and dreamlike. Finally, in Elgar's dramatic and programmatic works there can be found characters who pine for a distant homeland, for lost youth or for an idyllic landscape.

A still more extravagant collection of nostalgic impulses is evident in writings on Elgar by later commentators and critics and in independent artistic ventures inspired by him – plays, poems, novels, films and paintings. On one level, some find in Elgar's ceremonial idiom an echo of Britain's vanished imperial greatness. Others dismiss this view as superficial, and perceive in the music the sights and sounds of the English countryside, captured with unparalleled immediacy. Some are moved by a lament for a phase of civilisation which, it is said, in his day was passing and in ours is lost for ever. For others, in turn, Elgar's numerous pieces for or about children capture the freshness of youthful vision, and the composer's own childhood has become the object of wide interest. Others project a fiery, radical nostalgia onto Elgar. In this view, beneath the veneer of British Establishment values his music hints at a deeper, unruly kind of Englishness, connected to his home landscape but with ancient, pagan associations, resistant to all imposed authority.[9] Inevitably some versions of Elgarian nostalgia are whimsical; others lay themselves open to commercialisation. The Worcestershire authorities have not been slow to exploit the phenomenon in recent years, devising, amongst other attractions, a signposted 'Elgar route' for drivers exploring the local countryside. There is a market for domestic kitsch, exemplified by the mug and tea-towel set depicting the Elgar birthplace cottage and bearing a wistful utterance of the composer. Other, less profitable, items cater to the true Elgarian 'trekkie', for instance the book that lovingly documents his countryside cycling habits.[10]

The intensity and the extent of the nostalgia surrounding Elgar propels him into the midst of a fierce battle that has been raging in Britain and America for the past few decades, in which the very essence and the future direction of modern society are at issue. Those on the offensive in these 'nostalgia wars' have returned to Hofer's thinking and reconceived the condition as a disease, albeit now a social one. They detect a virulent plague of nostalgia sweeping across the population and consider it highly dangerous. The American social critic Christopher Lasch, though not one of their number, characterises the attitude well: 'To cling to the past is bad enough, but the victim of nostalgia clings to an idealized past, one that exists only in his head. He is worse than reactionary; he is an incurable sentimentalist.'[11] The cultural historian David Lowenthal has recorded some of the invective hurled at nostalgia in the 1980s alone: 'ersatz, vulgar, demeaning, misguided, inauthentic, sacrilegious, retrograde, reactionary, criminal, fraudulent, sinister, morbid'.[12] Here are some further representative examples. 'Nostalgia is sadness without an object, a sadness which creates a longing that of necessity is inauthentic because it does not take part in lived experience.' 'Nostalgia is to memory as kitsch is to art.' 'We are entering a future in which people may again die of nostalgia.'[13] To these can be added the charges that nostalgia is escapist and regressive – an evasion of adult responsibilities in favour of a return to infantile desires. Furthermore, numerous commentators have complained of nostalgia's implication in reactionary politics, alleging that it glosses over the deficiencies of the past in order to shore up the present power base of old elites. (Ronald Reagan's eulogising of the small-town America of his childhood during his re-election campaign would be one example.)[14] Feminists have charged nostalgic male writers with the glorification of the past in order to authenticate traditional gender roles and stifle criticism of them.[15] Theorists of postmodernism and of post-industrial society regard nostalgia as a typical mode of subjectivity in a world in which reality has dissolved and been replaced by 'hyperreality'.[16] For those on the traditional Left, nostalgia is dangerously open to commercialisation, and provides a useful tool for the forces of reaction – another opiate for the masses.[17]

In Britain, critics of nostalgia, especially in the sphere of Cultural Studies, have turned their ire above all on the so-called 'heritage industry' which is accused of sanitising and 'Disneyfying' the past, turning Britain into a theme park of country houses, railway preservation societies and insular local museums. Robert Hewison's *The Heritage Industry: Britain in a Climate of Decline* (1987) examines 'a country obsessed with its past, and unable to face the future'. The front cover illustration twists the map of the country into the shape of a flightless bird, labelled 'Dodo Britannicus'. Hewison hates the very idea of nostalgia, which 'deliberately falsifies authentic memory' and is 'profoundly conservative'.[18] In a similar vein the historian of American culture Michael Kammen complains that 'nostalgia ... is essentially history without guilt. Heritage is something that suffuses us with pride rather than with shame.'[19] The British historian David Cannadine complains of regular British 'nostalgia booms' at times of economic depression (the late nineteenth century, the inter-war years, the 1970s). At worst, Cannadine maintains (his scorn pouring over as the exaggerated alliteration of his prose), the idea of 'national heritage' can produce 'a neo-nostalgic, pseudo-pastoral world of manufactured make-believe, a picture postcard version of Britain and its past, titillating the tourist with tinsel "traditions" '.[20] Disapproval of nostalgia among intellectuals reached its height in the late 1980s, a time when it seemed that Britain was set for perennial Conservative government. When New Labour finally came to power in 1997, it made a concerted (though ultimately abortive) attempt to change Britain's collective self-image by 're-branding' the nation as 'Cool Britannia'. As Tony Blair put it, 'I want Britain to be seen as a vibrant, modern place, for countries wrapped in nostalgia cannot build a strong future.'[21]

In this context, Elgar's latter-day reception in Britain must fall under suspicion, for the recent growth of heritage culture closely corresponds to a pronounced rise in his popularity and profile. Today, public interest in Elgar in Britain has reached levels that could hardly have been predicted two generations ago. The inter-war period witnessed caustic attacks on him by progressive musical commentators, and in the mid-twentieth century mainstream critical opinion was largely indifferent to his work. But interest in Elgar among the broader public never declined altogether, and recent decades have been marked by a popular revival in all things Elgarian. Live performances, radio broadcasts and new recordings proliferate, while membership of the Elgar Society has grown healthily. Its journal and newsletter flourish, and its handsome website is packed with information for the aspirant devotee. The Elgar Birthplace Museum, in its delectable rural setting in the hamlet of Broadheath in Worcestershire, has been impressively modernised. Enthusiasts publish books and pamphlets on

Elgar's friends, Elgar's holidays, Elgar's hobbies, and Elgar's love affairs. Anthony Payne's popular realisation of sketches for a Third Symphony only hastened this trend. Even musicology, after decades of neglect during which Elgar research was left to journalists and unaffiliated scholars, is belatedly making amends with a number of conferences and publications. Detractors of the heritage industry would know exactly what to make of these phenomena. To them, such burgeoning interest in an icon of the Edwardian age, whose art makes reference to values of chivalry, monarchy, empire, Christianity and pastoralism by means of a conservative musical idiom, would signify collective cultural retrenchment of the first order.

It is hardly surprising, then, that when hard-edged nostalgia critique meets Elgarian nostalgia, sparks fly. Jeremy Crump, after exposing the political dimensions to the persistent image of Elgar as a bard of the English countryside, resorts to acerbic sarcasm. 'Before one is transported from suburban living room to the Malvern Hills in the golden glow of a late imperial afternoon, it may be of interest for the listener to reflect how it is that a complex series of sound patterns has so specific and literary a significance.'[22] A collection of photographs by Paul Reas entitled *Flogging a Dead Horse* (1993) – a withering assault on the heritage industry – includes an image entitled 'Elgar Country'. It portrays not the timeless rural scenes found in coffee-table favourites such as *The Malvern Hills: Travels Through Elgar Country*,[23] but the contents of a shop window – an Edwardian tailor's dummy and an old black-and-white photograph of cricketers – with the reflection of a gigantic McDonald's 'M' from a restaurant across the street superimposed on them. The accompanying text, which claims the shop to be near Malvern, Elgar's onetime residence, is itself superimposed on the first page of 'Land of Hope and Glory'. The identification of national heritage with cheap commercialism and fast-food consumption is plain.[24] The nostalgia wars reach even to the heart of Elgar scholarship. In a scathing review of the writings of the leading Elgar biographer Jerrold Northrop Moore, David Cannadine alleges that 'the author emerges as a man deeply into nostalgia, disillusioned by the darkening experience of contemporary living, disenchanted by present-day cults of speed and success, preferring England to America and Worcestershire to London'. Moore, he says, projects his personality onto Elgar and pursues this psychological complex for a thousand pages, badly distorting our view of the composer.[25]

But, despite the gravity of these charges, some credibility may yet be salvaged for Elgar and the Elgar revival. The anti-nostalgia and anti-heritage polemics of recent decades have not gone unchallenged. Christopher Lasch, for instance, has drawn attention to the canny tactics behind many of the attacks, which deploy *ad hominem* arguments that are difficult to answer. 'As an instrument of ideological warfare, [nostalgia's] usefulness lies . . . in the implication that [it] derives not merely from erroneous opinions but from emotional disability, a temperamental aversion to the rough and tumble, the complexity and turmoil, of modern life.'[26] Lasch calls for an explanation not of the supposedly nostalgic condition of society but of the preoccupation with it among intellectuals and the mass media. For him, this obsession is the work of a complacent intellectual elite that has lost faith in the very ideal of progress it supposedly advocates. The last resort is to portray this progress as inevitable (as opposed to desirable) and to paint those who question it as sick rather than just wrong. Trenchant nostalgia critique, Lasch concludes, mirrors nostalgia itself by burying the real past and trying to escape from it.[27] Lasch's strategy of turning the tables has been used to good effect by others who try to complicate the problem of nostalgia. Stuart Tannock points out that the feminist writer Gayle Greene, in advancing a stark opposition between contemporary nostalgia and a more bracing mode of 'feminist memory', unwittingly reveals a nostalgia of her own for the early days of radical feminism in the 1970s.[28]

This is not to say that we should endorse nostalgia indiscriminately, merely that each manifestation deserves a judicious appraisal. The first step in such a move must be to loosen the alleged ties between nostalgia and reactionary politics. Even Frederic Jameson, not normally an advocate of nostalgia, has recognised this point in connection with the philosopher Walter Benjamin. '[I]f nostalgia as a political motivation is most frequently associated with Fascism, there is no reason why a nostalgia conscious of itself, a lucid and remorseless dissatisfaction with the present on the grounds of some remembered plenitude, cannot furnish as adequate a revolutionary stimulus as any other.'[29] Patrick Wright, whose book *On Living in an Old Country* (1985) addresses the persistence of the past in 'everyday life' in Britain, likewise observes that 'there is also a nostalgia of the left . . . one which cherishes the romantic memory of a time when the working class could more easily produce its own meaningful world-view: the unproblematic community of the "general interest" '.[30] Indeed, a strong nostalgic impulse can be detected in a tradition of English radicalism extending back at least to the Civil War period and continuing through William Cobbett, William Morris and John Ruskin, which idealised the ancient English peasantry and lamented the effects of the Norman Conquest, the gradual enclosure of the land and the division of labour. Meanwhile the culture of heritage has received a robust defence from the

socialist historian Raphael Samuel, who contends that it is often a genuinely popular movement, supported by volunteers, conservationists and
the public, and decried only by snobbish intellectuals. He points out
that one of the early pillars of the preservationist movement, the Society
for the Protection of Ancient Buildings, was founded by William Morris.
The concept of 'green belt' land was introduced by the Labour-controlled
London County Council in the 1930s, while the National Trust was conspicuously sympathetic to the 1945 Labour government. British Communists
invoked the concept of national heritage as early as the 1930s. And, con-
versely, the Thatcher governments of the 1980s resisted conservationist
legislation in defence of private property rights.[31] There is, then, no easy
map from nostalgia to the political Right. Tannock adroitly disentangles the
issues: 'nostalgia approaches the past as a stable source of value and meaning;
but this desire for a stable source cannot be conflated with the desire for a
stable, traditional, and hierarchical society.'[32]

Nostalgic discourse is better understood first and foremost as a rhetorical
practice, for it draws on a collection of techniques for persuasion which
do not in themselves determine what kind of argument is advanced.
According to Tannock, 'In the rhetoric of nostalgia, one invariably finds
the three key ideas: first, that of a prelapsarian world (the Golden Age,
the childhood Home, the Country); second, that of a "lapse" (a cut, a
Catastrophe, a separation or sundering, the Fall); and third, that of the
present, postlapsarian world (a world felt in some way to be lacking,
deficient, or oppressive).'[33] The stories generated by these rhetorical techniques can be extremely seductive – but that is no reason to condemn them
outright. The nature of the prelapsarian world that the nostalgic subject
constructs and the subject's present relationship to it must be carefully
examined case by case. Is the nostalgia, as Tannock puts it, primarily a relief
from, or a resource for, confronting the subject's anxieties? Might the
longed-for past be regained through future endeavour? Does the nostalgic
impulse seem like an irresponsible disengagement from present struggles,
or can it be regarded as a productive critique of the present which might
stimulate change?

Approaching the issue from a different perspective, the cultural historian
Svetlana Boym presents a further distinction for the evaluation of nostalgias. What she calls 'restorative nostalgia' stresses the return home (*nostos*)
and seeks or promises to restore the old world in all its perfection and
purity. This kind of nostalgia does not recognise the distance between
desire and reality or acknowledge the active, shaping role of memory,
but claims to deal with objective truth. 'Reflective nostalgia', by contrast,

lingers in the pain (*algos*), highlighting the distance between the subject and the desired object, the dynamics of loss and longing, and the existential state of the homesick individual. Boym argues that the latter draws us into compassion for others through our shared condition of longing, regardless of its object, whereas the former divides us by reminding us of our different homes and those of the groups to which we belong. Restorative nostalgia is at the heart of many nationalist movements. 'The danger of nostalgia is that it tends to confuse the actual home and the imaginary one. In extreme cases it can create a phantom homeland, for the sake of which one is ready to die or kill. Unreflective nostalgia breeds monsters.'[34]

Nostalgia, then, is not just a tool wielded by a disgruntled social elite to hoodwink the masses, dampen class feeling, or encourage nationalism – though of course it may be that at times. Nostalgia in general is a multi-faceted phenomenon which refashions ancient sources in order to deal with physical and spiritual dislocation. Its evocative concepts and conventions can be put to work by individuals in numerous ways, according to personal agenda and cultural setting.[35] At the start of the twenty-first century these points have been recognised in writings on nostalgia in the fields of nineteenth-century literary criticism and studies of immigrant identities and diasporas. These writings are at ease with their topic and seldom engage in polemics. In 2004 a Cultural Studies journal ran an issue devoted to nostalgia that explicitly disavowed the one-sided political interpretations of the past.[36]

In this light, Elgarian nostalgia and the Elgar revival start to look more interesting and potentially complex phenomena. To be sure, there are some aspects that live up (or rather down) to the critics' caricature. Affluent patrons of the Last Night of the Proms who rent boxes to listen to 'Land of Hope and Glory' (and attend no other concerts in the season) delight in a nostalgia that is hardly 'reflective' in Boym's sense. The rural imagery surrounding Elgar is sometimes pushed to picturesque extremes, especially when used for promotional purposes, while the dubious practice of attributing to Elgar's music an essential 'Englishness' can easily go hand in hand with undesirable and unsupportable claims about a fixed and universal 'national character'. But on the whole these instances are easily identified and make soft targets for critical attack. To explain away Elgar's popularity as an ultra-conservative cultural backlash or a limp retreat from the contemporary world is too pat. A robust but balanced assessment of the nostalgias attached to his work is needed – an endeavour that promises to be more challenging and more rewarding.[37]

This book examines Elgar's music, its intellectual background and its varied reception history, seeking the reasons for its continuing appeal to today's listeners. Elgarian nostalgia, it is argued, touches on central themes in the British cultural response to post-Enlightenment modernity over the last two centuries. His art draws on ideas and tropes that were first advanced by the literary Romantics and were then taken up by the Victorians in their efforts to come to terms with the rapid changes affecting their world. Despite the obvious manifold differences in the concerns of the early nineteenth century, of Elgar's era and of our own, these Romantic ideas nevertheless established modes of expression and rhetoric that have persisted in British culture. Thus Michael Kennedy's observation that 'the nostalgia Elgar expresses is not our nostalgia' contains a half-truth – but only a half.[38] The nostalgias of individuals or generations may differ widely in their objects, yet maintain connections in their themes and rhetoric. And the differences between the objects decrease in significance the more reflective and the less restorative the nostalgias.

The existence of such connecting threads does not, of course, determine whether any of these nostalgias merit our approbation. Indeed the phrase 'nostalgic imagination' in the title of the book is deliberately double-edged. On the one hand, it indicates a response to the post-Enlightenment world (applicable equally to Elgar and to contributors to his reception) that may be active, original and thought-provoking. 'Imagination' in this sense would have been understood by the Romantics. But 'imagination' can also refer to a mental faculty producing illusory 'figments'. These may contribute to the perpetuation of tired myths or to the prettifying of unsightly ideology. Much of the book's task is to situate Elgarian nostalgia of various types in relation to these coordinates. On the whole, manifestations of the first kind of 'imagination' receive more attention; they cut against the grain of our expectations about nostalgia, and therefore, in the view taken here, are the more interesting.

The book's method is to isolate specific themes in Elgarian nostalgia, devote a chapter to each, and examine them from the perspectives of historical and cultural background, Elgar's own statements (especially when these evoke myths or literary conventions that resonate beyond the personal sphere), his compositional techniques, and his subsequent critical, literary and artistic reception. The precise approach varies according to the current state of discussion on the different topics. The book largely avoids the terrain of biography, or, when necessary, covers it briskly. Elgar's life and the development of his outlook have been well documented, whereas the social context for his attitudes and feelings and the manner of their expression have until recently received much less attention. Still, the book shares common ground with much of the biographical literature in so far as it adopts something of the tone of an apologia (as will be evident already). This defensive strategy is apparent in the trajectory of most of the chapters, which set up a foil (often a too-simple view of Elgar's nostalgia) against which to draw a more complex picture. There will however be no attempt to rebut every charge of political incorrectness or attribution of suspect ideology made by unsympathetic commentators down the decades – that would be both unnecessary and futile.

Chapter 2, 'Memory', examines thematic reminiscence in Elgar's mature instrumental works. Elgar's characteristic manner of preparing and leaving his reminiscences suggests a split between inner and outer spheres of consciousness, a split that is usually not healed in the course of a work, and often leaves a disturbing impression. Many examples invite interpretation by means of two metaphors for modern memory: haunting and epiphany. Chapter 3, 'Nobility', addresses one of the most controversial aspects of Elgar's work, and tries to tease out some complexities in his attitude and compositional practice. At its best, as many listeners have recognised, his longing for nobility is a reflective as much as a restorative nostalgia.

Chapter 4, 'Nature', is motivated by the persistent associations of Elgar's music with landscape and the countryside. Such notions are easy to mock either as fanciful or as transparent political constructions. The chapter reconceives the concept of nature in Elgar, turning attention away from biography and geography, and exploring literary contexts such as the pastoral tradition and Romanticism. This approach yields new perspectives on the music, especially the many passages that imitate the sound of wind. Chapter 5, 'Childhood', addresses a related and equally persistent topic. Some of the stories told about Elgar's childhood by himself and by others may well be fictitious, but they too show strong affinities with themes of literary Romanticism. Elgar's finest music of childhood avoids the dangers of irresponsible escapism by focusing on the adult's longing for innocence rather than its recovery, once again fashioning a reflective nostalgia.

Chapter 6, 'Identity', addresses the modes of rhetoric (both compositional and critical) that arise from the problem that one writer called 'the two Elgars'. The concepts that help to frame questions about the composer's personal identity also lend themselves to the discussion of national identity ('Englishness'). To this end the chapter draws attention to the 'imperialist nostalgia' in Elgar's cantatas of the 1890s and examines sympathetic responses to Elgar from two literary figures from the Left of the political spectrum, J. B. Priestley and David Rudkin. Chapter 7, 'Waters', acts as an epilogue, investigating three original contributions to Elgar's reception: C. Day Lewis's poem 'Edward Elgar' (1962), Norman Perryman's watercolour triptych *Elgar's Dream* (1996), and James Hamilton-Paterson's novel *Gerontius* (1989). Each draws together themes discussed earlier in the book under the flexible imagery of moving waters.

CHAPTER 2

Memory

Since nostalgia in its present-day sense refers primarily to the longing for a lost time rather than a lost homeland, it is appropriate to begin the study of Elgar's music and its impact in twentieth-century Britain with the topic of memory. References to memories abound in Elgar's letters and writings, especially from the second half of his career, while the texts he chose to set and the programmatic bases for several of his works provide plentiful evidence for his interest in recollections of the past. In the music, techniques for suggesting memory are common, and they draw attention to themselves as moments of special significance. Michael Allis aptly describes the evocation of the past in Elgar as a 'semantically charged area'.[1] Many passages that suggest acts of memory seem to demand interpretation in terms of a personal story or relationship, and would do so even had Elgar not made a habit of dropping hints as to the personal associations of certain moments in his music.

The musical 'past' in Elgar often seems imbued with values more positive than those of the 'present'. His substantial artistic investment in the processes and effects of memory is therefore fraught with risk. Since the sphere of memory is often figured as an idyll – involving a mixture of pleasure at the recollection of something precious and sorrow at its passing – any degree of compositional misjudgement is likely to bring into play some of the unattractive aspects of nostalgia that were outlined in Chapter 1. Elgar usually avoids these pitfalls quite deftly. Although his idyllic memories are treated fondly, in many cases they are exposed as either unreal or unattainable, and the final impression they leave is not comforting but disturbing or uncanny.

This chapter does not examine the content of Elgar's personal memories; nor does it probe the associations that certain passages carried for him or that prompted their composition in the first place, except when these help to illustrate a more general 'semantic charge'. Such aspects have been well covered in the biographical literature. Moreover, since it is the remit of later chapters to deal with phenomena of collective, cultural 'memory' (regarding nature, childhood, pseudo-medieval chivalry, and so on), those topics will likewise be absent. Instead the chapter is concerned with the forms and processes of personal memory in music: the way acts of memory are portrayed, the mechanism of recollection that supports those acts, and the mode of subjectivity thereby implied. Since there currently exists no systematic account of these processes in Elgar's music, the first half of the chapter is elementary in approach. The second half makes some bolder interpretative moves.

Of course, the evocation of memory through music was far from new with Elgar; he stands in a tradition with its origins in the early nineteenth century. The consistent use of thematic reminiscence in multi-movement instrumental works began with Beethoven,[2] and can be found in nineteenth-century instrumental compositions, both programmatic and 'absolute', by Schubert, Schumann, Mendelssohn, Berlioz, Liszt, Brahms, Dvořák, Franck, Smetana, Tchaikovsky and others. But thematic reminiscence was just one of many means available to nineteenth-century composers for representing memory. Recent studies of music from the 1820s have revealed a rich diversity of techniques from that decade alone. Charles Rosen has uncovered connections between memory and landscape in Beethoven and Schubert, and shown how memory can be suggested by various methods. In lieder, for instance, the singer may be restricted to a monotone or the piano made to play alone while the singer seems to meditate silently.[3] Schubert's instrumental music has become a particular focus for discussions of memory; contemporary scholars detect it everywhere in his compositions. As Carl Dahlhaus put it: 'In Schubert, unlike in Beethoven, the most lasting impression is made by remembrance, which turns from later events back to earlier ones, and not by goal-consciousness, which presses on from earlier to later.'[4]

For practical reasons this chapter restricts its coverage largely to cases of thematic reminiscence in Elgar's symphonic and multi-movement instrumental works.[5] 'Thematic reminiscence' is understood here to refer to instances of thematic return that are not obviously functional within a form or genre in a manner established by tradition (thematic return in ternary forms or sonata recapitulations, the use of leitmotivs in dramatic works). In nineteenth-century multi-movement works, non-functional returns may either be seamlessly integrated into the course of a movement or, alternatively, the incongruity and non-functionality of the return may be highlighted. In Elgar, the second case is more common, and certainly more characteristic. Often a theme from one movement, when reappearing in a later movement, will conspicuously break the 'frame' established by that movement, resulting in a moment of rupture or intrusion from 'without'. In most cases the worlds of past and present are not reconciled in any sort of synthesis, but are left in uneasy opposition.

Musical memory in Elgar reflects a number of trends and ideas that can loosely be described as 'modern'. The second half of the chapter explores modern forms of memory, sketching several areas of context within which to view Elgar's reminiscence techniques. They include the notions of ghosts and haunting that have formed key metaphors for memory since the late eighteenth century, and the idea of 'epiphany' through memory – a recurrent theme in European literature from Wordsworth to Proust and beyond. All these ideas recur in the later reception of Elgar. The final section of the chapter takes a single and somewhat anomalous instance of thematic reminiscence in Elgar and compares it to a particular mode of Romantic poetry that strikes another characteristically modern note: the Wordsworthian, solipsistic sublime.

THEMATIC REMINISCENCE IN ELGAR

The few instances in Elgar of a thematic reminiscence being relatively seamlessly integrated into a later movement come mainly from the first half of his career, and can be dealt with swiftly. The third movement finale of the *Serenade* for strings, Op. 20 (1893) begins in the 'wrong' key, G major (the first movement is in E minor and the finale ends in E major). The piece falls into two discrete sections, in G major 12/8 and E minor/major 6/8 respectively. The second section is entirely based on music from the first movement; several complete phrases from the first and the second thematic groups are used. However, the mood of the two sections is similar: both are graceful, subdued and largely diatonic, in *Allegretto* tempo and compound metre. The transition between the two is effected subtly, without much drama (Ex. 2.1). The dynamics drop to *ppp* and the tempo is slowed through a written-out *ritenuto*. After a long, sustained D in violas punctuated only by two soft chords, the first-movement material creeps in (bar 37). The fourth-movement finale of the Organ Sonata, Op. 28 (1895) twice recalls the main theme of that work's third movement, once at the opening of the development section and once in the coda, the latter marking the start of the final peroration (bars 137 and 305). These reminiscences are not prepared or presented in any distinctive way. They simply play their part in the argument of the finale and make a gesture towards overall unity in the sonata. Further examples of well-integrated thematic reminiscence are

Ex. 2.1 *Serenade* for strings, Op. 20, III, fig. O: 10–fig. P: 9

found in the 'Enigma' Variations (1899). Variation I includes an almost exact quotation of the melody of the theme, while Variation XIV (the finale) quotes Variations I and IX. All of these references may have programmatic significance; however, on a phenomenal level they do not suggest acts of memory. As will become clear later, Variation XIII is a more interesting case of musical memory despite the fact that it does not recall a theme presented earlier in the work.

The more characteristic type of thematic reminiscence – that which conspicuously breaks the frame established by the later movement – works quite differently. This type tends to be prepared through some technique that suggests a search for a half-remembered idea or the gradual disintegration of normal consciousness. Elgar sets up what Allis calls a 'narrative "haze",[6] usually through an unusual texture or timbre. Often these passages are harmonically static, and the functional status of pitches (the roles of chords in a key or notes in a scale) is thereby undermined. For instance, they may begin or end simply through the fading in or out of a single sound. Against this haze, the recollected material seems to speak out like a voice – usually softly and mysteriously. In addition to texture, other conventional means for marking out musical 'measure' or 'division' tend to disintegrate: metre, pulse or harmonic rhythm may lose their definition or break down altogether. As a result, time seems to stand still. The musical phrases or paragraphs that are recalled are seldom quoted complete; instead they tend to appear in fragmentary form. All these factors combine to imply the existence of two separate levels of consciousness, one external or public, one internal or private. This impression is reinforced by the fact that, on the level of form, reminiscences tend to occur at conventional sectional boundaries – during episodes placed between, say, the end of an exposition and the start of a development, or between the end of a recapitulation and the start of a coda. (In Elgar's later music, the latter technique becomes almost ubiquitous in finales: the 'penultimate' stage in the form is the place for reminiscence.) The latent world of memory pushes through the gaps, as it were, in the foreground layer of present consciousness. Finally, in most cases of this type of thematic reminiscence, the 'frame' of the movement is unambiguously reasserted by the end; the memories are confined within an interlude. In contrast to the *Serenade* or the Organ Sonata, any sense of continuity or synthesis between past and present is minimised.

The first case of thematic reminiscence in this stronger sense (considered chronologically) is found in the *Introduction and Allegro* for strings (1905). For present purposes the two parts of the piece will be regarded as separate movements, although some thematic material used in the Allegro is tested out in the Introduction first. There is one case of thematic return in the Allegro that carries a special impact: the reappearance of the theme that has become known as the 'Welsh tune' between the end of the exposition and the start of the fugue that serves as a development section (Ex. 2.2). When it appears in the Introduction, the Welsh tune is initially played by a solo viola – a soft, lyrical passage that stands apart from the grand rhetoric of the work's opening. In a programme note for the premiere, Elgar associated the tune with his own memories of hearing distant singing when walking in Cardiganshire and in the Wye valley, thus invoking a Romantic trope concerning distant, semi-audible music and its relationship with landscape and the infinite that dates back (in music) at least to Schumann and (in literature) to the Romantic poets.[7] In the Introduction, the choice of solo instrument helps to underline this sense of distance, making a virtue of the viola's relative lack of tonal projection. When the tune reappears in the Allegro, the sense of distance is underlined by means of a 'haze' achieved through a variety of string techniques: the four solo instruments play the

Ex. 2.2 *Introduction and Allegro* for strings, fig. 15: 1–12

tune in unison, *pp*, two of them *sul ponticello* and *tremolando*, and three of them with mutes. In the fifth and sixth bars of the tune, the orchestral violins add to the unusual effect, splitting into a five-part texture, *sul ponticello* and *tremolando*, and swelling sharply from *p* to *f* and back down to *ppp*. Moreover, the Welsh tune seems to emerge from the orchestral texture – just like the tune Elgar claimed to have heard emerging from a landscape – its opening motif A–F♯ echoing the persistent A–B–F♯ in the accompaniment. The placement of the passage likewise suggests the intrusion of something distant into present concerns (in the sense of both time and space). It appears just as energy dissipates after a vigorous climax at the end of the exposition – the formal juncture being clearly marked by the use of the Introduction's opening theme – and is accompanied by a gradual reduction in tempo, until after seven bars the tune dies away altogether, unfinished. The fugue then begins in a quite unrelated mood, style and tempo, with hardly any sense of harmonic continuity.[8] After this reference, the Welsh tune is heard just once more in the piece: in the final pages it returns as a glorious peroration in the tonic major. On that occasion, far from being fragmentary, it is played in full and with generous repetition of several phrases. This return is more overtly functional, and sounds less like a memory.[9]

Elgar tried some of these ideas again three years later in the First Symphony (1908). As in the *Introduction and Allegro*, the first movement is prefaced by an introduction, material from which recurs in the coda and, in fragmentary form, elsewhere in the movement. There are obvious differences, though: the introduction consists of a stately motto theme that is far too polished to sound improvisatory, while the music of the coda dies away after the climactic return, and the close of the movement leaves a number of issues (tonal and thematic) unresolved. However the recollection of the motto during the main Allegro section – in particular at the juncture between the exposition and development sections – makes a striking parallel with the *Introduction and Allegro*. Again the reminiscence emerges at a moment of stark contrasts. The exposition is predominantly stormy and is based on unstable chromatic harmony; it ends with a stabbing climax on brass. The recollection of the serene, diatonic motto represents an oasis of calm. It is given to muted horns *pp* doubled by violas playing *tremolando*, again suggesting a voice or song from afar. As in the *Introduction and Allegro* the tune is not stated in full; this time it fades away after eleven bars. A different mode of temporality is fleetingly evident. Perhaps, on some separate plane, the motto had been unfolding its long phrases and stately tread for ever, in endless repetitions, and had merely been 'forgotten' during the Allegro. When the storm abates it can again be heard faintly through the 'gap' between sections of the sonata form. That impression is supported by a second reappearance of material from the motto – this time in an even more fragmentary state – at the end of the development, just before the recapitulation: another sectional boundary and a lull. Furthermore, in the slow introduction to the finale – a traditional place for cyclic reminiscence and the breakdown of conventional formal rules ever since Beethoven's later works – the motto, along with other material from the first movement, reappears in mysterious guise (*ppp* with *tremolando* effects and the melody played by last desks of the violins only).

In the symphonic works following the First Symphony, the 'penultimate position' at the end of the finale becomes the favoured gap in consciousness through which memories float. The Violin Concerto (1910) is an obvious example. The cadenza of the finale, which is situated between the end of the recapitulation and the coda, has already been discussed in Chapter 1. A cadenza is a suitable position for the portrayal of a disordered state of consciousness by virtue of its traditional associations with free improvisation (or composed-out imitations of free improvisation) on themes from earlier in a movement. Here, though, Elgar deploys old conventions in the service of a distinctive form of memory. The approach to the cadenza makes use of thematic 'liquidation' combined with a gradual diminuendo and thinning of the texture. Material from the finale is gradually reduced to a rising semitone, which is tentatively repeated several times, before unfolding into the first theme of the first movement (Ex. 2.3). The process could be compared to the recollection of a memory through the association of ideas: part of one idea sparks off a dim recollection, and the subject searches for the full memory by fixing on that part of the idea and repeating it, trying to bring to mind its associations. The themes recalled in the cadenza are presented largely in fragmentary form, and alternate unpredictably with fast, virtuoso passagework, double-stopping passages and pauses. The cadenza deploys a variety of 'haze' techniques. At the opening, half the violins, violas and cellos play *pp*, *sul ponticello* and *tremolando*, while the other half of each section bow normally but use mutes. After the soloist's entry with the first 'Windflower' theme, the strings are instructed to play their chord 'pizz. *trem.*' at *ppp*, while the soloist runs through swift arpeggio figuration (see Ex. 4.5). In a note to the score, Elgar explained that 'the pizz. tremolando should be "thrummed" with the soft part of three or four fingers across the strings'. The thrumming sustains only a single chord through a long passage which lacks any regular pulse (and is

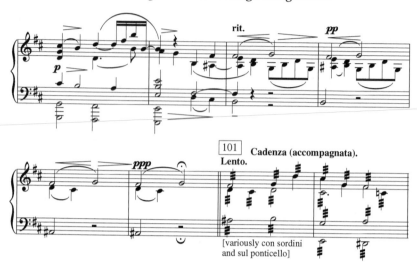

Ex. 2.3 Violin Concerto, III, fig. 100: 5–fig. 101: 2

notated without bar lines). Parameters such as metre, texture, phrase periodicity and harmonic rhythm thus lose much of their usual differentiation. As noted in Chapter 1, when the frame of the finale is finally reasserted for the coda, the world of memory is confined within a discrete interlude, and is unceremoniously swept away as the concerto ends with conventional, 'public' rhetoric, seemingly in a mood of triumph.

This finale could be said in some respects to fall back on a traditional practice: it is concerned with the demarcation of boundaries and with finding the 'correct' way to end. In this regard it is typical of Elgar's mature symphonic compositions, which display a commitment to formal closure unusual for their time, both in terms of tonality (the work must end in the key in which it began) and reassertion of the outer frame of a movement or work. But it would be a mistake to interpret that commitment as nothing more than conservatism. Closure is not the same as resolution, and Elgar often strongly asserts closure where there is palpably no resolution – a practice that leaves a most disturbing impression. In the Violin Concerto, Elgar refuses any synthesis between past and present. In Freudian terms the replacement of the cadenza by the coda represents an enforced forgetfulness akin to the process of repression.[10]

In Elgar's next symphonic work, the Second Symphony, thematic reminiscence occurs at a penultimate position in two movements. Like the First Symphony, this work contains a motto theme presented at the outset of the first movement, the significance of which is connected with the work's epigram from Shelley ('Rarely, rarely comest thou, / Spirit of Delight'). It therefore carries an immediate 'semantic charge'. This much – and the fact that the motto does indeed recur (but rarely) in the symphony – is a commonplace of the Elgar literature. However, the specific techniques of recollection in later movements – the Larghetto and the finale – repay close examination. In the Larghetto, which is cast roughly in 'slow-movement sonata form', the motto appears between the end of the recapitulation and the short codetta. As with the examples from the *Introduction and Allegro* and the First Symphony, the reminiscence emerges softly after a reduction in tempo and a process of dying away from a climax. (The practice of following a grand climax with fleeting moments of delicacy is common in Elgar's symphonic works, and in the literature is known as 'withdrawal'. It is discussed further in Chapter 6.) On this occasion the climax is especially luxuriant and the process of dying away extended. Eventually only strings remain, playing softly in their low registers in a purely diatonic Eb major. The reminiscence coincides with a sudden shift to C major, the submediant major of Eb (Ex. 2.4), and the introduction of the solo clarinet to play the motto underlines the sense of sudden freshness. As usual, unconventional string writing is in evidence: divided violins are marked *pppp*, cellos play *tremolando* and *sul ponticello*, and a solo double bass underpins the texture. This is the slowest and quietest moment in the whole process of withdrawal, but gives the impression of a ray of sunlight falling on a bleak funeral procession. Only a glimpse is permitted, however, before the melody peters out unfinished and the texture unravels, leaving a single, sustained D. The codetta reasserts the frame of the movement, invoking the original C minor funeral march and then the very opening bars of the piece, making a succinct close.

The recollection of the motto at the end of the finale of the Second Symphony is often noted in the Elgar literature, and this and later chapters will return to it. For the present, the manner in which the quotation of the motto is prepared and framed is the main concern. Again the reminiscence arrives during a process of withdrawal from a climax, this one still more grandiose than that in the Larghetto. That withdrawal is initially effected by means of descending sequences, before the finale's opening theme returns briefly to mark a formal boundary – the end of the recapitulation proper. The motto now enters in a mood of grand serenity and is repeated several times. However, when the softest, slowest moment finally arrives, it is not the motto that is quoted but the descending sequences, now *pp* on muted strings. The finale's opening theme briefly emerges once more (fig. 171) – again with the effect of formal punctuation, thus confining

Ex. 2.4 Symphony No. 2, II, fig. 86: 9–fig. 88: 2

the reminiscences to a penultimate position – and the movement closes undramatically with four long chords over a tonic pedal (avoiding a perfect cadence). This is the closest Elgar comes in his later multi-movement compositions to a synthesis between past and present. Although the passage in which recollection takes place is marked off as a discrete section by the two references to the finale's opening theme that sandwich it, seemingly ensuring the differentiation of past and present worlds, the motto is in fact not the only thematic material to appear in that section – the descending sequences are there too, providing a link back to the 'present'. The differentiation of the two spheres is further undermined by the integration of the motto into the long process of withdrawal from the climax: when that process is finally over, and a rapt, almost motionless, state is reached, it is the descending sequences, not the motto, that are recalled. Moreover, the reference to the finale's opening theme at 171 does not effect an abrupt change of mood that sweeps away (represses) the memories. Nor does the steady, pacing rhythm that sustained the theme for much of the movement restart. Instead the coda's overall mood of calm grandeur prevails, which thus transforms the profile both of the motto (memory) and of material from the finale (the present).

Elgar's last two major symphonic works do not continue the Second Symphony's tendency towards synthesis. Indeed, they press the disjunctions of the earlier orchestral compositions further than ever before, fully exploiting the potential for dramatic irony. *Falstaff* (1913), although not a multi-movement work, contains an episode near the end that is directly comparable to several of the examples above. The episode is dream-like, although the composer did not designate it a 'dream interlude' like two other sections in the work. It follows yet another process of withdrawal from a climax: the fading of the public procession through London to mark the crowning of King Henry V. The new king's public repudiation of Falstaff precipitates the old man's demise. His deathbed dream begins at fig. 140, prefaced by a sustained high F♯ on a solo cello (Ex. 2.5). The process of drifting into a reverie is conveyed by means of slow rising phrases on muted violins (fig. 140), which contain many parallel tritones: an interval that appears repeatedly in the episode as an image of decay.[II] Five themes from earlier in the work are quoted; all the references are fragmentary and are played slowly and softly. Continuity is achieved only in the most primitive fashion – by pauses or single sustained notes. A new motif is played by the clarinet at 146, a little like a speaking voice, before the spell is broken by long, ominous wind chords and a solo roll on a muffled side drum: an example of pitch and metre disintegrating into unpitched, unmeasured sound. This roll probably indicates the death of Falstaff, and certainly the moment of final disenchantment – the closing of the 'memory frame' and its confinement to a penultimate stage. The martial music of the

Ex. 2.5 *Falstaff*, fig. 139: 9–fig. 149: 4

king's procession now returns with a brief, brutal flourish in E minor, before the piece ends with a plucked C major chord: an image of closure (C minor is the main key of the work), yet one stripped of any functional harmonic meaning.[12]

The finale of the Cello Concerto (1919), a sonata form with rondo elements, contains another significant episode in the penultimate position (fig. 66–fig. 72). On this occasion there is no haze or unusual sound, but the drooping melody, chromatic harmony and slow tempo suggest anguished introspection. The contrast with the rest of the blustering finale likewise makes clear that this is an inner world, despite the initial lack of thematic recollection. After an impassioned climax there is a long withdrawal, with the tempo and dynamics gradually reduced and the chromatic phrases suffering such liquidation that they become little more than a long, descending chromatic scale: another image of decay (fig. 70: 3–fig. 71: 4). Near the end of the withdrawal, intensely expressive material from the slow movement of the work briefly reappears, like a momentary idyll (fig. 71: 5). Yet, like the recollection of the motto at the end of the Second Symphony, the reminiscence does not occur after the withdrawal process has finished; rather, it constitutes the final stage of that process. (Sentimental performances of the Concerto obscure this point.) The introspective gaze catches only a fleeting glimpse of a comforting memory, moments before its waning energy dissipates altogether. The 'dream' is then shattered by the return of the soloist's loud chords from the opening of the work. But this second case of inter-movement thematic reminiscence is hardly a memory in the same sense as the first. Instead it is the first part of the frame-reasserting process – a powerful signifier of the return of an 'outer' world. To complete that process the opening theme of the finale returns for a brief, strutting coda comparable in function to that of the Violin Concerto's finale, although shorter and with far more bitterness and irony. The sense of an empty gesture in the direction of convention is overt.

Even Elgar's greatest admirers admit that in places the Cello Concerto comes close to self-pity, and the final pages are not to all tastes.[13] The indulgent tendency is mitigated, however, by the fact that the thematic reminiscence is itself very brief – at least in comparison with those at the parallel stages of the Violin Concerto, the Second Symphony and *Falstaff*. In this most compact of Elgar's symphonic works, a single thematic reminiscence of five bars carries tremendous rhetorical force.[14]

To digress briefly from chronological sequence, these late works provide an interesting context for understanding memory in an earlier composition: the 'Enigma' Variations. If the thematic reminiscences in Variations I and xIV do not constitute memories in the sense under discussion here, the famous quotation from Mendelssohn's *Calm Sea and Prosperous Voyage* in Variation XIII is a stronger candidate, despite the fact that the tune does not appear earlier in the Variations. The quotation is prepared so portentously that it sounds like a spoken utterance from 'outside', and would do so even if the source were unknown – and even had Elgar not placed the first four notes within quotation marks in the score. A 'haze' is achieved through static harmony, a murmuring figure in the violas that blurs the metre, *ppp* dynamics and a timpani roll with side-drum sticks. The quotation swells briefly into a funeral march – the most sombre moment in any of the variations. It is no wonder that this variation has loomed large in the attempts to explicate the enigmas that may or may not lie behind the work: it practically demands extra-musical interpretation. But the mystery is confined to this variation – significantly, the penultimate one. The opening of the finale (Variation xIV) sweeps away the mood once and for all to close the work in vigour and triumph. Scott Burnham's judgement on certain passages in Schubert is relevant to this music. 'It is not so much that the content of these passages is somehow similar to the content of memories as that the attention these passages invite is similar to the attention invited by the act of remembering.'[15] Even though there is no thematic reminiscence, Variation xIII suggests the pensive inward gaze that is the hallmark of musical memory in Elgar.

Elgar used thematic reminiscence in two of the three chamber works he composed in 1918 and 1919: the Violin Sonata and the Piano Quintet. The sonata admittedly represents something of a throwback to Elgar's early practice. Although the reminiscence occurs towards the end of the finale – in the familiar penultimate position between the close of the recapitulation and the start of the coda – it is integrated into the movement without any special rupture. A lyrical tune from the central section of the slow movement returns in its original broad paragraphs with no suggestion of fragmentation. It receives no unusual preparation and carries little sense of mystery.

In the Piano Quintet, by contrast, a pattern of frame-breaking is set as early as the first movement, which begins with a slow introduction. Its thematic material, alternately jagged and mournful, reappears at several points in the following sonata form. Some of that material is used again in the slow introduction to the finale.[16] The work is therefore punctuated at various moments by 'alien' interjections that suggest a nagging memory of something sinister. The most interesting example occurs in the finale – not in the penultimate position this time, but in the development section, which is replaced almost in its entirety by an extended process of recollection. At figure 54, melody, motif and harmonic progression are abandoned for sixteen bars; interest is focused on texture and sonority through a variety of patterns that suggest a sound of faint rustling that moves up and down in waves (Ex. 2.6(i)). The whole passage unfolds over a C♯ pedal and the only harmonic change is the alternation of an F♯ minor chord with several 'neighbour-note harmonies' (such as the one five bars after 54) that highlight the sonorities of clashing semitones, major sevenths and minor ninths. This static rustling is followed by the quiet reappearance of the first theme of the first-movement introduction, now in the triple metre of the finale. It is followed by a longer version of the theme derived from the development section of the first movement, then by a series of fragmentary references to material from the second thematic group of the first movement, and finally by some harmonically and rhythmically unstable material from the finale, again played softly, with violins muted. The transition to the finale recapitulation is based on relatively static B♭ minor harmony (there are internal pedals on F and D♭), and uses *tremolando* in the viola to create a haze (Ex. 2.6(ii)). The minor key, augmented triads (fig. 59: 2–3 and later) and the steady, dirge-like tread convey a faint air of menace (the rhythm is similar to that of the march in 'Enigma' Variation XIII), but this music fades away and after a double bar and an abrupt modulation the recapitulation enters serenely in the tonic, A major. The reminiscences are entirely 'forgotten', and the movement surges to its bright, triumphant conclusion.[17]

Elgar's final exercise in thematic reminiscence in his instrumental music is found in a modest work from the end of his life: the *Nursery Suite* (1931). There are seven movements followed by a coda subtitled 'Envoy'. The seventh movement is a tender piece for strings (all muted) called 'Dreaming'. Its ending is an image of inconclusiveness: the final tonic chord is approached through unorthodox harmony, avoiding a perfect cadence (rather like the final E♭ chord of the Second Symphony), and the notes of the chord fade away one by one, starting with the lowest, so that finally only a solo violin remains. (The procedure is similar to that of the closing bars of Schumann's *Papillons* – a passage inspired by the Romantic idea of music fading into the distance until only one faint note is left.)[18] 'Envoy' opens with a cadenza for the solo violin, alternately virtuoso, capricious and pensive. Thereafter, cadenza-like passages alternate with reminiscences of earlier movements of the suite played in their original orchestral guises.[19] The final solo then breaks the frame of the piece in more radical fashion, quoting the opening theme of the first movement of the

(i) fig. 54: 1–8
Ex. 2.6 Piano Quintet, III

(ii) fig. 59: 1–9
Ex 2.6 (cont.)

Violin Sonata. This fragmentary music is ended by the return of the suite's first movement ('Aubade') in its original key and tempo, re-establishing steady metre and periodicity for twenty-two bars – the ultimate frame-reasserting gesture. The reminiscences are thus once again located in a penultimate position. The solo violin stands for the remembering subject – remembering its own youthful vigour through the cadenzas and wistfully recollecting the guileless tunes from earlier in the suite. On one level 'Envoy' simply revisits the idea behind the Violin Concerto cadenza; some of the virtuoso passages in the two cadenzas are even quite similar. It is far less sophisticated or intense than the earlier cadenza, although it thereby matches the unpretentious tone of the whole suite. Still, in a piece for children, 'Envoy' is the only section that children are unlikely to understand.

In summary, these examples of thematic reminiscence present a variety of moods, techniques and forms, but also some significant points of continuity. Most of them suggest, directly or obliquely, features of a familiar modern view of human identity, articulated most forcefully by Freud. In this view the mind is composed of an outer, conscious, or public aspect and an inner, private, and (generally) unconscious aspect. The latter is somehow more truthful, important and real, and is bound up with a unique personal history, yet for the most part it remains hidden and thus mysterious. The inner aspect may hold a secret clue to the individual. It is accessible only through memory – or, to put it better, through a suspension of the systematic process of forgetting that takes place in ordinary existence. In works such as the First Symphony and the Piano Quintet Elgar composes out a veritable dualism between inner and outer spheres. A second, hidden world exists alongside the conscious one and intrudes fleetingly when the subject drifts into a reverie or when normal temporality is suspended.[20] But Elgar's music does not, on the whole, constitute successful therapy. By the end of most of his later symphonic works (with the notable exception of the symphonies) the subject remains palpably split. In the concertos, indeed, the subjective contradictions arguably reach their greatest intensity only in the final pages. If the idyllic tone of these thematic reminiscences points to some form of nostalgia, Elgar nevertheless treats that nostalgia in a stark and unsentimental fashion. The past may seem to offer truth and meaning, yet it is ultimately brushed aside, either eerily, brutally, perfunctorily, or with bitter irony.

HAUNTINGS

Since Elgar's compositions usually insist on an abrupt return to the present after moments of reminiscence – a tendency pronounced in codas but present at other times too – the memories might be said to be killed off. They are no longer capable of participating in the musical argument of the main 'body' of a movement. On the other hand, at the very moment they intrude through gaps in the form, those memories seem very much alive, pushing their way to consciousness unsought for and unsummoned. In this respect they are ghost-like, for ghosts are similarly both dead and alive, and are fond of appearing at 'liminal' times and places – boundary points or thresholds in our world or in our lives. Memories in Elgar often assume the character of the 'uncanny' as theorised by Freud: the return of the repressed, the appearance of something eerily familiar that 'ought' to have remained hidden.[21] It is no surprise that ghosts and haunting figure prominently in Elgar's discourse on his own music as well as in reactions to it both critical and artistic.

The type of ghost under consideration here belongs to a specific modern literary genre: the gothic. The genre dates from the second half of the eighteenth century, when it emerged as a counterpoint to the values of the Enlightenment. Gothic simultaneously clarified and undermined the bourgeois categories of progress, reason, individuality and good taste, substituting tales of barbarity, superstition, disorientation and darkness, and narrating them in sensational fashion. The novels of Horace Walpole, Ann Radcliffe and Matthew Lewis explored contrasts between modern heroes and heroines and pre-modern villains. Feudal aristocrats and Catholic priests wielded power arbitrarily in gloomy southern European castles where the light of reason had not yet penetrated. Gothic 'repeatedly signalled the disturbing returns of pasts upon presents'.[22] Such literature persisted in modified forms throughout the nineteenth century, re-emerging powerfully in the period of Elgar's maturity to articulate late-Victorian fears about supposedly decaying urban civilisation and the 'racial degeneration' thought to accompany it. In the twentieth century, gothic came into its own in the sphere of popular culture. According to the critic Julian Wolfreys, 'the proliferation of phantoms and the effects of haunting are undeniable aspects of the identity of modernity'.[23] Like nostalgia, the gothic and its ghosts thrive within a negative space opened by the emergence of the ideal of progress.

Another critic, Terry Castle, goes further. In the novels of Ann Radcliffe, where all supernatural events ultimately receive a rational explanation, the apparitions illustrate a new metaphor of 'haunted consciousness'. When Radcliffe's heroines remember deceased friends or relations, those characters seem to appear before their eyes as ghosts, pointing to an experience with implications far beyond the literature of the supernatural. 'In the moment of romantic self-absorption, the other was indeed reduced to a phantom – a purely mental effect, an image, as it were, on the screen of consciousness itself . . . what mattered was the mental picture, the ghost, the haunting image.' The notion that recollected ideas, however mundane, can be said to haunt the mind eventually became normalised in twentieth-century speech. In this view gothic ghosts are 'the symptomatic projections of modern psychic life'.[24]

Ghosts figure prominently in Elgar's literary sources of inspiration. In *Scenes from the Saga of King Olaf* (1896), based on a text by Longfellow, the wraith of Odin returns to haunt Olaf's hall after the king banishes the pagan gods from Norway. The two short pieces entitled *Dream Children*

(1902) refer to a story by Charles Lamb in which an old bachelor beholds two children who gradually fade from his view, whispering 'we are nothing, less than nothing, and dreams. *We are only what might have been.*' Elgar's later part-songs, such as *Death on the Hills* (1914), *The Wanderer* (1923) and *The Herald* (1925), are filled with ghostly presences. In his final years Elgar himself declared his intention to haunt a particular place in Worcestershire, and told a friend that if, after Elgar's death, he should hear someone whistling a theme from the Cello Concerto on the Malvern Hills, 'don't be alarmed, it's only me'.[25]

Still more significantly, Elgar used spectral vocabulary with reference to passages from two of his major works. The most celebrated instance occurs near the start of the development section of the Second Symphony's first movement. On an early sketch of this passage Alice Elgar wrote 'ghost'. Elgar later explained in letters that 'I have written the *most extraordinary* passage I have ever heard – a sort of malign influence wandering thro' the summer night in the garden'; 'there's one *passage* . . . which might be a love scene in a garden at night when the ghost of some memories comes *through it*; – it makes me shiver.' To Alfred Littleton he described the same music and the tune played by the cellos at fig. 28 as 'remote & drawing some one else out of the everyday world' – a formulation reminiscent of the dualist model suggested above to explain Elgar's manner of thematic recollection.[26] Jerrold Northrop Moore's interpretation of the symphony draws deeply on the metaphor of haunting: for him the music tells of ghosts, apparitions, spectres, even 'wraiths of Delight'. For Peter J. Pirie, the whole of the symphony is haunted by a 'spectral menace', the 'veiled terror' of a 'twilight wraith'. And James Hepokoski maintains that in both Elgar's symphonies 'ghosts of unsustainability, regret, and loss of innocence lurk everywhere'.[27]

Eight years after the composition of the Second Symphony Elgar wrote to Ernest Newman of the first movement of the Piano Quintet: 'It is strange music I think & I like it – but – it's ghostly stuff.'[28] The mood of the piece is linked to an unsettling spot in the Sussex countryside near the cottage (Brinkwells) where Elgar composed it; Elgar's musical response was probably mediated through the imagination of his friend Algernon Blackwood, an author of spooky stories who was known to his friends as the 'ghost man', and who visited Elgar at Brinkwells. Furthermore, Michael Allis may well be correct in discerning a programme behind the quintet derived from Edward Bulwer-Lytton's supernatural novel *A Strange Story*.[29] Whatever the truth about these extra-musical associations, the work's critical reception has been guided by the allegedly spectral qualities of some of its music. Moore once again uses the vocabulary of haunting throughout his account. Ivor Keys argues provocatively that Elgar's music from the Brinkwells period marks the return of the composer after a compositional 'death' earlier in the 1910s. 'We are dealing with a huge ghost: the resurrected, post-mortem composer himself.' This is 'the extraordinary ghost of Elgar Redivivus'. More specifically, the thematic reminiscences at the centre of the finale have attracted interest. Diana McVeagh speaks of a 'ghostly presentation of the second subject from the first movement', Ivor Keys hears 'a ghostly waltz', while Daniel Grimley refers to the 'ghostly return of the first movement'.[30]

The momentum that this topos has gathered and sustained can be attributed not just to the mysterious or eerie atmosphere of the passages in question but also to their formal function – or non-function. In both the Second Symphony and the Piano Quintet the 'ghostly' music does not participate fully in the overall musical argument of the respective movements – the processes of thematic development and large-scale intensification and release. It just appears – and disappears. More generally, then, Elgar's thematic recollections can be said to assume something of the character of apparitions on account of their confinement within discrete episodes within a form and their marginalisation with regard to the broader argument. From this perspective, the Violin Concerto cadenza might be deemed a veritable Victorian seance in music: a translation into sound of the theatre of the darkened room and the pathetic, melancholy voices struggling to make themselves audible to the living, before fading away, impotent.

Aside from musical criticism, ghosts have a prominent role in the imaginative literature inspired by Elgar. This is especially the case in plays, where the act of haunting can be portrayed dramatically. In David Pownall's stage play *Elgar's Rondo* (1993; discussed below), the ghost of the deceased A. J. Jaeger twice returns to Elgar, urging him to take a radical path in his future work. Pownall's later radio play *Elgar's Third* (1994) has the ailing composer repeatedly disturbed by the voice of his late wife, Alice. In James Hamilton-Paterson's novel *Gerontius* (1989; discussed in Chapter 7), Elgar's late friend Alfred Rodewald makes a return, and Elgar later becomes convinced that the whole world is populated by ghosts. Occasionally Elgar himself does the haunting. In David Rudkin's television play *Penda's Fen* (1974; discussed in Chapter 6), the main character, a troubled adolescent in 1970s Worcestershire, suffers a series of disturbing dreams and visions which include a meeting with Elgar that transforms his self-understanding. Alick Rowe's radio play *The Dorabella Variation* (2003) likewise casts Elgar in the unlikely role of therapist for a contemporary teenager; in this case the composer dispenses his opinions on twenty-first-century life from a windy spot on the Malvern Hills.[31]

Among these instances, *Elgar's Rondo* contains perhaps the most genuinely Elgarian kind of haunting, for Jaeger's importunate speeches are in vain. The play's two settings correspond with Elgar's recorded references to spectral qualities in his music. They are, respectively, Elgar's composing studio in 1911 shortly after the premiere of the Second Symphony, and the garden of Brinkwells in the summer of 1918, just before the composition of the Piano Quintet. In the first scene Elgar is moody and self-pitying, having been disappointed by the symphony's reception. He has fled a party in his honour, and several friends enter the studio to persuade him to return, without success. Jaeger understands Elgar better than the others, and, just as in life, urges him to more and greater works – specifically, more symphonies. He is fascinated by what he perceives as the proto-modernism of the Second Symphony's Rondo, and even plays Elgar a few snatches of Alban Berg to encourage him. Elgar, though, declares his Rondo demonic and recoils from it. The German Jaeger accuses Elgar of surrendering to a well-meaning but philistine circle of English friends and wasting his talent on 'quatsch'. He instructs Elgar to return to the inspiration of his boyhood, and at the same time to take further the implications of the Rondo – in other words, to bypass the suffocating effects of English society. In Act II Jaeger returns again, this time in a mud-spattered German soldier's uniform, which represents, among other things, his fight against artistic trivia. He is disappointed by Elgar's wartime output, and belittles even the chamber music that Elgar has been composing in Sussex. He again urges Elgar to write symphonies, but leaves without winning an assurance.

Thus Jaeger, in his role as Elgar's artistic conscience, fails to loosen the grip of polite English society and fails also to release Elgar's (allegedly) dwindling creative energies. The play ends with the sound of the opening of the Cello Concerto, Elgar's final major work. The audience is invited to consider Elgar's compositional career after 1911 as a failure of nerve that leaves the radical implications of the Rondo unfulfilled. To be sure, the views of the real Jaeger, had he lived, are unlikely to have corresponded with those of Pownall's Jaeger (he was no Schoenbergian), and the story Pownall tells about the Rondo and Elgar's subsequent compositions is highly contestable. Nevertheless, the fate of Jaeger's ghost can be viewed as an appropriate commentary on Elgar's art, for, like Elgar's supposedly demonic impulse in the Rondo, and so many of the thematic reminiscences in his other works, Jaeger must simply withdraw, allowing the plot to take its own course, his mission unfulfilled.

EPIPHANIES

Pownall's play neglects to mention that the Rondo's unsettling quality is partly attributable to thematic reminiscence. The well-known section at the centre of the Rondo in which hammering percussion violently drowns out the rest of the orchestra quotes the cello tune from the 'ghost' music of the first movement. The treatment of the reminiscence is typical of Elgar's later practice in that it gradually fades away, after which the 'ghost' music plays no further part in the symphony. On the other hand, it is atypical in so far as the original atmosphere of mystery attaching to this music is thoroughly dispelled in the Rondo; the effect is nightmarish but not exactly uncanny. To interpret this passage, the concept of memory must be somewhat expanded – an approach that will enhance understanding of other works by Elgar as well.

If one form of modern memory can be identified through the imagery of ghosts and the gothic, then a second, related form is connected to the notion of epiphany. As a literary mode, epiphany took shape only slightly later than gothic, and likewise enjoyed a strong legacy throughout the modern period, albeit in 'higher' genres. In its original, religious meaning, epiphany stood for a manifestation of the divine in a body, or, more generally, for a manifestation of the spiritual in something material. But, rather than being felt as mysterious, that manifestation is recognised by the subject as a moment of revelation, which, though transient, leaves an abiding impression, and may effect a fundamental spiritual reorientation. The Romantics revived epiphany, but in a secularised and internalised form. They generally needed no supernatural agent to bestow grace; the divine was associated with heightened subjective experience. A sudden transcendent feeling might be provoked by a mundane object or a humble event or place. Coleridge's 'flashes', Shelley's 'best and happiest moments', and Keats's 'fine isolated verisimilitude' were followed in the Victorian period by Browning's 'infinite moments', Arnold's 'gleaming' moments, and a host of other examples. The experience survived into the twentieth century in Conrad's 'moments of vision', Wallace Stevens's 'moments of awakening', Virginia Woolf's 'moments of vision' and Joyce's theorising in *Stephen Hero* (1944) – the text which coined the term epiphany for modern critical usage.[32] Most significantly for this chapter, Wordsworth located the sources of epiphany in the history of the subject and its memories, an idea illustrated by the famous 'spots of time' episode in *The Prelude*, and extended by Proust with his 'mémoires involontaires' in *A la recherche du temps perdu*. In this version, epiphany through memory yields the key to self-understanding and the resolution of a narrative. Strong claims have been made for epiphany in its secular guise. The critic M. H. Abrams spoke of it as the 'modern Moment'. Robert Langbaum argues that 'the epiphanic mode is to a large extent the Romantic and modern mode – a dominant modern convention'. It has 'pervaded poetry and determined its structure since Wordsworth', shaping, among other genres, the Victorian dramatic monologue, the modern short story, and the movements of Imagism and Symbolism. For Ashton Nichols, 'in so far as the roots of modernism are contained in Romantic and Victorian poetry, they are contained to an important extent in the structure of epiphany'.[33] In literature, subjective epiphany was a crucial means for uncovering meaning in the disenchanted modern world.

Among the many variants of epiphany, the most appealing to Elgar was perhaps what might be termed the 'Shelleyan variant', in which the ephemeral character of the experience is underlined and any lasting effects are downplayed. The posthumous *Song* that Elgar quoted at the head of the Second Symphony describes this type of epiphany. Yet the *Song*, while familiar to Elgarians, merely echoes a greater poem, the *Hymn to Intellectual Beauty* (1816):

> The awful shadow of some unseen Power
>> Floats through unseen amongst us, – visiting
> This various world with as inconstant wing
>> As summer winds that creep from flower to flower. –
> Like moonbeams that behind some piny mountain shower,
>> It visits with inconstant glance
>> Each human heart and countenance;
> Like hues and harmonies of evening, –
>> Like clouds in starlight widely spread, –
>> Like memory of music fled, –
>> Like aught that for its grace may be
> Dear, and yet dearer for its mystery.[34]

The poem later describes Shelley's youthful search for inspiration and meaning in traditional sources such as 'God, and ghosts, and Heaven'. When these fail, he is thrown back on an alternative: the mind itself. Yet the spirit of 'intellectual beauty' is frustratingly elusive, casting its enchanted light upon the objects of the material world unpredictably and fleetingly. This is the price of internalising epiphany. In his essay *A Defence of Poetry* (1821) Shelley accounts for the process of artistic creation in similar terms:

[T]he mind in creation is as a fading coal, which some invisible influence, like an inconstant wind, awakens to transitory brightness; this power arises from within like the colour of a flower which fades and changes as it is developed, and the conscious portions of our natures are unprophetic either of its approach or its departure...

We are aware of evanescent visitations of thought and feeling, sometimes associated with place or person, sometimes regarding our own mind alone, and always arising unforeseen and departing unbidden, but elevating and delightful beyond all expression: so that even in the desire and the regret they leave, there cannot but be pleasure, participating as it does in the nature of its object.[35]

The examples of thematic reminiscence from Elgar's *Introduction and Allegro*, First Symphony first movement, and Second Symphony second movement – moments when time seems to stand still, yet which come and go without obvious rationale – fit the Shelleyan model for epiphany.

Other examples in Elgar point more directly to epiphany through memory along the lines of Wordsworth and Proust. One of these is the E♭ minor music in the finale of the First Symphony, a pivotal passage at the end of the development section which coincides with a turning point in the work's tonal and emotional trajectory.[36] Up to that point the outer movements of the work have unfolded a dichotomy between the serene order of the motto theme in its diatonic A♭ major, and the Allegro sections, based around A minor or D minor but highly chromatic and filled with complex textures and dense motivic working. The E♭ minor music coincides with the final turn to the tonal sphere of the motto's A♭ major, where most of the recapitulation remains, leading to the motto's final triumphant return in its home key. Moreover, this passage effects another, equally potent, kind of resolution – a revelation of kinship amongst seemingly disparate materials. A little earlier in the movement, the conclusion (and climax) of the exposition is marked by a short-winded, stabbing march tune, which confirms the D minor tonality and provides the raw material for much of the subsequent development section. In the E♭ minor passage this march reappears transformed – one might even say transfigured. The orchestration is luminous and the mood impassioned yet elevated. The fevered energy of the preceding pages is converted into a calm, ordered rhythm of long phrases. The generous span of the curving melody and the relative stability of texture and tonality are all qualities that in the outer movements are largely confined to the presentations of the motto. If the motto and the march tune can be regarded as 'antagonists' in some kind of drama – an interpretation that the symphony almost irresistibly invites – then the E♭ minor music mediates between them. For almost the first time in the symphony, the antitheses established in the outer movements threaten to dissolve altogether.[37]

The process of dissolution gives the impression of being effected through the agency of thematic reminiscence. Three bars before fig. 129 the development is brought to an abrupt halt by a kind of 'call to arms' in bass instruments followed by a reference to the motto (Ex. 2.7(i)). But although the two-part counterpoint of the motto is unmistakable, the precise contours of the parts are significantly modified. The bass follows the rhythm and melody of the finale's march tune (the reference is easy to discern as the motto's bass and the march are both based on regular, detached notes with occasional pairs of notes of twice the speed). At fig. 129 the melody of the motto enters, but not on the usual $\hat{3}$ of a major scale; the first three notes unfold a minor third, and in retrospect it becomes clear that the initial C♭ is $\hat{6}$ of E♭ minor. This is the first time in the symphony that the harmonisation of the motto has clearly indicated a minor key. The affinities between the motto and the march are thus pointed out in an almost didactic fashion. Later, at one of the climaxes in the E♭ minor music, another connection is made; this time the motto – again in E♭ minor – emerges through the counterpoint. Its first phrase and the first part of its second phrase appear in different voices; the counterpoint is arranged so that the notes that suggest the second phrase are in the voice that contains the transformed march tune (its seventh to tenth notes). Thus the motto is heard, as it were, 'through' the march. (Ex. 2.7(ii) illustrates the point by showing the second violin and flute parts, omitting all doubling.) The music of Ex. 2.7 (i) and (ii) reveals that the two themes are both based on patterns of stepwise motion, first descending, then ascending. Yet at this point both are transformed.[38] The E♭ minor music can be regarded as an epiphany through memory in so far as the 'inner' or spiritual world of the motto becomes manifest in the 'outer' or material world of the Allegro (represented by the march) by means of a process of association and recollection. During the extended 'moment' that it takes to perform, the temporality of the Allegro is suspended and that of the motto is substituted. Thereafter, although the Allegro resumes for the sake of the recapitulation, the experience of its music is permanently transformed, and the work seems impelled to its triumphant conclusion.[39]

The epiphany in the First Symphony's finale provides a useful perspective from which to view the reappearance of the 'ghost' in the Rondo of the Second, for there are some striking similarities as well as significant differences. The main similarity is the care with which a resemblance is gradually revealed between the contours of the opening theme of the Rondo and the recollected ghost theme: this is another case of recollection through association. After what sounds like a trio in a scherzo movement (starting at

(i) fig. 128: 5–fig. 129: 10

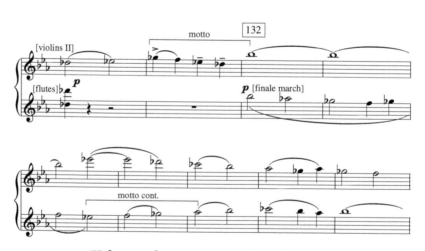

(ii) fig. 131: 9–fig. 132: 7 (second violin and flute parts)
Ex. 2.7 Symphony No. 1, IV

fig. 106), the movement's opening theme reappears in the woodwind as though to start the third part of a ternary form (fig. 116). However, its continuation is sidetracked, and eventually gives way to the outburst of the ghost. Violins shadow the woodwind, yet they pick out just a few notes of each phrase, revealing a hidden contour 'behind' the theme (Ex. 2.8, fig. 116–fig. 117). The woodwind then drop out of the texture, allowing the first five bars of the violin's new melody to stand in relief (fig. 117). This short phrase is repeated again and again, but with the first of its syncopations removed, bringing it still closer to the ghost theme (fig. 117: 5). The memory thus seems somehow to be prompted by the Rondo music, yet at the same time it drives that music out of consciousness. As in the First Symphony finale, an outer world gives way to an inner world through recollection. On this occasion, however, the epiphany is negative: a case perhaps, of what one literary critic has called 'demonic epiphany'.[40] It provides not a glimpse of the divine but a glimpse into the abyss. The second difference is that the recollection of the ghost in the Rondo reverts

Ex. 2.8 Symphony No. 2, III, fig. 116: 1–fig. 117: 9 (selected violin and woodwind parts)

to the typical Elgarian pattern of 'inconstancy' in the sense of Shelley – it eventually fades away and the return of the Rondo music continues almost as though nothing had happened.[41] Inevitably the mood is clouded on this second hearing, given the violence of the ghostly interjection, but there are no structural alterations as substantial as the reorientation of tonality in the First Symphony finale.

Elgar's epiphanic mode has not elicited a great deal of commentary, but there is one intriguing literary response that deserves mention. The playwright and author J. B. Priestley – a sensitive critic of Elgar's music, whose writings will be examined in Chapters 5 and 6 – refers to one of Elgar's special moments to convey the experience of a secular epiphany in his novel *Festival at Farbridge* (1957). The subject is Laura Casey, a secretary who turns co-founder and organiser of an arts festival in a fictional English town. Near the end of the book, when the festival week finally arrives after long preparation, Laura stands in a deserted, shady place outside the town's concert hall looking down some steps into bright summer sunshine. The street below is 'brilliant, warm, alive with every passer-by on the pavement caught in that brief clarity which is at once beautiful and melancholy, as if it were an image of Time itself'.[42] Indeed time seems to stand still, and she is greeted by several friends, whose actions are accidentally coordinated so as to seem almost choreographed. And she hears music.

Then came stealing through the open doorway, from the orchestra waiting to rehearse on the platform far down the hall, the sound, remote but clear, of the first violin, and then the viola, idly playing the second theme of Elgar's 'Introduction and Allegro'; and it was as if far-away voices, noble and dreamy, were pronouncing the benediction she had already vaguely felt, were blessing for ever, so that she could never forget, the brilliant warm street and its image of Time.[43]

By 'second theme' Priestley almost certainly means the 'Welsh tune'.[44] Although the players are only warming up, the experience – time standing still, attention focused on something distant yet clear – is remarkably similar to the impression given by the first appearance of the Welsh tune in the piece itself. In fact, the reference to 'far-away voices' suggests that Priestley knew Elgar's account of the genesis of that music. Luckily for Laura, and in contrast to many of Elgar's compositions, she is able to cling to the memory of the moment with some success:

And she never did forget it. Many a time afterwards, in a dark hour, with hope fading, existence a sad desert, she returned in memory to that time, that place, caught and held once more that very moment, and felt the stream of life running free again, flashing in the sun, as it had done in that high summer of the Festival.[45]

AUTUMNAL HARMONIES

Most instances of thematic reminiscence in Elgar's later multi-movement instrumental works can be regarded either as hauntings or as epiphanies of some kind (or as both). Only one passage remains to be accounted for, which is exceptional in several respects. As indicated above, the recollection of the 'spirit of delight' motto at the end of the Second Symphony's finale is a rare case among Elgar's later symphonic works where thematic reminiscence supports some degree of synthesis between past and present. As might be expected, then, the impression of this coda is far from uncanny, and there are significant differences from the fleeting visitations of the spirit that take place earlier in the symphony. Yet this passage too can be understood as a form of modern memory – at least, if the freedom of a little speculation may be allowed.

Since Elgar's death a tradition has grown up that interprets the end of the Second Symphony as elegiac – a farewell to the hopes and ideals of the Victorian and Edwardian eras. Perhaps Elgar lacked the vocabulary to articulate this idea himself, or was reluctant to admit that the Second Symphony ended less positively than the First, but it is notable that he used a rather different range of epithets for the finale. He wrote to Alfred Littleton: 'the whole of the sorrow is smoothed out & ennobled in the last movement, which ends in a calm &, *I hope & intend*, elevated mood.' 'The last movement speaks for itself I think: a broad sonorous, rolling movement throughout – in an elevated mood.'[46] As will become clear in the next chapter, the concept of nobility in Elgar certainly does not exclude the elegiac. In this case, though, an analysis in terms of thematic reminiscence helps to show how the two might be related, and Elgar's vocabulary reconciled with that of his interpreters.

Since much of this chapter has been concerned with parallels between musical and literary modes, it seems appropriate to seek literary parallels for the ending of the Second Symphony. The last stanza of Shelley's *Hymn to Intellectual Beauty* takes a turn which strikingly anticipates that ending. The frustration at the spirit's inconstancy is now a thing of the poet's youthful past; the future can be met with a steadier gaze:

> The day becomes more solemn and serene
>   When noon is past – there is a harmony
>   In autumn, and a lustre in its sky,
> Which through the summer is not heard or seen,
> As if it could not be, as if it had not been!
>   Thus let thy power, which like the truth
>   Of nature on my passive youth

> Descended, to my onward life supply
>   Its calm – to one who worships thee,
>   Whom, SPIRIT fair, thy spells did bind
> To fear himself, and love all human kind.[47]

The glowing, autumnal mood of the stanza speaks of joy remembered and sublimated, finally reconciled with the passing of time. Still, the precise operation of memory is not described in the poem. In this regard it may be helpful to consider one of the main precursors of this final stanza: the third section of Wordsworth's *Lines Composed a Few Miles above Tintern Abbey* (1798), one of the most famous 'elevated' passages in English Romanticism. The poem contains an early statement of Wordsworth's belief in the constitutive role of memory in the shaping of subjectivity. In the second half of the poem, however, having returned to a picturesque viewpoint that he last visited five years before, the subject finds that he regards the prospect through more mature eyes. The 'aching joys' and 'dizzy raptures' of his youthful response to nature have dissipated, but he finds 'abundant recompense' in calmer, grander thoughts:

>   For I have learned
> To look on nature, not as in the hour
> Of thoughtless youth, but hearing oftentimes
> The still, sad music of humanity,
> Nor harsh nor grating, though of ample power
> To chasten and subdue. And I have felt
> A presence that disturbs me with the joy
> Of elevated thoughts; a sense sublime
> Of something far more deeply interfused,
> Whose dwelling is the light of setting suns,
> And the round ocean and the living air,
> And the blue sky, and in the mind of man,
> A motion and a spirit, that impels
> All thinking things, all objects of all thought,
> And rolls through all things.[48]

Here again the subject achieves reconciliation with time: the former heady delights are replaced by an intellectual and religious attitude. But the mood of calm is shot through with sadness, a consequence of the loss of immediate pleasures and the awareness of human suffering that flows from the philosophical perspective. The factors mediating between the earlier and later states of consciousness are the particular landscape and the subject's memory of it; recollection merges with present perception to illuminate the difference in experience. It seems plausible to attribute a similar function to the coda of the Second Symphony's finale, as the spirit of delight is recollected in tranquillity. This reading has the virtue of going some way to accommodating both Elgar's description of the entire finale as 'ennobled' and 'elevated' and numerous listeners' subsequent perception of the conclusion as valedictory.

That is not of course to insist that Elgar had either of these passages in mind as he composed the symphony, although his fervent literary aspirations and the status of the Romantic poets in his day make it almost certain that he would have known them. Rather, the symphony mirrors a characteristic Romantic pattern in moving, as it would seem, from sensation to intellect, from energy to calm, from unreflective joy to tempered sadness. The poems quoted here fix on the problem of meaning for the modern subject; they solve it without recourse to religious doctrine, transferring authority to the human mind. Both reject any return to comforting old certainties, yet also try to avoid giving way to despair. The alternative they find is a form of sublimated consciousness achieved with the help of personal memory. The price of this alternative is Romantic solipsism, for the spirit of intellectual beauty and the 'presence that disturbs' are both predicated on the individual subject. It is in one respect unsurprising that Elgar found a parallel solution for the end of his symphony, for by 1911 the triumphant conclusion of the First Symphony seems no longer to have been available to him, while the irony, anger and even nihilism detectable in the conclusions of *Falstaff* and the Cello Concerto were still in the future. In the recollections of the Second Symphony's coda Elgar's lingering commitment to the ideal of nobility guided him down a singular path.[49] The next chapter will examine more closely that ideal and its formative effect on Elgar's art.

CHAPTER 3

Nobility

There is no shortage of evidence for Elgar's fascination with the concept of nobility. His early passion for Scott and Longfellow; his choice of subjects for major compositions;[1] his penchant for the expression marking *nobil-mente*; his famous marches; his pleasure at mixing with royalty and his eagerness to dedicate works to monarchs; his love for the subject of heraldry; his military appearance; all these aspects testify to a sustained interest in the Victorian revival of medieval chivalry and the concomitant idealisation of the 'gentleman'.[2] However, the topic of nobility is discomforting for the modern Elgarian, for the idea has not aged well. The very aspects of his personal image and musical style that appealed to audiences at the turn of the twentieth century soon fell under suspicion. In the course of that century the 'English Gentleman' became an object of scorn rather than of admiration, and today the social type is virtually extinct. Elgar's liking for nobility in all its forms has provided his detractors with useful ammunition.

The criticisms levelled at Elgar on this score might be distinguished roughly as follows. First, and most obviously, Elgar – both the man and the composer – aims to be noble, but manages only to be pompous. Secondly, the music of his noble style is said to be complacent: its tone is too unruffled and is achieved too easily for the modern listener's comfort. That point is related to a broader complaint about the society of the Edwardian period – the familiar allegation that it was an irresponsible age hurtling unconcernedly towards the catastrophe of 1914. In this view the cult of chivalry promoted by schools, churches and political parties, which reached its peak at the start of the Great War, had the gravest of consequences. Its stirring images of knights and dragons must be held partly responsible for the eager idealism with which thousands of young men threw themselves into the conflict. The celebration of the chivalric codes of the middle ages was not passive escapism, but a pernicious form of restorative nostalgia. Ancient standards of behaviour were co-opted for modern purposes, idealised, and then fashioned into an unwise model for future conduct. Seen from this perspective, Elgar was not just a snob, but an eloquent mouthpiece for ideas which had calamitous results.

Such charges, being relatively specific, can be met by citing carefully chosen writings and utterances of Elgar and by making intelligent critical observations on the music that seek to draw out its complexities – and that is what Elgar's defenders have generally done.[3] But, whatever the merits of their arguments, in a broader perspective Elgar's preoccupation with nobility still seems troubling. Writing in the late 1970s, the nadir of Britain's economic and post-colonial decline, the historian Martin J. Wiener diagnosed a fatal defect in the national mentality, which had emerged in the mid-nineteenth century and sapped the dynamic expansion and enterprise of the mid-Victorian period. Ever since then, he contended, it had fostered an atmosphere of retrenchment. Despite leading the world into the Industrial Revolution and pioneering modern trade and commerce, by the late nineteenth century the British began to fashion a self-image as a people distrustful of progress, hostile to materialism, slow moving in thought and action, and deeply attached to tranquillity and stability. Wiener attributed this paradoxical state of affairs to a collective failure of nerve on the part of the British middle class. Never having effected a bourgeois revolution, they were faced with residual traces of pre-modern society in their midst, and responded not by confronting the aristocracy, but, as far as possible, by aping its manners, lifestyle and attitudes. Wealthy Victorian industrialists tried to turn themselves into country gentlemen. They built rural mansions, behaved as though they were ashamed of benefiting from commerce, and sent their sons to public schools for a classical education and a route into the professions. Science, technology and all pursuits judged merely 'utilitarian' were denigrated in favour of a life of style and leisure. In the twentieth century, both the political Right and Left perpetuated elements of this passive mentality. If Wiener is correct then Elgar's attempts to achieve nobility in his music could be regarded as the manifestation of a common impulse that has proved detrimental to British society.[4]

Although Wiener's argument has been disputed,[5] it gives the present topic an undeniable relevance, for it places nobility, gentlemanliness and the desire to aspire to those conditions centre stage in the debate over modern British identity and consciousness. It may, then, be worth reviewing some relatively well-known texts from the anti-Elgar reaction of the 1920s in order to clarify where the battle lines are drawn in his case. Most of these attacks employ irony or even withering sarcasm in order to deflate

Elgar's pretensions (as they are seen) to nobility. Two instances refer primarily to the man rather than the music. In his autobiography of 1949, Osbert Sitwell recounted (and perhaps embellished) his memories of an afternoon of 1927 when he attended Frank Schuster's celebration of Elgar's seventieth birthday. In his lengthy and morbid account of the proceedings, the 'Angel of Death' hovers over Elgar's ageing friends as they honour 'the prosperous music of the Master'. The composer appears as a 'plump wraith . . . who with his grey moustache, grey hair, grey top hat and frock-coat looked every inch a personification of Colonel Bogey'. Sitwell does not conceal his indifference to the fact that these 'floccose herds of good-time Edwardian ghosts' will soon be dead and gone.[6] 'Prosperous' and 'good-time' are the keywords, for they conjure up familiar images of pre-war complacency, here identified with the Angel of Death. A second hostile commentary on Elgar the man is found in a diary entry from 1922 by Siegfried Sassoon. This account is more succinct than Sitwell's but also more injurious, coming as it does from a fellow artist, an architect of the twentieth-century literary reaction to war, and a decorated army officer who condemned the manner of prosecution of the Great War and narrowly escaped court martial. Sassoon confided that 'Elgar is, outwardly, a retired army officer of the conventional Victorian type. He prides himself on his conventional appearance. I have often heard him use the phrase "A Great Gentleman". It is his sublimity of encomium – his encomiastic apex. No doubt he sublimates *himself* as a G. G. – the Duc d'Elgar.'[7] Sassoon's war poems and memoirs took savage aim at the army Staff and at complacent civilians at home; his sketch of Elgar, both in its content and its ironic tone, seems to place the composer uncomfortably close to those targets.

As for nobility in the music, two memorable responses of this period come from book-length surveys of the contemporary musical scene by the critic Cecil Gray and the composer Constant Lambert. In both cases the writer seeks to expose the limitations of Elgar's preoccupation with nobility by comparing him with other composers. According to Lambert's *Music Ho!* (1934), 'the aggressive Edwardian prosperity that lends so comfortable a background to Elgar's finales is now as strange to us as the England that produced *Greensleeves* and *The Woods so wilde*. Stranger, in fact, and less sympathetic. In consequence much of Elgar's music, through no fault of its own, has for the present generation an almost intolerable air of smugness, self-assurance and autocratic benevolence.'[8] At least Lambert does not pin the blame wholly on the music: he takes account of the perspective – and perhaps partial blindness – of contemporary listeners. Gray, in his chapter on Elgar in *Survey of Contemporary Music* (1924), likewise admits that the anti-Elgar reaction is a symptom of a wider impatience with all things Victorian. But he goes on to explain that the great artist, while expressing his age, will also rise above it, and this Elgar fails to do. 'He never gets entirely away from the atmosphere of pale, cultured idealism, and the unconsciously hypocritical, self-righteous, complacent, Pharisaical gentlemanliness which is so characteristic of British art in the last century.'[9] Many of the best artists of the Victorian period were 'tainted with this spirit', 'this pervading, subtly insinuating atmosphere of gentility'. Gray's verdict is that Elgar 'might have been a great composer if he had not been such a perfect gentleman'.[10]

How damaged is Elgar by all this spleen? In the end, probably not too badly, for, although some of the points hit their mark (especially as regards the personality of the later Elgar of the post-war years), much of the rhetoric comes across with a hint of adolescent posturing by the younger generation (with the exception of Sassoon, whose remarks were private). It is notable that neither Elgar nor his adherents bothered to respond publicly to the plentiful barbs in Gray's chapter, though there was a full decade before his death in which to do so. The situation was different with a further notable instance of hostile criticism of Elgar – the comments on the composer in the weighty *Handbuch der Musikgeschichte* (1924) by the Cambridge academic, distinguished author and critic and President of the International Society for Contemporary Music, Edward J. Dent. When they were first noticed by loyal Elgarians (in late 1930 after the publication of the second edition), they provoked a storm of protest, including an indignant letter to German and British newspapers signed by leading musicians and cultural luminaries. Dent's remarks have passed into Elgarian legend, and even down to the present his biographers find it hard to report them without indignation. Dent was a well-respected musical figure both nationally and internationally, and his brief, dismissive lines on Elgar in a foreign publication seemed to some like treachery. (That the book was in German was still worse, for it reawakened old anxieties about the supposedly derisive German reception of British music in the late nineteenth century.) Here are the relevant passages from Dent's article:

He was a violinist by profession, and studied the works of Liszt, which were an abomination to conservative academic musicians. He was, moreover, a Catholic, and more or less a self-taught man, who possessed little of the literary culture of Parry and Stanford ...

To English ears Elgar's music is too emotional and not entirely free from vulgarity. His orchestral works, two symphonies, concertos for violin and cello, and several overtures, are vivid in colour, but pompous in style and of a too deliberate chivalrousness [*Ritterlichkeit*] of expression.'[11]

It is easy to see why the outcry occurred. On one reading, the privileged insider accuses the self-taught shopkeeper's son of studying abhorrent music, of being Catholic and (thus?) of being vulgar. Furthermore his music is pompous and ill-judged. Finally, the English are said to dislike Elgar – a point which his supporters hotly contested.

More recently there have been efforts in turn to defend Dent's remarks. Philip Radcliffe has suggested that Dent was mocking the fastidious 'English ears' and Brian Trowell has argued that each of his sentences can be read as a genuine statement of fact or as an objective remark that was not implausible at the time of writing (the early 1920s).[12] Such attempts are undermined, however, by another of Dent's contributions to a continental publication, an entry on English music in *La musica contemporanea in Europa* (1925). Here his true colours are revealed. 'In England the best musicians have a real horror of him (Liszt). The only composer who shows traces of his influence is Elgar, and Elgar, despite his brilliant style, is repugnant to many English musicians, by reason precisely of that chivalrous rhetoric which badly covers up his intrinsic vulgarity.'[13] Moreover, Radcliffe attributes to Dent the following judgement: 'when Elgar is outright vulgar he is at his best; when he wishes to be noble he makes me uncomfortable.'[14] By putting the three extracts side by side, Dent's view of Elgar and nobility becomes clear. Elgar tries to adopt a high style, but, on account of his essential vulgarity, is unable to do so properly. Thus he writes pompous music whose expression of chivalry is exaggerated and rhetorical. A musician of taste instantly sees through this pose.

Dent's view is worth considering further because it refers obliquely to a problem that dogged the Victorian discourse on nobility and the gentleman. Is the prized quality of 'gentlemanliness' primarily an inward or an outward matter? Must a gentleman possess elegant manners, meticulous dress and refined speech, or is the true gentleman one who acts well, regardless of how shabby or roughly spoken he may be? This point is of vital importance, for it determines the extent to which the idea of the gentleman is based on class; the degree to which, to use Cecil Gray's term, it is confined to a 'Pharisaical' clique. Most Victorian writers who addressed the question steered a middle course between the two kinds of gentleman, extolling moral behaviour but never fully relinquishing the connection to outward decorum. Thus a social outsider could join the ranks of gentlemen, but only at the expense of copying their manners to the letter. (This could create agonies for the aspirant gentleman, as Elgar himself must have experienced keenly during his early years.) In the eyes of Dent – who had a far more privileged background – Elgar's adopted nobility is of a distinctly superficial variety. Elgar perceives only the outward appearance of nobility, and compounds the felony by aping it poorly.

It is easy to identify in Elgar's music the kind of 'chivalrous rhetoric' that Dent disliked: a rhetoric whose vocabulary is based on pacing rhythms and the imitation of courtly gestures. The former are familiar and require no illustration. In cases of the latter, a melodic line suggests an elaborate courtly bow by dipping gently before rising swiftly with a flourish, generally through larger intervals. Ex. 3.1 shows four such gestures, each of which has an explicit connection with chivalry. Ex. 3.1(i) portrays the gentler side of a medieval knight after his jousting and galloping is finished; Ex. 3.1(ii) is sung by King Olaf when extending hospitality to a stranger at his feast; Elgar described the effect of Ex. 3.1(iii) as 'ritterlich' (chivalrous); while in reference to Ex. 3.1(iv) he wrote that 'Prince [Hal] is suggested in his most courtly and genial mood'.[15] Many similar melodic shapes can be found throughout Elgar's oeuvre. From Dent's perspective it could be argued that such phrases, with their leaping and plunging and their often highly coloured orchestration (Lisztian, as he might have perceived it) are the musical equivalent of an inflated literary style.

The answering of these charges is not straightforward, and requires some care. One strategy would be to try to make a virtue out of Elgar's alleged vulgarity. According to this way of thinking, his view of nobility is a commoner's view – a view from below. Bold, picturesque and unreal, it springs from his childhood imagination, which, stimulated by books, was always ready to seize on a vivid stimulus. Ernest Newman made this argument in his attempt to explain the meaning of Elgar's ubiquitous *nobilmente* marking. Newman argued that the term does not mean 'this theme is noble', but that Elgar had seen his subject as noble. He continues:

He was a man of enormous vitality, for all his sensitiveness and occasional valetudinarianism. That nose of his, with its boldness and mass, and the exceptionally large nostrils that, even when he was lying pitiably weak in his last illness, seemed to be distended in a passionate effort to draw all life into them and make it part of himself, were the outward symbol of a constitution and a mind of unusual strength. He saw the outer world as a magnificent pageant, every line and colour of which thrilled him.[16]

Newman describes Elgar's visceral reactions to sights such as a military display and Roman ruins. Although given to dark moods as well, 'he

(i) *Froissart*, fig. I: 1–5 (clarinet part)

(ii) 'The Wraith of Odin' (*Scenes from the Saga of King Olaf*), fig. F: 1–8 (alto part)

(iii) Violin Concerto, III, fig. 71: 1–fig. 72 (first violin part)

(iv) *Falstaff*, fig. 4: 1–4 (cello part)
Ex. 3.1 Elgar's 'chivalrous rhetoric'

mostly saw life in terms of chivalry, of brave pageantry, of a line that was at once bold and sensitive' (compare with the melodic lines in Ex. 3.1). This predominantly sensory response to the world – encapsulated by the symbol of the nose – would perhaps be classified by Dent as uncultured. Newman certainly does not take that view, but his account nevertheless runs the risk of turning Elgar into an overgrown child. In dispelling the 'misunderstandings' of Elgar's *nobilmente*, he strips nobility of its moral aspects and makes it purely aesthetic; thus Elgar cannot be held responsible for any discomfort listeners might feel at his attempts to achieve nobility in music.

Instead of turning Elgar into a child, the rest of this chapter seeks to uncover some complexities in his approach to nobility. The following section provides some immediate – indeed family – context by exploring the aesthetics of Elgar's wife, Alice. Her equation of nobility with 'the ideal' partially overlaps with her husband's view, and reveals a dimension independent of the 'rhetoric' identified by Dent. Yet Alice's writings in turn neglect the quality that Elgar's advocates have always regarded as the saving grace of his noble style when it works well: its emotional ambiguity. The note of resignation they hear points to a reflective rather than a restorative mode of nostalgia. The penultimate section analyses passages from Elgar's symphonic music with these points in mind, while the final section returns to one of Elgar's post-war critics for a more generous view of his nobility.

THE IDEAL IN THE PRESENT

When Cecil Gray identified the aspects of the Victorian age that Elgar failed to 'rise above', his reference to 'unconsciously hypocritical, self-righteous, complacent, Pharisaical gentlemanliness', is relatively straightforward to understand. Even today, aspects of Elgar's style may grate on the sensibility, and we can recognise how irritating they might have been for the post-war generation, regardless of whether we agree with the substance of Gray's charges. However, the first part of the sentence from which that phrase comes – the allusion to an 'atmosphere of pale, cultured idealism' is less easy to grasp intuitively. It is not immediately clear how such an atmosphere relates to Elgar's alleged self-righteous gentlemanliness. A few clues can be gleaned from Elgar himself (to be explored later), but these are hard to interpret in isolation. However, the writings of his wife Alice on aesthetics lay out an 'idealist' position at length, and in this regard provide some context in which to locate her husband's ideas and music.

Alice Elgar is an easy character to ridicule. A staunch upholder of conventional morality, religion and social propriety, a true-blue Tory (at least latterly), maternally protective of her younger husband, and unshakeably convinced of his genius, she appears to embody a host of unfashionable values. There is some truth to this picture, and the reminiscences of Elgar by his younger female friends have their fun with Alice.[17] Yet as her biographer Percy Young has shown, at times she tugged forcefully against the values and routines of her upper-class Worcestershire family (she was the daughter of a major-general, and her family claimed descent from royalty).[18] The most obvious example is the very fact that she married Elgar the shopkeeper's son, for which she was disinherited by a wealthy aunt – one of her closest surviving relatives. In her earliest adult years she acquired a lively interest in the science of geology, and kept in touch with developments in the contemporary arts. She was a published writer, and several of her literary works from the period prior to her marriage deal with pressing Victorian social issues. The hero of her two-volume novel *Marchcroft Manor* (1882) espouses radical solutions to those problems of a kind that would have been roundly rejected by most of her social peers. Although marriage marked the end of her own artistic ambitions she continued to write occasional poetry and to reflect on the arts in prose.

Some time in the 1890s, Alice Elgar wrote her most substantial piece of criticism: an essay on contemporary art, literature and music entitled 'The Ideal in the Present'. The essay was not published, and in the manuscript that survives (about 2,700 words) some sections are unpolished.[19] But the text gives a clear picture of her ideas about aesthetics and elucidates terminology that she later used in diary entries relating to Elgar's music.

'The Ideal in the Present' begins by posing the question: 'How will the latter half of the 19th century be characterized by the historian of the future?' Alice's answer is that it will be viewed as practical, realist and materialist – qualities she lists regretfully, even while acknowledging the great benefits they bring to the comfort and convenience of everyday life. The great thinkers of the modern age do not, according to Alice, uncover abstract, universal principles as did Copernicus, Galileo and Newton, but contribute to the rapid advancement of practical spheres such as transport and communication. An obvious materialist aspect to the age that the historian of the future will note is the pursuit of wealth, which, Alice claims, is unsurpassed by any other period in history. Here the values of her class – the representatives of inherited wealth – are all too evident in a note of weary disdain and a distinct ambivalence towards the aspirations of working people:

In all fields of labour, of trade, of speculation, the eager crowd rushes surging onwards in its wild efforts to clutch the gold, the key to open the treasure house of their hearts desire. And against the full tide of daylight in which the struggle takes its course, a new shadow appears – Demos, – claiming his share and insisting that all practical efforts shall be made to give room and space for him also, that he too, may reap and enjoy.[20]

This dispiriting analysis of the present prompts Alice to take up a familiar philosophical-cum-literary theme which had appealed to critics of modernity since at least the days of Rousseau, and which had become a veritable institution in nineteenth-century Germany – the theme of nostalgic philhellenism:

Our existence affords a striking contrast to the old life of Greece where the citizens lived untroubled by the problems which assail us, where thoughts concerning the education and raising of the masses had no place. There[,] presence and urgency seemed hardly to belong to the clear days steeped in sunshine when the townsmen, spending a great portion of their lives out of doors, strolled and conversed, 'ever delicately walking in most perfect air', and transferring their worship from sculpture to painting, from painting to the drama, and so back to sculpture. Then, (in intervals of political peace) one of their most stirring events would have been a new play given in the open air, when the glorious thoughts and marvellous words of their great poets mingled in an intoxicating rapture of sunlight and blue heavens.[21]

These sentences, despite their reliance on commonplaces of sentiment and style, are the most eloquent passage of the whole essay. They function as the keynote, sounding a lament for political innocence and the dignity of art with which the rest of the work tries to come to terms. Alice does not altogether give way to despair, however, for, 'in the midst of our hurried life and massive incomprehension of lofty art, we must remember with joy and astonishment that there is an ideal side even to this age, weary, worn out and sordid as it seems in many respects'. She explains that 'above all this endeavour to attain luxury in the most practical manner, the Ideal is still manifested in art. It is one of the glories of the time and a hope of salvation amongst the darker aspects of the age that this is true, though alas! Its influence is far from all pervading.'[22] She seeks the contemporary ideal in the paintings of Edward Burne-Jones and George Frederick Watts, in novels by John Henry Shorthouse and Mrs Humphrey Ward and in the music of Brahms and Max Bruch.

Alice's concept of the ideal in art strongly suggests the influence of German aesthetics. She was familiar with German culture and a fluent speaker and reader of the language (one friend observed that she was probably more comfortable in Munich than in many places at home).[23] Hegel's system of Absolute Idealism (a phrase to which Alice makes passing reference) is the most obvious context, although she does not appear to work within Hegel's system. A more likely model for Alice's essay can be found in the aesthetic writings of Schiller, whose ideas became a touchstone for thinking on the arts in later German culture. In *On the Aesthetic Education of Mankind* (1795), written in the wake of the Terror following the French Revolution, Schiller addressed the pressing question of how to be free in the modern world. The advances of latter-day civilisation, he complained, driven by the utilitarian interests of science and the state, had split human nature, dividing sense from intellect and mind from matter, and forcing the individual into specialisation in work and education.

Modern life can be compared unfavourably with that of ancient Greece, where, according to Schiller, humanity had been at one with nature and with itself. The only way for humanity to reclaim its wholeness and freedom is first to become aesthetic, that is, for individuals to strive to realise the ideal inner human being that lies dormant within them. This self-fashioning is an 'art of the Ideal' – an art which 'must abandon actuality, and soar with becoming boldness above our wants and needs'.[24] The critic Constantin Behler refers to Schiller's outlook as 'nostalgic teleology': the positing of an idealised past and an alienated present along with the goal of a future synthetic third stage in which the original state is recaptured but in some heightened form.[25] Schiller's term 'ideal' is the adjectival form of 'idea', used substantively and referring to the realm of Ideas in a Platonic sense, that is, an unchanging, supersensuous reality in contrast to the world known empirically. Schiller often uses 'ideal' interchangeably with 'noble' or 'ennobling', indicating the state of those who take steps towards the realisation of the ideal within themselves. Thus 'ennobling' refers primarily to the achievement of a state of universality.[26] Alice Elgar likewise treats these terms practically as synonyms: for her, 'ideal' 'noble', 'lofty', 'sublime' and 'elevated' mean much the same and can reinforce one another for rhetorical effect when necessary.[27]

Alice discerns two painters of what she calls the 'absolutely ideal' in the late nineteenth century: Edward Burne-Jones and George Frederick Watts (Rosetti is discounted after consideration). She discusses five works by the former and four by the latter. She introduces them with a vivid analogy for the difference in effect of the real and the ideal: 'Step for a moment aside out of the roar and hurry of London streets full of the excitement and anxiety of life; – enter a quiet gallery. A magic presence seems to banish the noise and rush of town from the mind and excitement and anxiety fade as a refreshing touch seems to reach the jaded spirit.'[28] She begins her inspection of this imaginary gallery by considering Burne-Jones's celebrated painting *The Golden Stairs* (1872–80), observing that 'the picture represents no love story, no legend of any age, you are lifted into a world of pure imagination, the maidens are rapt and content in their own existence, fulfilling some law unknown to us – we know not whence they come or whither they go'.[29] She quotes verses of her own composition dating from a viewing of the painting in 1880:

> In other world than thine we dwell
> And morn and eve our praises swell
> As climbing slow the amber stair
> We reach a pure serener air.

> But not for thee to know our life
> Where sheltered well from heat and strife
> We pass adown the Golden Stair
> Nor time nor age can touch us there.[30]

The picture reveals to Alice that there is 'a world beyond the dusty present', and proves that the viewer can be transported there for a while. She concludes that 'We must leave them, grey-cloaked, pensive and serene, but in our minds remains a pure streak of golden sun beam, a glimpse of ideal ministry to the inner Ideal of the good and beautiful which lies dormant in the souls of every one of us'.[31] The 'inner Ideal of the good and beautiful' recalls the Greek concept of *kalokagathia*, the unity of moral and physical beauty in the human being. Under the influence of Schiller and his late eighteenth-century contemporaries, the realisation of this ideal (or rather, a certain interpretation of it) in each individual later became an important part of the self-identity of the German cultural elite.[32]

Alice next discusses Burne-Jones's *The Days of Creation* (1877); *Chant d'Amour* (1868–73); *Love Among the Ruins* (1894); and *Hesperus: The Evening Star* (1870), using a similar vocabulary and tone. When she moves on to Watts, Alice intensifies her rhetoric, declaring:

The whole aim of the work of this great master seems stretching after, and pointing to, an Ideal, vast and sublime, yet tempered with the grace and beauty and touching subjects, in most instances, so near our human hearts and souls that they can dwell in our thoughts and leaven the dull and narrowed atmosphere which only too often heightens its hold upon us.[33]

Watts, though well known for his portraits of Victorian luminaries, produced many symbolist paintings with titles such as *Love and Death, Life, Death and Judgement, Love and Life*, and *Hope*, in which allegorical figures are portrayed in dramatic situations. Alice discusses the latter pair. In *Love and Life* (Fig. 3.1), for instance, she discerns 'the ideal of Love in its best and highest influence, saving, leading and raising its fellow soul through the difficulties and over the stony and steep paths of the world.'[34] Both the picture and Alice's commentary suggest the scaling of Mount Purgatory. In fact, her writing in this essay frequently refers to ascending paths, difficult journeys under the guidance of an escort, and the search for the pure air of Idealism. In this analogy, the sin to be purged by the ascent is the tendency to cling to realism and materialism. The essay is prefaced by a quotation from the *Purgatorio*:

> The high heavens call you and about you wheel,
> Showing eternal beauties to invite you;
> But all you see's the earth beneath your heel.[35]

Fig. 3.1 George Frederick Watts, *Love and Life* (1893; oil on canvas)

Alice thereby exhorts her nineteenth-century contemporaries to turn their gaze upwards – a task that is eased with the help of artists such as Watts.

Alice deals more swiftly with literature – or seems to, since pages appear to be missing from that section of the essay. The main trends in English literature of recent decades fill her with indignant rage: 'Never it will be said, has such a wide stream of unwholesome, loathsome, impurities been poured out, glossed over as the work of a new art and with a new prefix to the indispensable "ism".' Only the now little-remembered Henry Shorthouse, author of *John Inglesant* (1881) and *Sir Percival* (1886), along with Mrs Humphrey Ward, author of *Robert Elsmere* (1888), receive commendation, the latter with reservations on account of her book's questioning of traditional Christianity.

When she turns to music Alice makes a passionate case for absolute music. Her prose now starts to sound similar to that of Hubert Parry, who, in his prolific writings and lectures, championed the cause of German abstract instrumental music, especially Beethoven and Brahms. For Parry, terms such as 'noble', 'exalted', 'purifying' and even 'ideal' were common currency.[36] Alice claims that the art of music has recently entered a new phase, following the example of Beethoven, who nevertheless remains unsurpassed.

Music's exponents have attempted to attain spheres hitherto undreamed of & to express feelings, thoughts & passions & to portray histories & tragedies of life in an entirely new method. This new direction, however immensely expanded in our own days, cannot be said to date from our own age but was inaugurated by Beethoven. But instead of a rapid progression in the direction of the Ideal, we may say that nothing so nearly approaching it has been written as his C minor Symphony. The music working through successive phases of beauty to the inspired climax in which all personal longings & passions are forgotten in the vast enthusiasm of reconciled & rejoicing humanity.[37]

The ideal does not reign supreme in the new world of music, however; opera and programme music are far removed from it. Nevertheless, Alice singles out two contemporary composers for praise: Brahms and Bruch. Once again she deploys the image of the purgatorial ascent:

Brahms attains to a pure intellectuality based on no romance nor calling in the aid of any of the scenes which might be called from the world around us. We are led into a region of pure and abstract thought. Into the same region are we led also by the noble, inspiring strains of Max Bruch to a sphere in which everything ignoble must be lost to sight and the soul can be steeped & strengthened anew for its onward journey.[38]

This is the Romantic aesthetic of absolute music given an overtly moral twist. In strong versions of that aesthetic, the finest music is absolute both in the sense of being wordless and in the sense that to its hearers it opens the realm of the infinite.[39] To Alice Elgar, this revelation is at the same time a process of purification and ennoblement.

The conclusion to the essay is a disappointment: an overwritten tirade against the modern age and the masses which shows Alice in an unflattering light.[40] And, to be sure, the whole essay could be dismissed as the reflections of an earnest, upper-class, but newly impoverished Victorian lady who was attached to old forms of propriety and resented 'new money' and the aspiration to acquire it ('wild efforts to clutch the gold'). Martin Wiener would know exactly what to make of her longing for the vanishing ideal, and would lament the fact that so many of her contemporaries and successors felt its siren call, especially those who wielded the new money themselves. On the other hand, Alice's trenchant views have their appealing aspects. Her sense of a shining ideal existing beyond the petty concerns of the present more than likely contributed to her desire to marry Elgar, thereby precipitating her financial disinheritance in the first place – surely an impulse that could appropriately be called 'noble', and one that few women in her position would have countenanced, let alone carried through. And her nostalgia is not wholly an escapist fantasy, for her robust criticism of the present is complemented by the conviction that traces of the ideal remain and can be recaptured by genius.

The extent to which Alice's attitudes overlapped with her husband's is of course another matter. There seems no doubt that Elgar was emotionally and intellectually drawn to the ideas articulated in her essay, partly on account of the dignity they confer on the art of music. His enthusiasm is most apparent in some of his grand public statements – statements such as public lectures and overtly public musical utterances. He ended his inaugural lecture as Professor of Music at the University of Birmingham with a call for the students to adopt 'a higher ideal', and cited E. T. A. Hoffman at length – one of the best-known purveyors of the notion of absolute music:

'We speak a loftier language than mere human speech, in the wondrous accents of Music.'

'It is as if we mortals were wafted upward in some condition of mystic consecration, on the pinions of the tones of the golden harps of the Cherubim and Seraphim, to the realms of light, where we learn the mystery of our existence.'[41]

(He followed up these sentences with several more in the same vein.) Later in his lectures, Elgar boldly championed the causes of absolute music and the symphony. Here, perhaps, his enthusiasm was misplaced, for his remarks embroiled him in controversy and a messy public debate, and were at odds with his own compositional practice at that stage of his career (1905). Among his works, the First Symphony, which self-consciously aspires to advance the German symphonic tradition in its most heroic manner, seems to realise something of Alice's aesthetic. On its completion she called it 'noble and beautiful'.[42] Elgar drew on a similar vocabulary – albeit reluctantly – when he told Ernest Newman, 'the opening theme is intended to be simple &, in intention, noble and elevating (I do hate to attempt to describe what I feel): the sort of *ideal* call – in the sense of persuasion, not coercion or command – & something above the everyday & sordid things.'[43] The 'ideal call' suggests the vocation of one of the Grail knights so beloved of Victorian poets and painters, while 'everyday and sordid things' sounds like Alice's 'present'. A little later Elgar wrote to Walford Davies, 'There is no programme beyond a wide experience of human life with a great charity (love) & a *massive* hope in the future.'[44] By restricting the programmatic element to the portrayal of this subset of the cardinal virtues, Elgar calls to mind the titles of Watts's symbolist pictures. Indeed it is tempting to imagine the motto theme of the symphony in the role of Love in Watts's *Love and Life*, coaxing the soul upwards and away from the vain materialist strivings of the main themes of the outer movements. The manner in which the motto theme returns during those outer movements – softly but firmly interrupting the unfolding of energetic sonata-like forms – recalls Alice's literary conceit of inviting the reader to step into a quiet gallery from a busy London street. In this view, the highly chromatic, rhythmically turbulent, brilliantly orchestrated material of the fast sections evokes a modern musical 'present', which presses to the future in a way similar to Alice's 'eager crowd . . . surging onwards'. Against that musical present, the motto's diatonic harmony, periodic phrase structure, and suggestions of species counterpoint patterns could be understood as the memory of some older set of values, now facing a challenge but not yet vanquished. (In the symphony, those old values finally triumph.)

However, despite these connections, Elgar's compositional practice reaches beyond the scope of his wife's aesthetics in important ways. First, in Alice's essay (as far as it goes), the ideal and the real are antithetical principles which remain unmediated. By contrast, Elgar's noble idiom is intimately connected with the physical motions of pacing and gesture, and is thus well positioned to accomplish precisely that mediation. Secondly, and related to the first point, nobility for Alice almost always refers to a positive frame of mind. The ideal leads onwards and upwards: there is no place for the dying fall so essential to Elgar's expressive world. As a shining beacon glimpsed from the forsaken world of the present, the ideal seems untouched by sorrow or resignation. (Whatever Alice's debt to Schiller, she seems not to have been drawn to his distinction between the 'naïve' and the 'sentimental', which might have led her in interesting directions.) Ironically, then, Alice's position has something in common with those of Elgar's post-war critics, despite their opposing judgements on his music, for all are inclined to read nobility 'straight' – a reading which, at its best, Elgar's art eludes.

It is not easy to gauge Alice's reaction to Elgar's finest compositions (which post-date 'The Ideal in the Present'), since most of the surviving evidence is found in her diary entries, which are too brief to permit extended commentary. However, the few glimpses that are available do not suggest a substantial reorientation in her aesthetic values. For instance, a diary entry penned when her husband's Second Symphony was nearing completion hints at a sorrowful response to the music's 'sublime' qualities, but then makes what seems today a curiously trite evaluation of the work's conclusion. 'It is really sublime – no one with any feeling c[oul]d hear it without an inward sob – It resumes our human life, delight, regret, farewell, the saddest word & then the strong man's triumph.'[45] Elgar's own description of the symphony for Alfred Littleton (discussed in Chapter 2) echoes these words in its emphasis on nobility, yet leaves open the possibility of a negative interpretation of the end of the finale rather than foreclosing it, as Alice's does. To be sure, her verdict (like her response to the First Symphony cited above) was written before she had heard the work in orchestral performance. But if anything that fact emphasises the sense in which her words constitute a formulaic reaction, partly preordained by her aesthetic viewpoint. Rosa Burley's description of Alice's behaviour when the symphony was played confirms this impression: 'At the first performance I sat with Alice, whose rather exaggerated appreciation of Edward's work, expressed in sighs, shakings of the head and appealing looks, tended to disturb one's own response to the music.'[46]

NEGATIVE NOBILITY

'Heroic melancholy' (W. B. Yeats), 'noble resignation' (Anthony Payne), 'stately sorrow' (Ernest Newman, after Elgar himself), 'crippled splendour' (Peter J. Pirie): such near-oxymorons seem to gather around Elgar's music and capture something salient about the way that people have come to hear his expressive idiom.[47] They form part of a broader discourse, familiar to anyone conversant with literature on Elgar in the later twentieth century, according to which his music intones 'the funeral march of a civilisation', sounds 'a note of recessional', captures a 'sunset quality', or conveys the equivalent of Edward Grey's famous utterance on the eve of the Great War: 'the lamps are going out all over Europe; we shall not see them lit again in our lifetime'. (The most eloquent advocates of this view are Ernest Newman, J. B. Priestley and Michael Kennedy.)[48] Elgarian nobility is thereby subsumed within the category of the elegiac and the accusation of complacency is easily met. This strategy of attributing a negative aspect to nobility – hearing it somehow undermined even as it is affirmed – is attractive to modern listeners sympathetic to Elgar and today is virtually received wisdom.

The popularity of the idea doubtless owes something to the political conditions of post-colonial Britain, yet its application to Elgar is hardly anachronistic. The Victorian interest in chivalry was multifaceted, and not all of its manifestations were prescriptive or patrician. (After all, two of its main advocates, Charles Kingsley and John Ruskin, were, in their different ways, socialists.) Indeed the cult included an influential strand, exemplified by Tennyson's *Idylls of the King*, according to which practically all knights were melancholy, all noble ideals doomed, and Arthur's passage to Avalon inevitable. Decline from grandeur was a theme familiar to all Victorians who knew Edward Gibbon's *Decline and Fall of the Roman Empire*, and found new expression in the nineteenth-century interest in Venice and its allegedly melancholy condition – epitomised by Turner's paintings and Ruskin's *The Stones of Venice*. Venice in its heyday had been worryingly similar to contemporary England – an independent, mercantile, naval empire, fiercely protective of its island identity – yet had succumbed to foreign domination, leaving its artistic and architectural wonders to convey to the modern viewer only a pale reflection of its former glories. In this way of thinking, chivalry was invoked not in a spirit of facile affirmation, but in order to express an unhealable alienation from the present. A longing for lost nobility or grandeur could help to outline a contemporary sense of belatedness, disillusion or unease.

There are a host of ways in which Elgar's 'chivalrous rhetoric' can be subtly distorted or destabilised, and it would be tedious to catalogue them in full. Anthony Payne pointed to the 4–3 appoggiaturas that saturate Elgar's music, especially within 6 or 6/5 harmonies. He finds that these sighing figures 'embody resignation in the face of ... decay'. Moreover Elgar's favourite instrumental combination of horns, bassoons and clarinets in their low register gives a 'hollow ring', especially when 'the timbres are constantly added and subtracted from the melodic line to work directly on the nerves' ends'. When this happens in the second movement of the Second Symphony, 'ceremony is transcended'.[49] Payne, Kennedy and others have drawn attention to the process of 'withdrawal' that often follows climaxes in Elgar's symphonic works – a tendency that was noted in Chapter 2 and will be discussed at greater length in Chapter 6. In such cases – the second movement of the Second Symphony could be cited again – the tender introspection of the 'withdrawn' music tends retrospectively to sap the climax of its positive value. Finally, Elgar's noble idiom usually is based on diatonicism, and his diatonic writing in general paradoxically derives much of its characteristic tone from infiltration by elements that would normally be deemed chromatic, chiefly the diatonic augmented fourth. When a diatonic passage reaches a 6/3 chord with an augmented fourth or a diatonic half-diminished seventh chord, the moment is frequently milked for its expressive potential by means of dynamics, texture, pauses or other means of emphasis. The mood conveyed by this 'inflected diatonicism' is usually double-edged in some way, and it can be effectively combined with the flourishes of Elgar's chivalrous rhetoric.[50] The characteristic progressions involving the diatonic augmented fourth may also serve an apparently self-conscious process of allusion, suggesting memories of parallel instances throughout Elgar's oeuvre. An example of inflected diatonicism is the sweeping lyrical theme from the orchestral prelude to *The Music Makers*, which presents a largely diatonic sequence of courtly bows that rises by step in a long crescendo before pausing on a diatonic half-diminished seventh chord (Ex. 3.2). The tension of the augmented fourth is resolved via a 4–3 appoggiatura and the melodic line plunges down again. The heroic aspiration of the sequence thus dissolves and fades almost before it reaches fulfilment. This is fitting music for the lonely music makers, the 'movers and shakers / Of the world forever', who nevertheless find no reward in the present, but 'dwell, in our dreaming and singing, / A little apart from ye'.

The partial undermining of Elgar's noble idiom is perhaps most subtly achieved in the two symphonies. The coda to the Adagio of the First Symphony (1908) is a good example, and one which brings into focus the role of nobility in mediating between musical versions of the real and the ideal. For the circle of German and German-orientated musicians amongst whom Elgar moved during the 1900s, adagio movements in a post-Beethovenian manner, and symphonic adagio movements above all, represented music in its highest state. (Hans Richter and A. J. Jaeger both eulogised the Adagio of the First Symphony with reference to Beethoven.)[51]

Ex. 3.2 *The Music Makers*, fig. 2: 1–12

It is interesting, then, to examine the way the coda transforms the work's motto theme – its 'ideal call'. The motto replicates the gentle dip and sudden leap of the extracts in Ex. 3.1, but without their rhythmic flourishes. This could be considered a semi-idealised version of Elgar's favourite chivalrous gesture (only semi-idealised because the marching bass retains a tenuous link with a 'reality principle'). The motto's two-part counterpoint is almost uniformly diatonic, but contains two notable augmented fourths, one sounding between the two parts, the other emerging from an implicit multi-voice texture outlined by the bass (Ex. 3.3(i) and (ii) respectively). Both progressions are commonplaces of Elgar's style.[52] The second is emphasised through a slight dynamic swell, but the first is left for the moment unarticulated either by dynamics, spacing of the parts or any other obvious parameters. This means that the realisation of its full expressive potential can be saved for later – and that occurs in the coda of the Adagio. The motto now undergoes a transformation. The tempo is slower; the marching bass is absent and the metre is unstressed; the texture is fuller and is no longer based on two-part counterpoint. The third note of the melody is transposed up an octave and the fourth note rises by step rather than falling – a catch of the breath. Yet the correspondence with the underlying voice-leading of the opening of the motto is unmistakable (compare the outer parts in each case). The motto's third note is now supported by a widely spaced II^7 chord, and its octave transposition means that the sonority is approached via a rising seventh (Ex. 3.3(iii)). Again both

(i) I, bars 3–4

(ii) I, fig. I: 4–7

(iii) III, fig. 104: 1–2

(iv) III, fig. 104: 5
Ex. 3.3 Symphony No. 1

features are Elgarian fingerprints.[53] The motto's first augmented fourth is now absent (the seventh of the II[7] formation resolving upwards to an octave rather than downwards to a sixth). Yet to a listener experienced in Elgar's diatonic idiom and attentive to the rest of the symphony that unstable interval still sounds in the voice-leading 'background': the notes that are present seem like a deformation of a more basic model. The second augmented fourth is more decisively articulated by means of a pause and hairpin dynamics (Ex. 3.3(iv)). A 9–7 voice exchange means that the augmented fourth sounds first in the outermost parts, then between the two lowest parts. In this rapt, intense music, the transformation of the motto gives the impression of a discovery of hidden emotional depths in material that had seemed familiar. This is a second stage in the idealisation of Elgar's noble idiom: both courtly gestures and march rhythms are dissolved so that the 'motions' suggested by the music are inward ones. The new version of the motto gives the music a chance to break free, as it were, from its lingering shackles in material reality (a freedom vividly conveyed through the orchestration), yet that freedom is at the same time a turn to introspection and sadness.[54]

James Hepokoski has written with reference to Elgar's symphonies that

> In this valedictory world the magnificent, *fortissimo* moments of attainment and affirmation seem simultaneously to be melting away, and Elgar often shores up such moments with rises and underswells in unexpected places, as if he were trying to sustain an illusion forever slipping away from his grasp. In such an environment of dissolution, diminuendos and simple descending sequences can take on enormous expressive significance.[55]

In the Second Symphony, the dissolution that Hepokoski senses reaches its final phase near the end of the finale with an especially subtle use of a diatonic augmented fourth progression (Ex. 3.4). Instead of being articulated by means of increased dynamics or instrumental forces, the progression marks the moment of greatest withdrawal in a phase of waning energy after a great climax. That climax (fig. 165 + 8) follows what might be termed a long 'processional' section in the recapitulation deploying all the resources of Elgar's chivalrous rhetoric: leaping and flourishing motifs, diatonic harmony, a steady marching bass and conspicuous brass. The descending sequences that follow, which employ no less than eight

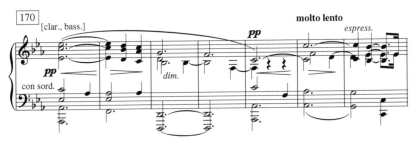

Ex. 3.4 Symphony No. 2, IV, fig. 170: 1–7

4–3 appoggiaturas, begin an answering 'recessional', which, as noted in Chapter 2, spills into the coda. When the 'spirit of delight' motto returns – in elegiac mood and lush orchestral colours (fig. 168) – its first statement takes a harmonic course familiar from the first movement: a D♭ draws the music towards subdominant harmony. The hushed final statement receives a very different treatment, however. Woodwind instruments gradually drop out of the texture, leaving only muted strings holding a diatonic 6/3 chord which swells slightly before dying back – another sigh. A D♮ is now softly introduced. For the first time in the work, the subdominant tendencies of the motto (represented by D♭) are directly contradicted; the D♮ helps to fix the music in the tonic in advance of the final cadence. But it simultaneously implies the very same harmonic progression encountered in Ex. 3.2 and in Ex. 3.3(ii) and (iv), the D♮ supplying the requisite augmented fourth. Thus, for the experienced listener, the belated harmonic straightening of the motto within a diatonic E♭ major is drained of any sense of affirmation by a flood of memories of other unsteady passages of inflected diatonicism in Elgar's music. There are further aspects that lend a quality of negation to this moment: it is the point of greatest enervation in the dynamic trajectory of the movement and of maximum motivic dissolution in the coda. During the 'sigh', musical time, which for most of the movement has been divided by a regular pulse and by repetitive rhythmic patterns and sequences, seems for once to stand still. The augmented fourth progression is presented as a pure voice-leading pattern, without melodic elaboration. Thereafter, thematic definition is re-established only haltingly by means of a hushed repetition of the descending sequence that began the recessional, now played *molto lento* on muted strings. As in the Adagio of the First Symphony, then, the material aspect of nobility is negated; here, though, it is simply dissolved rather than transformed. Neither Elgar nor his wife did justice to this entropic process with their verbal accounts of the finale of the symphony. Alice at best touched a note of elevated calm in the manner of Wordsworth (appropriate enough for the recollections of the spirit of delight, along the lines argued in Chapter 2), but she would or could not evoke in words Hepokoski's 'environment of dissolution' or the coda's negation of the earlier processional music.

For the most part these examples from the symphonies capture well Elgar's mature treatment of nobility, which mediates between certain concepts of the real and the ideal and, more broadly, between his wife's positive aesthetic and a melancholy Tennysonian fatalism. He never ventures as far as a direct critique of nobility – through irony, for instance. Still, there is one work where the idea of nobility comes perilously close to unravelling: *Falstaff*. In this 'symphonic study', noble elements usually bring with them some form of their own negation, and in the course of the work nobility differentiates itself into two distinct and incompatible forms, the one calculated to enlist pity, the other, at best, grudging respect.

At the outset, Falstaff and Prince Hal are companions in revelry and adventure, even conspiring in an absurd heist. Later they split apart in person and in outlook, Hal rejecting Falstaff and embracing the duty and responsibility of kingship, Falstaff falling into undignified decline and death. But it would be a mistake to view Hal's mode of nobility as authentic and Falstaff's as reprobate: Elgar was adamant that Falstaff should be regarded neither as a buffoon nor a rascal.[56] He wholeheartedly endorsed the account of the character by the eighteenth-century critic Maurice Morgann, who found Falstaff fraught with intriguing paradoxes: 'He is a character made up by Shakespeare wholly of incongruities; – a man at once young and old, enterprising and fat, a dupe and a wit, harmless and wicked, weak in principle and resolute by constitution, cowardly in appearance and brave in reality; a knave without malice, a liar without deceit; and a knight, a gentleman and a soldier, without either dignity, decency or honour.'[57] 'A knight, a gentleman and a soldier. That's it,' Elgar told his friend and biographer Basil Maine.[58] He also pointed to a judgement by Kenneth Deighton, Victorian editor of the Henry IV plays:

He had been page to the Duke of Norfolk, a fact which certifies to his respectability of position and inferentially to his possessing the instincts of a gentleman; had associated with John of Gaunt, who certainly would have had nothing to do with a poltroon; had served for many years in the army and earned knighthood, then a purely military title ... takes his soldiers into the thick of the fight where they are soundly peppered, and he himself must have been in great danger, earns from the Prince who supposed him to be dead, a tribute of regret he would hardly have bestowed on one whose cowardice he despised.[59]

The views of Morgann and Deighton may be contestable as Shakespeare criticism, but Elgar was convinced by them. Moreover, on this basis he described Falstaff as 'one of the most truly English characters ever created' – a remark that, on Elgar' lips, must be taken as a tribute.[60] Perhaps the point is that while Falstaff possesses all the impulses of a genuinely noble character, the defects that inevitably accompany those impulses are, in him, overt. In this sense, Falstaff's is a more truthful nobility than that finally practised by Prince Hal, which enforces the order of outward appearances and denies the secret, uproarious past that he shared with Falstaff.

The work employs chivalrous rhetoric sparingly – Prince Hal's 'courtly and genial' theme (Ex. 3.1(iv)) is a relatively isolated instance. The marking *nobilmente* is absent from the score, and even the note of heroic melancholy is seldom struck. The only instance of inflected diatonicism occurs in the first 'dream interlude' (Ex. 3.5), as Falstaff, in a drunken stupor, dreams of his youth as page to the Duke of Norfolk – 'the courtly period of his youth', as Elgar's commentary on the work has it.[61] This much-discussed passage presents an oasis of diatonic A minor/C major that contrasts with the restless, shifting chromaticism of much of the rest of the work. Elgar wrote that, 'simple in form and somewhat antiquated in mood, it suggests in its strong contrast to the immediately preceding riot, "what might have been" '.[62] The rhythm of the dream interlude's tune, as Aidan Thomson points out, suggests a kind of gavotte.[63] Courtly gestures are in evidence, but their motions are modest and reserved, lacking the ostentatious flourishes that characterise, for instance, the melodic lines in Ex. 3.1. The old man thus attributes a pure form of nobility to his youthful self – an ideal which, as an adult, he has failed to realise. Diatonic augmented fourths and diminished fifths are highlighted in the widely spread 6/3 chords for the harp (Ex. 3.5(i)) and later in descending melodic figures in the violins and cellos (Ex. 3.5(ii)). But these inflections suggest regret on the part of the

(i) fig. 77: 1–5

(ii) fig. 78: 5–6
Ex. 3.5 *Falstaff*, first 'dream interlude'

dreamer rather than any intimation of melancholy in the page. The image of nobility purified only in dream and memory can be compared with a moment from Falstaff's death scene, when Prince Hal's courtly theme is recalled sweetly, softly and slowly. This recollection makes a sharp contrast with the rest of Hal's music during the second half of the work, which is strident and at times militaristic. At figure 127, for instance, even the courtly theme is blared out *fff grandioso*, with brass prominent. By the end, as Elgar puts it, 'the man of stern reality has triumphed'.[64] What is to be called noble in the new 'reality' of King Henry's reign is presented as distinctly unappealing, perhaps violent. In both of Falstaff's recollections, by contrast, the idealised nobility is palpably *un*real. Yet the symphonic study can hardly be said to unfold a rejection of present reality in favour of the ideal in the fashion of Alice Elgar's writings. Falstaff's recollections stand in ironic contrast to his degraded physical condition on each occasion; he is in no position to realise the imagined ideal within himself. Nobility has here lost its power of mediation; it splits into the mutually exclusive forms of authoritarian display and passive escapism. Although the dream interlude is a beautiful section of the work and Elgar's sympathies clearly lie with Falstaff, the fact remains that both options are unpalatable.

Falstaff was not the first of Elgar's works in which a rupture between inner and outer worlds deepens in the closing stages, as Chapter 2 illustrated. But the close identification of that rupture with the theme of nobility was novel. Basil Maine, to whom Elgar confided his ideas on the character of Falstaff at some length, concluded his account of their discussions by referring to what he called 'the growing scepticism of Elgar's attitude to life'. According to Maine 'it is one of the many contradictions that are to be discerned in his character, that this scepticism exists in him together with an intense and noble idealism. The problem is to discover which of the two is the more deeply rooted.'[65] *Falstaff* is exceptional for its frank exploration of that contradiction; Elgar attempted nothing comparable thereafter.

FAITH AND RUIN

In the light of these analyses it may be useful to return to the post-war criticism of Elgarian nobility. Most of the comments cited in that connection (by Sitwell, Lambert, Gray and Dent) can be read outside any broader context without greatly distorting their meaning. Siegfried Sassoon's account of Elgar is different. Read on its own, his unflattering sketch of the 'Great Gentleman' is an uncomplicated piece of 1920s anti-Victorianism by one who could attack the values of the older generation from a position of moral authority. Yet Sassoon was in fact a passionate lover of Elgar's music, who responded to it in verse. The keyword for understanding his attitude to Elgar is the qualifying term 'outwardly' ('Elgar is, outwardly, a retired army officer of the conventional Victorian type'). For, having known the music for some years – *The Apostles* and the Violin Concerto being his particular favourites – Sassoon was puzzled and disappointed when he finally encountered Elgar in person. The sarcasm of his diary entry is a reflection of that disappointment and of Sassoon's perception of the gap between Elgar's public persona of the 1920s and the artist who had created such moving compositions.

Sassoon returned to the theme of Elgar the man on several occasions in his diary during the early 1920s. In September 1921 he attended perform-ances of *Falstaff, The Apostles* and the Cello Concerto, but was appalled by what he saw as Elgar's shameless snubbing of Frank Schuster when the latter took Sassoon backstage after a concert. And when he encountered Elgar in person in a hotel lobby a few days later, he pondered 'Could this possibly be the man who composed that glorious work [*The Apostles*] – this smartly dressed 'military'-looking grey-haired man, with the carefully-trimmed moustache and curved nose?'[66] On that occasion Elgar was friendly with him, and Sassoon almost wished for that very reason never to speak to him again. But a year later, at Schuster's house, Elgar again disgraced himself in Sassoon's eyes. This time 'the Order of Merited composer who masquerades as a retired army officer of the country con-servative club type' was so upset at the suggestion that he might compose music for Queen Mary's Doll's House that he delivered 'a petulant tirade which culminated in a crescendo climax of rudeness aimed at Lady M[aud Warrender]'.[67] Once again, Sassoon found it hard to reconcile the behav-iour of the man with his own experience of a recent performance of *The Apostles*. Several months later he noted that Elgar was 'a disappointing man', always looking out for potential insults to himself.[68] In July 1924 Sassoon enjoyed being treated to Elgar playing the piano in Schuster's music room, and momentarily forgot 'the "other Elgar" who is just a type of "club bore" '. At lunch, the composer adopted his garrulous persona, and Sassoon felt that 'the real Elgar was left in the music room'.[69]

On 23 January 1917, while Sassoon was on sick leave from the war, he heard a performance of Elgar's Violin Concerto in Liverpool, and it prompted a poem. By this time Sassoon had long abandoned the unreflective patriotism with which he, like so many others, had entered the war, and had published poems attacking the sanitised picture of life at the front that was promoted at home and the platitudes uttered by the representatives of organised religion. In only six months' time he was to make his famous 'Soldier's Declaration', withdrawing his services and alleging that the war was being deliberately prolonged by politicians. But the concerto was a rare feature of civilian life at this time that did not elicit his scorn. Instead it drew his imagination back to his comrades at the front, telling a truth – surprising as it might seem – about their lives there. He explains: '*pp nobilmente* etc made me glorious with dreams to-night. Elgar always moves me deeply, because his is the melody of an average Englishman (and I suppose I am more or less the same).'[70] Sassoon quotes a snatch of music, possibly from fig. 94 of the concerto.[71] His thought continues with further unembarrassed reference to nobility, and leads to an extraordinary vision:

In all the noblest passages and the noblest strains of horns and violins I shut my eyes, seeing on the darkness a shape always the same – in spite of myself – the suffering mortal figure on a cross, but the face is my own. And again there are hosts of shadowy forms with uplifted arms – souls of men, agonised and aspiring, hungry for what they seek as God in vastness.[72]

The conception is not quite as egotistical as it might seem at first sight. The imagery of Calvary was common in First World War literature including that of Sassoon. Sometimes the ordinary soldier is portrayed as Christ-like; in other cases the roadside shrines and crucifixes that dotted Flanders and that made a deep impression on British troops are used for dramatic purposes. In Sassoon's 'Christ and the Soldier', for instance, a single private stops on his journey and holds a conversation with Christ. In his diary entry Sassoon may have been reflecting on his relationship with the men he commanded and their search for a replacement figurehead at which to direct their still lingering religious impulses ('what they seek *as* God in vastness'). After all, he had a reputation for outstanding bravery and was greatly admired. This interpretation finds resonance in the poem that follows, although here the sight of his own face is not implied:

THE ELGAR VIOLIN CONCERTO

I have seen Christ, when music wove
Exulting vision; storms of prayer
Deep-voiced within me marched and strove.
The sorrows of the world were there.

A God for beauty shamed and wronged?
A sign where faith and ruin meet,
In glooms of vanquished glory thronged
By spirits blinded with defeat?

His head forever bowed with pain,
In all my dreams he looms above
The violin that speaks in vain –
The crowned humility of love.

O music undeterred by death,
And darkness closing on your flame,
Christ whispers in your dying breath,
And haunts you with his tragic name.[73]

The poem points to a spiritual state induced by the war, a state in which religious aspirations, which have been heightened through suffering, yet deprived of old assurances of salvation, confusedly seek fulfilment. This is a region of 'vanquished glory' where 'faith and ruin meet'. Those who inhabit it are 'blinded' – perhaps with overtones of the literal blinding of soldiers by mustard gas, but with the metaphorical meaning of spiritual disorientation. The last two stanzas clarify the analogy between the figure of the suffering Christ and Sassoon's hearing of the music: both combine high spiritual values with a sense of doom. The music is strangely 'unde-terred' either by death or by the darkness that closes upon it, yet it has reached its 'dying breath' and the violin 'speaks in vain'. These Christ-like qualities are the reason why he 'haunts' it and why Sassoon's vision arises on hearing it. That vision is bleak, for the last word is with death – there is no mention of hope for resurrection or redemption.

Sassoon is strongly affected by the element of negativity that he hears in the concerto's nobility. Faith and ruin; glory and defeat; love and death; hopeless determination; these are the music's contradictory qualities. His description of them echoes not the scornful wit of his contemporaries Gray and Sitwell, but the nuanced responses to Elgar's music of Yeats, Payne, Newman, Pirie and Kennedy, who hear in his noble style an underlying strain of melancholy, unease or sorrow. At a historical moment that has been seen by subsequent generations as marking an epochal loss of inno-cence in modern Britain, Sassoon found something worth salvaging in Elgarian nobility.

CHAPTER 4

Nature

Of all the associations that have grown up around Elgar in the course of the twentieth century, perhaps the most securely established concerns nature and a sense of place. Biographies and popular literature on Elgar stress his love for the countryside, especially his native Worcestershire. There is a familiar Elgarian iconography based around the Malvern Hills, the view of Worcester Cathedral across the river Severn (used for the 1999 issue of the Bank of England £20 note), and the picturesque Elgar birthplace cottage at Broadheath. Book illustrations, CD booklet covers and television and radio programmes reinforce these references. Elgar enthusiasts frequently return to the issue, sometimes claiming to perceive Elgar's home landscape in the notes themselves. The group of artists calling themselves the 'Ruralists' (initially known as the 'Broadheath Brotherhood') take Elgar as one of their main sources of inspiration.[1] The topic of nature, then, is crucial to an understanding of the status and meaning of Elgar in twentieth- and twenty-first-century Britain – and in fact it looms large in all the remaining chapters of this book.

However, there are complications. On close inspection, the significance of nature for Elgar's music as opposed to his life can seem tenuous, to say the least. He deliberately refrained from aligning his work with the younger generation of English 'pastoral' composers, whose writings (and the titles of their compositions) thematise the country far more systematically than he ever did. And, whereas with a composer such as Vaughan Williams it is easy to point to rural signifiers in the scores – the melodic contours of folksong, for instance, or a solo violin imitating the song and flight of a lark – it has in practice proved much trickier to make a link between Elgar's personal attachment to nature and the actual fabric of his music (despite numerous attempts). When viewed soberly, the connection with nature threatens to dissolve into hopeful assertions that gain credibility only through constant repetition.

It would be plausible, then, to dismiss the topic as evidence of escapist tendencies within a largely urban society. This is a familiar story to tell about the role of the countryside in modern British culture.[2] Chapter 1 cited the historian Jeremy Crump, who issued a memorable warning against enthusiastic responses to Elgar from the suburban living room. Crump argues that it was only in the 1930s that Elgar's supposed 'Englishness' was defined by commentators in predominantly rural as opposed to ceremonial or other terms, and he implies that the association with nature must be explained with reference to the history and politics of that period rather than any intrinsic properties of the music. By the 1930s Elgar's links with militarism and imperialism had become embarrassing and were downplayed. Listeners disturbed by contemporary ills such as industrial strife and economic depression were comfortable with a pastoral Elgar, through whose music they could happily recollect the pre-war era as an idyll. 'In this guise,' Crump concludes, 'Elgar's music could provide a refuge for those whose nostalgia for the Edwardian years was essentially conservative.'[3] Furthermore, he points out that the modern 'canon' of Elgar masterpieces was first defined at this very time: a selection centred on the symphonic works and notably excluding the patriotic wartime music. In his view, the responses to Elgar of late twentieth-century listeners are a legacy of the inter-war period.

Crump's position must be taken seriously. That period witnessed a heightened popular consciousness of the English countryside and its supposedly enduring values. Public musical discourse frequently linked the music of native composers – not just Elgar – with landscape when attempting to establish its genuine Englishness.[4] And there is much at stake, for the ruralist impulses of the time were significantly politicised. The leaders of both political parties played on the theme, Elgar's Worcestershire countryman Stanley Baldwin with particular success. Baldwin's bucolic rhetoric ('England is the country and the country is England')[5] struck an emollient note that probably helped to keep the Conservatives in government for most of the inter-war period despite profound unrest in much of Britain. Although ruralism was certainly not confined to the Right, some 'preservationist' literature nevertheless echoed the body-worship and 'blood and soil' ideology of continental Fascism.[6] Indeed, the preoccupation with the countryside in this period resonates uncomfortably with the prevailing atmosphere of isolationism and insularity in the 1930s, and thus, ultimately, with the policy of appeasement towards Nazi Germany that the National Government adopted towards the end of the decade. The fact that Elgar's associations with nature and landscape gathered so much momentum in the 1930s gives them a faint air of disrepute.

But things are not quite as simple as Crump's argument would have them. Although certainly selective in regard to Elgar's life and work, the viewpoint of the 1930s cannot be reduced entirely to posthumous construction and illusion. The connection between Elgar and the landscape of Worcestershire had been established in interviews with Elgar from the late 1890s onwards, several of which opened with lyrical evocations of the landscape near his home in Malvern.[7] The composer was said to take inspiration directly from his surroundings. When he received an honorary doctorate from Cambridge University in 1900, the orator made much of these themes. Elgar's private letters are littered with self-conscious references to nature and landscape and their impact on his art, while his Inaugural Lecture as Professor of Music at the University of Birmingham in 1905 called for an 'out-of-door' spirit in English music.[8] Most subsequent writings on Elgar and nature preface themselves with quotations from these sources. The discourse was thus in place from an early stage of Elgar's public career, and ever since has shaped itself around his own verbal utterances.

The force and persistence of that discourse result not from any particular depth or coherence in what Elgar had to say about nature, but from *how* he said it. His statements are poetic in tone, yet sufficiently terse and epigrammatic to bear endless repetition in programme notes, radio broadcasts and popular literature. 'My idea is that there is music in the air, music all around us' he told an interviewer in 1896, 'the world is full of it ... and – you – simply – simply – take as much as you require!'[9] 'This is what I hear all day – the trees are singing my music, or have I sung theirs?' he pondered in a letter to A. J. Jaeger, quoting a snatch of the 'Woodland Interlude' from his cantata *Caractacus*.[10] Conversations and private communications such as these appear to expose the intimate sphere of the composer's imagination and cast light on the genesis of his music.

Elgar scholarship has responded by identifying and describing the locations associated with his works. Sometimes the connection is relatively straightforward. Herefordshire Beacon on the Malvern Hills first suggested *Caractacus*; it was then believed to be the site of the eponymous hero's preparations for his last stand against the Roman invaders. The woods around Birchwood Lodge, Elgar's summer cottage on the north side of the hills, were in his mind when composing the Woodland Interlude of Scene III. The Bavarian mountains and the Italian Riviera provided the stimulus for compositions with distinct 'picture-postcard' elements: *From the Bavarian Highlands* and *In the South*. More often, however, locations are significant for Elgar's music not as settings for action or objects for depiction but as sources of general inspiration or prompting. Many ideas for the oratorio *The Apostles* were conceived whilst sitting alone in the vicinity of Longdon Marsh in Worcestershire. As explained in Chapter 2, the 'Welsh tune' from the *Introduction and Allegro* stemmed from the composer's experience of hearing distant singing on holiday in Wales. And the late chamber music was stimulated by the country life that Elgar led in a cottage in Sussex that he rented for several summers after 1917. The identification of these cases, however, invites a further question. Did the landscapes merely set the creative juices flowing, or can we detect in the finished music the presence of an elusive *genius loci*?

Some Elgarians tend towards the latter. Elgar's friend the violinist W. H. Reed heard in some passages an 'indescribable something hidden in the sound somewhere that only Elgar, of all composers, could produce ... something imbibed in the air of the Malvern Hills and the countryside around his birthplace at Broadheath during his childhood'.[11] According to Diana McVeagh, a certain phrase from the third movement of the Second Symphony is 'one of those fragments that breathe the scent of Severnside to those who know it'.[12] (Notice, though, that she leaves open the possibility that the listener brings the association to the music rather than simply finding it there.) Michael Kennedy goes further. 'No technical analysis can discover for certain just how he took something from the air of the Malvern Hills, from the banks of the Teme and Severn, from the cloisters of Worcester Cathedral, and turned it into music which speaks immediately and directly of these things to his fellow-countrymen. Walk in Worcestershire and the music of Elgar is in the air around you, fantastic as this may seem to the prosaically minded.'[13] At least Kennedy recognises that his claim might seem far-fetched. By contrast, the author of a tourist guidebook to Elgar's favourite haunts states unequivocally that 'Elgar has done for Worcestershire what Constable did for Suffolk by reflecting so vividly in his work the landscape beauty of his "home" county'.[14] This kind of thinking has been given an air of respectability by the latest book on Elgar by Jerrold Northrop Moore which pursues a 'quest for the essential Elgar' and 'links the composer to the English landscape that informed all of his work from his earliest years'. 'In its pages Elgar is revealed for the first time [*sic*] as a pastoral visionary to set beside Shakespeare and Milton, Turner and Samuel Palmer.'[15]

Unfortunately these approaches tend to treat nature as unmediated, neglecting the long and complex history of the idea of 'nature' in human culture. This chapter therefore adopts a different perspective and asks a different set of questions. While rejecting the idea that nature in Elgar points unswervingly to a mid-twentieth-century Conservative ideology, it also avoids taking Elgar's statements at face value. To be sure, he may have believed the stories he told about himself to be true on some level and thought that his music embodied the spirit of certain places. But at the same time some of those stories clearly represent attempts to fashion a public or semi-public image, while others owe their existence to the literary games Elgar liked to play with correspondents.[16] An investigation of the manner in which he recounted those stories can lead to a richer concept of nature structuring both his music and latter-day responses to it. Many of Elgar's ostensibly biographical remarks function also as specific literary tropes that suggest a range of meanings in the context of Edwardian culture. Those meanings in turn derive from the Western pastoral tradition and from English Romanticism. In this chapter the enquiry is limited to those of his pronouncements that refer specifically to wind – among reeds, pine trees, and across the strings of an Aeolian harp. In each case, passages from Elgar's music can be identified in which the imitation of the sound of these winds – carefully positioned within the course of a movement or episode – serves some broader idea of nature. This approach by no means exhausts the possible meanings of nature in Elgar, but for the purposes of this book it usefully draws together his music, his words, some literary antecedents and some key themes in his reception in a way that lays the ground for later chapters.

THE RURAL PAN

Of all Elgar's recorded comments on nature, perhaps the most evocative is found in a letter of 1921 to his friend Sir Sidney Colvin. 'I am still at heart the dreamy child who used to be found in the reeds by Severn side with a sheet of paper trying to fix the sounds & longing for something very great – source, texture & all else unknown. I am still looking for This – in strange company sometimes – but as a child & as a young man & as a mature man, no single person was ever kind to me.'[17] The image of the child by the river has caught the imagination of Elgar's admirers: McVeagh counts the first words of the lines to Colvin as one of Elgar's utterances that 'everyone knows'.[18] Many books use it to frame their narratives or discussions. Kennedy put it at the very opening of the first chapter of his *Portrait of Elgar* (1968). Robert Anderson's *Master Musicians* volume on Elgar takes its epigraph from a poem by C. Day Lewis which begins 'A boy among the reeds on Severn shore' (the poem is discussed in Chapter 7). The Severn reedbeds opposite Worcester Cathedral, near Elgar's childhood home, are illustrated on the first page of the tourist guidebook mentioned above, with

Elgar's childhood memory quoted beneath. The book by Moore that claims Elgar to be a 'pastoral visionary' includes as its frontispiece a sketch entitled 'Elgar Dreaming Beside the River' by the Ruralist artist Graham Ovenden. Even the editors of the recent *Cambridge Companion to Elgar* use the letter to Colvin near the beginning of their Introduction to bring into focus some key issues in Elgar's life.[19] The dreamy child is a favourite image for literary works on Elgarian themes. In David Pownall's *Elgar's Rondo* (see Chapter 2), the ghost of Jaeger exhorts Elgar to abandon the trappings of worldly success and search within himself for the boy by the river, the source of his true inspiration.[20]

The story of the child at the riverbank has usually been taken as pointing to a historical truth, despite the many years that intervened before its telling; after all, as an adult Elgar was much given to riverside walks and outings. The tale can also be cited as a key to Elgar's character: it reflects the high-minded ideals he inherited from his mother ('longing for something very great') as well as the chip that he seems always to have had on his shoulder ('no single person was ever kind to me').[21] Yet the story's lasting fascination can best be explained through the way it brings together some venerable but still potent literary images. Elgar could have relied on his correspondent Colvin, a friend of the late Robert Louis Stevenson and a student of the English Romantic poets, to be alert to these resonances.[22]

By locating the early source of his own music in a bed of reeds, Elgar, whether consciously or otherwise, was invoking an ancient tradition of myth and speculation surrounding the question of the origin of music. The image of the wind blowing through reeds ultimately refers to the legend of Pan and Syrinx. Pan was said to have pursued the nymph to the banks of a river, whereupon she appealed in desperation to the gods, who took pity on her and turned her into a reed. In his frustration, Pan could only clasp the reeds in the bed in which she now stood, and as the wind blew through them he heard an echo of his own sorrow. So he constructed the 'pan-pipes' or 'syrinx' by binding together reeds of various lengths and continued the music himself. According to some versions of pastoral legend, Pan then bequeathed music to humanity by teaching Daphnis to play the pan-pipes.[23] Ancient writers who tried to take a more rigorous approach to the question of music's origin retained the motif of the reeds. Diodorus Siculus believed that music had been invented in Egypt, where people had imitated the sound of the wind in the reeds on the banks of the Nile. Lucretius likewise thought that human beings had first made music by imitating natural sounds, though he included bird calls along with the reeds.[24] When, in the seventeenth and eighteenth centuries, the origin of music again became a hotly debated issue, these classical sources were widely cited and discussed by such music historians and lexicographers as Athanasius Kircher, Jean-Jacques Rousseau and Sir John Hawkins.[25]

Rustling reeds had also long been a stock image of pastoral poetry. They represented the voice of a quasi-animate nature, which could alternatively be personified by Pan with his pipes. By the turn of the twentieth century, all kinds of English literature could invoke winds moving through reeds, trees and various other vegetation. Collections of verse appeared with titles like *Reeds Shaken with the Wind* and *The Wind in the Trees*. In 1899 W. B. Yeats published *The Wind among the Reeds*, and Kenneth Grahame had considered giving a similar title to the book that eventually became *The Wind in the Willows*.[26]

The figure of Pan captured the imaginations of the late Victorians and Edwardians. To be sure, many cultures have felt the tension between country and city life, with urban dwellers gripped by a yearning for a supposedly lost innocence and simplicity: that is partly why pastoral has been such an enduring literary genre. But by the late nineteenth century the beginnings of modern suburban sprawl and the realisation that the depopulation of the countryside was irreversible left English intellectuals with an acute awareness of this divide.[27] On one level, then, Pan symbolised a desire to escape progress and the urban, industrial future. On another, he promised spiritual relief from the Victorians' protracted religious controversies. His very name, usually taken to mean 'all things', matched the synthetic tendency of many Edwardian intellectuals, who valued unity, wholeness and relationship, and shunned division and dissolution. ('Only connect', as E. M. Forster put it.) And as a deity of fun, freedom, and the outdoors, Pan seemed the embodiment of favourite Edwardian pastimes such as sport, recreation, children's games and the Boy Scout movement.[28]

Literary manifestations of Pan were abundant and diverse.[29] Aubrey Beardsley emphasised Pan the rapacious faun, scourge of polite Victorian mores. In Arthur Machen's novella *The Great God Pan* (1894) and in short stories by Saki and E. M. Forster, Pan was the dreadful god of 'panic' who according to legend could cause armies to flee just by stamping his hoof.[30] In children's literature such as J. M. Barrie's play *Peter Pan* (1904) and Rudyard Kipling's *Puck of Pook's Hill* (1906), whimsical Pan-like figures stood somewhere between a child and a fairy. Above all, however, Pan was the god of the secluded riverbank, who might be sensed fleetingly by the solitary rambler. This was the vein of Kenneth Grahame's essays 'The Rural Pan' and 'The Lost Centaur', and especially of the seventh chapter of *The Wind in the Willows* (1908), 'The Piper at the Gates of Dawn'.[31]

Much of this literature, especially in the latter mode, sounded a note of lament even as it invoked magic, freedom, or the rural idyll. After all, the pagan Pan was said by Plutarch to have died at the moment of Jesus' birth. (In Christian iconography he had later become the devil.) To call on Pan was in part a nostalgic attempt to reconnect alienated, modern humanity with nature, to 're-enchant' the world and endow nature with personal significance, so that it seems to 'speak' once again.[32] As Oscar Wilde put it in his 'Double Villanelle' (1891):

> O Goat-foot God of Arcady!
> This modern world is grey and old,
> And what remains to us of Thee?
> [. . .]
> And dull and dead our Thames would be
> For here the winds are chill and cold,
> O Goat-foot God of Arcady!
> [. . .]
> Though many an unsung elegy
> Sleeps in the reeds our rivers hold,
> O Goat-foot God of Arcady!
> Ah, what remains to us of Thee?[33]

On this occasion the reeds withhold their music. A similarly melancholy mood is evoked by Charles Sims's painting *The Beautiful is Fled* (1900), in which a small faun sits huddled on a branch overhanging a river swollen by November floods, his pipes hanging silently beside him (cover illustration).

Not everyone despaired, though. In an influential essay entitled 'Pan's Pipes', Robert Louis Stevenson urged that 'Pan is not dead, but of all the classic hierarchy alone survives in triumph; goat-footed, with a gleeful and an angry look, the type of the shaggy world: and in every wood, if you go with a spirit properly prepared, you shall hear the note of his pipe'.[34] Science, Stevenson maintained, cannot wholly explain the reality of the experience of nature. Modern people, so many of whom live humdrum urban lives untouched by imagination, should strive to recapture the heady mixture of delight and terror that awaits them when they return to nature in the sense of obeying their instincts. Many Edwardians took this message to heart – especially in so far as it involved revelling in long walks and riverside jaunts. The experience was exemplified by Grahame, who put the emphasis on the delight of nature rather than its terror. In 'The Rural Pan', he described the god (and his human imitators) 'prone by the secluded stream'. In solitary backwaters, he 'sits and dabbles, and all the air is full of the music of his piping'. 'Remote in other haunts than these [London] the rural Pan is hiding, and piping the low, sweet strain that reaches only the ears of a chosen few.'[35]

It is perhaps in 'The Piper at the Gates of Dawn' that Grahame comes closest to the sentiments of Elgar's story of childhood. Here he infuses the sound of the reeds with something of the same sense of mystery, elusiveness and longing ('trying to fix the sounds and longing for something very great – source, texture and all else unknown'). In this chapter, intended as the spiritual heart of the book, the 'wind in the reeds' of the original title mingles with Pan's piping as, in his role as protector of animals, he guides the protagonists Rat and Mole to the lost son of their friend Otter. As dawn breaks, issuing in a hot summer's day, the pair, who have been up all night scouring the river, hear an imperious summons which must be obeyed:

A bird piped suddenly, and was still; and a light breeze sprang up and set the reeds and bulrushes rustling. Rat, who was in the stern of the boat, while Mole sculled, sat up suddenly and listened with a passionate intentness. Mole, who with gentle strokes was just keeping the boat moving while he scanned the banks with care, looked at him with curiosity.

'It's gone!' sighed the Rat, sinking back in his seat again. 'So beautiful and strange and new! Since it was to end so soon, I almost wish I had never heard it. For it has roused a longing in me that is pain, and nothing seems worth while but just to hear that sound once more and go on listening to it for ever. No! There it is again!' he cried, alert once more. Entranced, he was silent for a long space, spellbound.

'Now it passes on and I begin to lose it,' he said presently. 'O, Mole! The beauty of it! The merry bubble and joy, the thin, clear, happy call of the distant piping! Such music I never dreamed of, and the call in it is stronger even than the music is sweet! Row on, Mole, row! For the music and the call must be for us.'

The Mole, greatly wondering, obeyed. 'I hear nothing myself,' he said, 'but the wind playing in the reeds and rushes and osiers.'[36]

After Pan has revealed himself (a solemn passage couched in quasi-biblical language), he makes sure the animals forget their experience so that they remain carefree. The whole episode thus acquires a dreamlike quality. Yet, as they row home in the morning, with the young otter safely returned to his father, they hear once again the music of the reeds, ever-changing and impossible to pin down:

'hark to the wind playing in the reeds!'

'It's like music – far-away music,' said the Mole, nodding drowsily.

'So I was thinking,' murmured the Rat, dreamful and languid. 'Dance-music – the lilting sort that runs on without a stop – but with words in it, too – it passes into words and out of them again – I catch them at intervals – then it is dance-music once more, and then nothing but the reeds' soft thin whispering.'[37]

The Wind in the Willows was published thirteen years before Elgar's letter to Colvin. Although there is no record of Elgar having read the book, it is possible that by 1921, when his Christian faith had faded, he had come to share something of Grahame's riverbank paganism. His early biographer, Basil Maine, who spoke to him at some length, wrote of his 'pantheistic bias'.[38] On his deathbed Elgar asked at one stage for his ashes to be scattered at the confluence of the rivers Severn and Teme.

But what of Elgar's music: can Pan's pipes ever be heard in it? The texts of the solo song 'The Pipes of Pan' (1900) and the part-song 'After Many a Dusty Mile' from the *Greek Anthology* settings Op. 45 refer to Pan's music, although in both cases the scoring allows little scope for the composer to suggest it in tones. Another possibility is suggested by Alice's reaction in verse to a performance in 1888 of the early *Suite for Strings*. The first movement, she writes, tells of 'rivers fringed with wavering reeds'.[39] The *Suite*, now lost, was probably an early version of the *Serenade* for string orchestra, Op. 20. Nevertheless, there are no specific riverside associations with that work, and the scoring once again precludes the direct imitation of piping.

More suggestive are passages that highlight woodwind instruments. In Elgar's 1917 ballet score *The Sanguine Fan*, the worlds of eighteenth-century France and mythological Arcadia collide, as the courtship of a modern couple is disrupted by Pan and Echo, with tragic consequences. Pan carries a set of pipes, and Elgar personifies him with a clarinet, reserving a flute for Echo.[40] Another possible instance, this time featuring two clarinets, is found in 'Fairy Pipers' from the first *Wand of Youth* suite. In the scenario of the children's play that the music was supposedly to accompany, some fairies appear aboard a boat on a stream that separates the adult world from fairyland. The children's parents, who have been lured across a bridge, are 'charmed to sleep'.[41] The mood and texture suggest a barcarolle, but the fact that the adults stand on an enchanted riverbank implies a link with the Edwardian world of Pan.

However, there is one moment in Elgar's music where the story of the 'dreamy child' seems to find fulfilment. In August 1907, as he was working on ideas that would later become the First Symphony, Alice recorded in her diary: 'E. wrote *lovely* river piece. You cd. hear the wind in the rushes by the water.'[42] There are several seemingly pastoral episodes in the symphony to which this might apply, but the most obvious candidate is a delicate episode in the scherzo-like second movement (Ex. 4.1). The middle section of a minuet or scherzo movement was the place in the four-movement Classical symphony where rustic or pastoral associations were most likely

Ex. 4.1 Symphony No. I, II, fig. 66: 1–12

to be found (this was true to an extent even in the nineteenth century, for instance in Bizet's Symphony in C). The association is confirmed by a remark Elgar made to the London Symphony Orchestra as they were rehearsing this very section. The leader of the orchestra, W. H. Reed, recalled that 'the passage at Fig. 66 in the second movement was being played in too matter-of-fact a manner to please him, [so] he stopped and said, "Don't play it like that: play it like" – then he hesitated, and added under his breath, before he could stop himself – "like something we hear down by the river".'[43] The opening part of the movement is a fast, brittle march with chromatic tendencies; the delicate episode – which is conspicuously diatonic – makes a sharp contrast. The relationship of the march to the 'river music' is that of harsh reality to the magic of the rural retreat: a contrast analogous to those set out by Stevenson and Grahame. Elgar certainly knew that feeling. From London he once wrote to Sidney

Colvin's wife: 'My labour will soon be over & then for the country lanes & the wind sighing in the reeds by Severn side again.'[44]

The scoring of Ex. 4.1 and subsequent bars clinches the association with Elgar's childhood tale. The delicate melody for a pair of flutes suggests ethereal piping, while the accompanying harp triplets and string figures provide a murmuring background. All bass instruments are silent. Typically for Elgar, the orchestral palette is constantly changing, resulting in a range of subtle variation in instrumental colour: sometimes the flutes are joined or replaced by clarinets, sometimes they merge briefly with strings. The flutes' melody is generally highlighted, but on occasion seems muffled by the indistinct 'rustling' of the accompaniment. The harmony is static and the tune never achieves a cadence. The sense of a 'voice' of nature alternately condensing out of sheer noise and then fading back into it parallels the perceptions of the animals in 'The Piper at the Gates of Dawn' (published the same year as the symphony's premiere) and also recalls the efforts of the child Elgar to 'fix the sounds'. The episode conjures up an enchanted world that can be sensed fleetingly, but whose music remains elusive.[45]

THE WIND AMONG THE PINES

Along with the story of the child by the riverbank, perhaps the most widely disseminated Elgarian nature image is found in Cardinal John Henry Newman's poem *The Dream of Gerontius* (1866).

> The sound is like the rushing of the wind –
> The summer wind – among the lofty pines;
> Swelling and dying, echoing round about,
> Now here, now distant, wild and beautiful;
> While, scatter'd from the branches it has stirr'd,
> Descend ecstatic odours.[46]

When Elgar set Newman's lengthy text he made substantial cuts, and retained only the first two lines of this passage. But they appear to have had special significance for him and have subsequently made a considerable impression on his biographers.

At the time Elgar was born, his parents' cottage at Broadheath, now the Elgar Birthplace Museum, was known as 'The Firs' after a nearby clump of Scots pines. The family moved back to Worcester long before Edward was old enough to form a memory of his surroundings, but he later spent a childhood holiday at the cottage and retained a great affection for it, often revisiting it in later life. The idea of Broadheath haunted Elgar for decades. The pine trees in particular seem to have been a recurring motif in his life. Many decades later he wrote to a friend who had been to Worcestershire to see his birthplace: 'So you have been to B. – I fear you did not find the cottage – it is nearer the clump of Scotch firs – I can smell them now – in the hot sun. Oh! how cruel that I was not there – there's *nothing between* that infancy and *now* & I *want* to see it.'[47] One of the several Catholic schools to which the young Elgar was sent was at Spetchley Park, a few miles west of Worcester. The schoolhouse was set in an estate belonging to an old Catholic family, and the spacious grounds again contained tall pine trees. Almost ninety years later, the critic Ernest Newman recalled: 'Elgar told me that as a boy he used to gaze from the school windows in rapt wonder at the great trees in the park swaying in the wind; and he pointed out to me a passage in *Gerontius* in which he had recorded in music his subconscious memories of them.'[48] And nearly fifty years after his schooldays, Elgar revisited Spetchley Park, where his Catholic hosts asked him to write in their score of *Gerontius*. He turned to the passage about the 'lofty pines' and wrote 'In Spetchley Park *1869*'.[49] Another memory dates from the time when, as a young man of 23, Elgar went to Paris for a few days with his future brother-in-law. Once again, many years later (in 1933), after he had returned from a visit to France, he recorded: 'In passing through the pine-scented forest of Fontainebleau I had come to a road leading to Barbizon. The scent recalled a romance of 1880, and I nearly – very nearly – turned to Barbizon.'[50]

As noted in Chapter 2, for Elgar the recollection of the distant past – in words or music – was usually bound up with matters of intense personal significance. So it is unsurprising that commentators have seized on allusions to pines in Elgar's works and erected a veritable thicket of them around his music. Act II of the play *The Starlight Express*, to which Elgar contributed incidental music in 1915, was set on the edge of a pine forest. Moore suggests that this would 'revive Edward's private memories of Broadheath, Spetchley, [and] Fontainebleau'.[51] Robert Anderson observes of the part-song 'After Many a Dusty Mile' that 'as the traveller rests, a wind passes through Elgarian pine trees'.[52] The image has been wholeheartedly taken up in the popular Elgar literature; *The Malvern Hills: Travels through Elgar Country* includes a photograph taken near Birchwood Lodge where he composed *Gerontius* showing Worcestershire pine trees outlined against a red sunset, with Newman's words about the lofty pines as the caption.[53]

It seems likely, however, that the motif of rustling pines had resonance for Elgar beyond the purely biographical. The 'music' of these trees is present at the beginning of the Western pastoral tradition. The first of Theocritus' *Idylls* opens by comparing a shepherd's music with that of a tree: 'Some sweet whispering, goatherd, that pine by the spring plays, and you too pipe sweetly.'[54] Later, this would become a conventional device in Greek bucolic poetry for calling the herdsman to song. Longus has Daphnis play the syrinx (the skill he learned from Pan) in competition with the pines.[55] Even Newman's epithet has a long history: Arthur Golding's 1567 English translation of Ovid's *Metamorphoses* refers to 'the loftie Pynetree', and it soon became a conventional tag in English pastoral literature.[56] By Elgar's day the tradition had hardly abated. Rustling pines are a recurrent theme in the writings of Algernon Blackwood, on whose work the scenario of *The Starlight Express* was based.[57]

There are further literary and mythological contexts that reach beyond the pastoral tradition in significant ways. In many cultures across the globe, wind and breathing are closely connected etymologically with spirit or soul. *Spiritus*, for instance, can mean wind, breath or soul, and much the same applies to *anima*, *pneuma*, and the equivalents in Hebrew, Sanskrit, Arabic and Japanese. Creation myths, including that of the Old Testament, often speak of a god 'breathing' life into the world. The original meaning of 'inspire' was 'breathe into', and both the Classical and the Judeo-Christian traditions conceived prophets or oracles as being filled with divine breath. Perhaps the best-known example occurs in Acts 2: 1–4 when, on the day of Pentecost, 'suddenly there came a sound from heaven as of a rushing mighty wind'. The Apostles are filled with the Holy Spirit and speak in tongues to the people gathered in Jerusalem.[58]

This idea of wind as a spiritual force was a commonplace in nineteenth-century English literature, since it had been thoroughly exploited – albeit in a secularised mode – by the Romantic poets. As M. H. Abrams has shown, the image of 'air-in-motion' thoroughly informs the poetry of Coleridge, Wordsworth, Shelley and Byron, being used to reflect a transformation in the poet's inner condition whereby a mood of depression or a state of creative impotence is overcome: 'The rising wind, usually linked with the outer transition from winter to spring, is correlated with a complex subjective process: the return to a sense of community after isolation, the renewal of life and emotional vigour after apathy and a deathlike torpor, and an outburst of creative power following a period of imaginative sterility.'[59]

The reinvigoration of the imaginative faculty was a central Romantic theme (a variety of epiphany, in fact), and examples of energising winds can be found in Coleridge's *Dejection: an Ode*, Wordsworth's *The Prelude*,

Shelley's *Adonais* and *Ode to the West Wind,* and elsewhere. At the beginning of *The Prelude,* Wordsworth jettisons the traditional invocation of a Muse, replacing it with a reference to the creative stimulus of moving air:

> O there is blessing in this gentle breeze
> A visitant that while it fans my cheek
> Doth seem half-conscious of the joy it brings[60]

Later he compares himself to a priest or prophet as the gust induces a spiritual wind within:

> For I, methought, while the sweet breath of heaven
> Was blowing on my body, felt within
> A correspondent breeze that gently moved
> With quickening virtue ...[61]

One of the two famous 'spots of time' – indelible memories of childhood incidents – that according to Wordsworth sometimes nourished his imagination when it was flagging, involves 'the wind and sleety rain'. As a consequence, the adult poet explains, even to this time

>   at noon-day,
> While in a grove I walk, whose lofty trees,
> Laden with summer's thickest foliage, rock
> In a strong wind, some working of the spirit,
> Some inward agitations thence are brought,
> Whate'er their office, whether to beguile
> Thoughts over busy in the course they took,
> Or animate an hour of vacant ease.[62]

The Romantics, then, updated a trope of Classical pastoral poetry in aid of their theories of the creative imagination.

These Romantic antecedents may help to explain why Newman introduced the motif of the rustling pines into his mystical poem, which at first sight is far removed from the pastoral genre. Newman was familiar with Romantic poetry (especially Wordsworth) and it seems plausible that his choice of image in *Gerontius* indicates a spiritual renewal or reawakening within the protagonist. The lines are uttered by the soul of Gerontius just after entering the House of Judgement but not yet having reached the 'Presence-chamber' where a face-to-face meeting with God awaits. Moments earlier the soul and his Guardian Angel have heard the second in a succession of choirs of angels intoning the hymn 'Praise to the Holiest in the Height'. It is this angelic music that the soul likens to the rushing of a summer wind.

Elgar too knew the Romantics well and would have appreciated their insight into the psychology of creativity: his own compositional behaviour was characterised by bursts of activity alternating with bouts of depression or total indifference. The part-song 'O Wild West Wind', Op. 53 No. 3, sets lines from Shelley's *Ode to the West Wind*, describing a typical Romantic gale. Other songs have titles such as 'Weary Wind of the West', 'It's oh! To be a Wild Wind', and 'The Wind at Dawn'. The central climax of *The Kingdom* (1906) concerns the inspirational events of Pentecost, and Elgar made full use of his orchestra to suggest the 'rushing mighty wind', as tongues of fire descend upon the Apostles (fig. 76–9). The orchestra for *The Starlight Express* includes a wind machine to evoke the semi-personified winds of Algernon Blackwood's imagination, which serve to enhance the magic of childhood vision in contrast to the mundane outlook of adulthood.

In fact, Elgar's setting of the lines describing the lofty pines surpasses Newman in its evocation of Romantic 'wind poetry'. Elgar captures precisely the typical emotional trajectory in which dull dejection is followed by quickening imaginative revival. And he expands on Newman's single reference: the music associated with the wind is heard on three separate occasions in the orchestra, each time heralding a decisive change of mood in which a subdued passage, or even a sense of foreboding, is replaced by the glowing affirmation of the angelic choirs' hymn 'Praise to the Holiest in the Height'. These transformations take place at evenly spaced intervals in the course of the first half of the overall set-piece chorus known itself as 'Praise to the Holiest'. An imitation of natural sounds thus helps to structure a broad span of music.

Newman's poem includes five choirs of 'angelicals' and one choir of 'Angels of the Sacred Stair'. Each choir's contribution is framed at its beginning and end by words of praise, while in between they comment on the Christian story or on doctrine. There are occasional interjections: the soul sometimes reacts to the choirs' words, and the Guardian Angel pauses to explain some finer points of doctrine. Elgar cut much of the choirs' commentary and the Angel's explanations but kept most of the words of praise. The musical result is a long chorus of roughly bipartite structure with a central climax. In the first part, the chorus sings the hymn in Ab, Eb and C (figs. 61, 69 and 74), each time with more voices and greater force, so that the overall effect is a great crescendo to the *fortissimo* central climax. The music strikingly conveys the gathering crescendo of voices around the soul and the Angel as they penetrate ever deeper into the House of Judgement, and it is in this first part that the three instances of the wind music are heard. (The second part is firmly based around C major and contains the rest of the fifth choir's words plus a second grand statement of the hymn and an extended, climactic coda, both in C.)

In Elgar's version of the text, the soul's lines about the wind in the pines do not directly follow the words of any of the angelic choirs. Instead, they become a response to the Angel's words 'We have now pass'd the gate, and are within / The House of Judgement' (Ex. 4.2). They then lead directly into the second statement of the hymn of praise. Unlike many of the lines

Ex. 4.2 *The Dream of Gerontius*, Part II, fig. 67: 4–fig. 69: 5 (selected parts)

Ex. 4.2 (cont.)

Ex. 4.2 (cont.)

in *Gerontius* that refer to music or sounds, they do not receive a memorable melodic phrase. Indeed, the contour of the tenor part is determined by the accompanying instrumental patterns, which imitate the rushing wind. Those patterns had already been introduced at the start of the whole chorus, and they also appear a little later, just before the first grand C major statement of the hymn. The first instance (fig. 60) occurs immediately after the Angel's morbid description of the stigmata of St Francis (an attempt to illustrate to the soul how the presence of God will both 'gladden' and 'burn' it). The description is cast as a soft, slow recitative, accompanied by the solemn 'judgement' theme, which was first heard in the opening bars of the Prelude.[63] The passage, which begins *pp*, ends with the marking 'rit. e dim.', before flutes, harp, violins and violas enter *ppp* with the 'rushing' music. In similar fashion, the second appearance – the one that accompanies Gerontius's utterance of the lines themselves – directly follows a soft, slow passage (see Ex. 4.2). The Angel's 'We have now pass'd the gate' occurs just after the markings 'dim. molto' (from *pp*) and 'rit.', and coincides with a pronounced descent in register and a slowing of harmonic rhythm. The 'rushing' music is now played by harp, violins and violas, accompanied by the organ. On both these appearances it mingles with soft choral singing (omitted from Ex. 4.2), which then grows into the hymn. The final instance (fig. 73) likewise heralds a transformation in mood, register and dynamics, though this time it is part of a larger process of crescendo and acceleration, which leads to the central climax. A few bars earlier a powerful sense of foreboding had been established by harmonic progressions based on stepwise voice-leading motion and featuring the low brass: a passage illustrating the soul's cry 'But hark! A grand mysterious harmony: / It floods me like the deep and solemn sound / Of many waters'. After several abortive crescendos, the 'rushing' music arrives on woodwind, harp and strings, a little more forcefully than on the two previous occasions. It again coincides with the notional crossing of a boundary, this time the entrance into the Presence-chamber itself. The Angel sings 'And now the threshold, as we traverse it, / Utters aloud its glad responsive chant'. Each time it is heard, then, the 'wind music' signals an emotional transformation and a gathering of impetus, and leads to a choral affirmation. It may also denote a clarification of spiritual understanding, as foreboding gives way first to a confused perception of angelic singing (the 'rushing') and then a clear one (the hymn). The cumulative effect over the first part of the whole chorus fully justifies the tremendous climax at its centre.

Elgar's musical interpretation of Newman's poetic wind may indeed, as he and his biographers have suggested, have been shaped by a memory of childhood. But if so, it is not just a recollection of the historical childhood of Elgar himself, recoverable through biography, but touches on 'childhood' in the sense of the Romantic poets – that is, a state of heightened imaginative vision and spiritual freshness that can occasionally be recaptured in those moments of poetic inspiration that the Romantics evoked through the imagery of wind. (The Romantic attitude to childhood will be explored further in Chapter 5.) In fact, as will become clear in the next section, Elgar drew heavily on a further central image for the 'music of nature' in nineteenth-century literature, and did so in contexts which appear to have no connection with his own past.

AEOLIAN VISITATIONS

In 1904 Elgar's friend Arthur Troyte Griffith made him an Aeolian harp, which he placed by a window in the study at 'Plâs Gwyn', his house in Hereford. He was fascinated by its sounds, and drew them to the attention of visitors. The Aeolian harp, or 'wind harp', consists of a wooden box containing a number of taut strings placed very close together. The strings are of equal length and are tuned to the same pitch, but they are of different thicknesses. When moving air passes over the harp, the vibrating strings together set up complex patterns of harmonics, and as the force of the wind changes, the sounds fluctuate fitfully and unpredictably. Despite being restricted to the harmonic series of a single fundamental tone, the Aeolian harp can sometimes produce sounds astonishingly reminiscent of some of the harmonic and melodic progressions of Western classical music. At other times, it simply makes an ethereal, harmonious humming noise with little connection to human music. The construction of the instrument was first described in the seventeenth century by Athanasius Kircher, and it became a popular domestic toy in the second half of the eighteenth century, especially in England and Germany. Aeolian harps were placed on window ledges where the breeze could catch them, and sometimes hung in trees in public parks or in the grottoes of private grounds. Scholars meanwhile debated the scientific explanation of the harp's music. But by the end of the nineteenth century the fashion had passed, and in Elgar's time the instrument was already something of an antique curiosity.[64]

The rise and decline of the Aeolian harp's popularity was mirrored by its appearances in literature.[65] In the late eighteenth and early nineteenth centuries it was the subject of numerous lyric poems and was a commonly invoked trope in larger works. Most of the poets who mention the harp were from England and Germany – Wordsworth, Coleridge, Shelley, Tennyson, Goethe, Schiller, Novalis, Jean-Paul Richter, Mörike – although towards the end of its lifespan the image crossed the Atlantic to appear in the verse of Emerson, Thoreau and Melville. Initially its fascination for poets was the interplay it represented between the natural and the artificial. The instrument was produced by an ingenious craftsman, but the 'player' was the wind and the performance a capricious improvisation (suggestive perhaps of the eighteenth-century 'free fantasy'). In *The Castle of Indolence* (1748) James Thomson heard in the harp's sounds 'wild-warbling Nature all above the reach of Art!'[66] To some, this natural music was a faint echo of the music of the spheres and promised an escape to an enchanted world. By the turn of the nineteenth century, the image had acquired additional significance, coming to stand as an analogy for the poetic mind and taking pride of place among the Romantics' wind images. According to Shelley, 'Man is an instrument over which a series of external and internal impressions are driven like the alternations of an ever-changing wind over an Aeolian lyre which move it by their motion to ever-changing melody.'[67] In *The Prelude* Wordsworth draws an analogy between the awakening of the poet's imaginative faculties and the wind across the Aeolian harp's strings:

> It was a splendid evening, and my soul
> Once more made trial of her strength, nor lacked
> Æolian visitations . . .[68]

Similar conceits are found in poems such as Coleridge's *Dejection: An Ode* and *The Eolian Harp* and Shelley's *Ode to the West Wind*. In the first of these, the poet, languishing in a state of bitter ennui, and having lost his 'shaping spirit of imagination', recovers some of his vitality just as a violent storm breaks out and provokes the Aeolian harp beside his window to a 'scream of agony'.[69]

Some clues as to how the Aeolian harp might have sounded to nineteenth-century ears can be found in a treatise by Georges Kastner entitled *La harpe d'Eole et la musique cosmique* (1856) – probably to this day the most comprehensive work on the subject.[70] The author, who had evidently listened long and carefully, tried to record the harp's music in conventional Western notation (Ex. 4.3). Kastner hears what might be called a typical musical 'utterance' of the harp as an overall dynamic swell, beginning and ending very softly, though with the possibility of local dynamic modifications (Ex. 4.3(i)). This reflects the changing strength of a single gust of wind. The rise and fall of the dynamics is accompanied by a rise and fall in pitch levels, as the higher tones in the harmonic series become audible, before dying away again. Kastner is particularly impressed by the *perdendosi* effect that occurs at the end of each utterance. Sometimes all the tones in the harmonic series are sustained and die away in descending order. On the other hand, according to Kastner it sometimes happens that each note falls silent as soon as the next is sounded, resulting in a kind of melody. Both types are illustrated in Ex. 4.3(i). Indeed, the harp is apparently capable of remarkable variety and complexity, including shifting textures and even the suggestion of counterpoint. Kastner notes several interesting patterns that may occur momentarily in the course of an utterance. Sometimes there is the impression of a melody moving in thirds and also doubled in thirds (Ex. 4.3(ii)). A single high note may be sustained, as though marked *tenuto*,

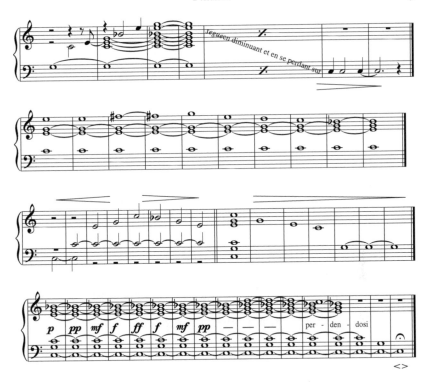

(i) Typical examples of a single 'utterance'

(ii) Melodies in doubled thirds

Ex. 4.3 Georges Kastner, *La harpe d'Eole et la musique cosmique* (1856), illustration of Aeolian harp effects

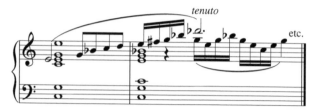

(iii) Sustained high note with figuration beneath

(iv) 'Louré'
Ex. 4.3 (cont.)

while swift, elaborate patterns take place beneath (Ex. 4.3(iii); Kastner admits that this example merely 'gives an idea' of the effect, which may have been too complex to notate reliably). One of the harp's most characteristic sounds, though audible only in very quiet passages, is a tremor or throbbing in which one note in a texture is repeated – or at least reinforced, since there may be no absolutely clear attack – in a regular pulse, while the rest are sustained. Kastner calls this 'louré' (Ex. 4.3(iv)).

When the Elgars' friend Dora Penny visited Plâs Gwyn in 1904, Alice directed her to the study.

I opened the door and went in. I was greeted with a burst of music! But what curious music it was, and the sound rose and fell in arpeggios of intervals of thirds – minor or diminished. It was very strange and rather eerie – in an empty room. I walked forward and saw that one of the windows which looked on the veranda was only partly open and a framework with vertical strings was fixed in the opening. I wondered if it was an Aeolian Harp – I had never seen or heard one. The Lady [Alice] had come in after me and was now beside me.

'Edward loves it. He thinks it is so soothing!'

'I don't think it would "soothe" me,' I said; 'it varies too much; but I call it most fascinating.'

A little breeze sprang up and it seemed as though a second harp joined in with the first.

'That's jolly. What does it do when there is a high wind? I should think it would get tremendously excited.'

'We don't generally have that window open when it blows, and if it gets excited Edward takes it down. The cadences are lovely, aren't they, dear Dora? So ethereal and mystic!'[71]

The 'minor or diminished' thirds that Penny reports are evident in Ex 4.3(ii): E to G and G to B♭ respectively (on an Aeolian harp the B♭s in these examples would sound slightly flat). Alice's casual remarks, though, are not a reliable guide to her husband's attitudes. The violinist W. H. Reed's reactions to hearing it were more considered, and probably come close to Elgar's own response. The harp, he said,

produced a shimmering musical sound of elfin quality, the strings being tuned to concordant intervals; therefore the effect, when the velocity of the wind varied and swept across the strings, was entrancing.

All the resultant harmonics and overtones rose and fell as the wind pressure changed; sometimes rising to extreme heights, and then falling rapidly if the wind dropped suddenly. One never knew what it was going to do next. The variety and delicacy of the tone were indescribably beautiful: almost inaudible at one moment, then swelling out to intensity in the next. Altogether, it was most fascinating; and Elgar never tired of listening to its fairylike improvisations.[72]

Reed's description of the rise and fall of the overtones, and the swift, unpredictable changes in tone and dynamics accord well with Kastner's transcriptions. Reed identifies several moments in Elgar's music that imitate the harp:

Æolian harp passages abound in [Elgar's] works. I can always hear these delicate rising harmonics in No. 1 of the *Sea Pictures* at the words 'like violins' [Ex. 4.4(i)]. In the *Introduction and Allegro* for Strings, when the *tremolo* in the violins begins against the second subject-tune in the quartet, the *crescendo* and *diminuendo* in the *tremolo* give an exact impression of the minstrelsy of that harp in the window [Ex. 4.4(ii)].

Much the same effect is produced by those widely extended chords shimmering in the divided strings (***ppp***) in *Gerontius*, beginning at the fourth bar after Fig. 25 at the words 'strange innermost abandonment', and again two bars later. The orchestral harp thrumming the repeated notes in triplets is really an Æolian harp [Ex. 4.4(iii)].

In the first movement of the Violin Sonata the *arpeggios* in the second page of the violin part rise and fall – dwelling on a note here and another one there (*tenuto*). When playing or listening to this section of the movement, or its repetitions later on, I always hear the rise and fall of the wind over the strings of a harp [Ex. 4.4(iv)].[73]

Although the harmonic progressions in most of these extracts are too complex to be produced by an Aeolian harp, other aspects of the music, such as melodic contour, dynamics and texture, invite comparison with Kastner's examples. Reed correctly pinpoints the dynamic swell in Ex. 4.4(ii) as characteristic of an Aeolian harp. The rising and falling arpeggios of the orchestral harp in Ex. 4.4(i) (also with a swell) and in the piano part of Ex. 4.4(iv) recall the typical pitch contours of Kastner's

(i) 'Sea Slumber Song' (*Sea Pictures*), fig. E: 1–2
Ex. 4.4 Aeolian harp effects in Elgar's music according to W. H. Reed

(ii) *Introduction and Allegro* for strings, fig. 15: 10–11

(iii) *The Dream of Gerontius*, Part I, fig. 25: 4–5 (reduction as in vocal score)

Ex. 4.4 (cont.)

Aeolian harp utterances. The throbbing of Kastner's *louré* is suggested by the violins' *tremolo* in Ex. 4.4(ii), although the correspondence is even more marked in Ex. 4.4(iii), where the orchestral harp's repeated notes set against the wide string chords are strikingly reminiscent of the textures of Ex. 4.3(iv). Finally, in Ex. 4.4(iv) the violin's arpeggios, with the notes in the highest voice strongly articulated, invite comparison with Ex. 4.3(iii) (where the sustained note in the upper voice is marked *tenuto*). Having heard Elgar's instrument at first hand, Reed appears to have become remarkably sensitive to any potential Aeolian harp effect in his friend's music.

(iv) Violin Sonata, I, fig. 5: 9–16
Ex. 4.4 (cont.)

Strangely, however, Reed does not mention Elgar's most substantial
Aeolian harp passage, from a work with whose gestation he was intimately
connected. On 18 September 1910, Elgar wrote to Ernest Newman about
his recently completed Violin Concerto, for which Newman was contributing an 'analysis' to be published prior to the first performance. Elgar
explained that in the accompanied cadenza near the end of the finale, 'the
sound of distant Aeolian harps flutters under and over the solo'.[74] As
explained in Chapter 2, in parts of this cadenza Elgar asks the strings to
play soft, sustained chords 'pizz. *trem.*', while the soloist plays virtuoso

Ex. 4.5 Violin Concerto, III, fig. 102

arpeggios alternating with long high notes and double stops (Ex. 4.5). Elgar's instruction that the instruments should be ' "thrummed" with the soft part of three or four fingers across the strings' echoes Reed's use of the term 'thrumming' to describe the orchestral harp's repeated notes in the *Gerontius* excerpt (Ex. 4.4(iii)). The Aeolian harp effect is unmistakable. Although the exact layout of the first inversion minor triad in the orchestral strings could not be realised on the instrument, the hushed pizzicato/*tremolando* imitates the indistinct murmur of the harp when touched by a gentle breeze, possibly with a rapid *louré*. Dynamic swells in the strings, beginning and ending very softly, are in evidence both here and in later passages in the cadenza. And although Elgar stated that harps are heard 'over and under the solo', the solo violin itself contributes to the imitation, suggesting sudden bursts of harmonics provoked by a gusting wind. Rising and falling melodic contours are complemented by rising and falling dynamic levels, while note values are shorter during crescendos than the ensuing diminuendos, the descending gestures tailing off into long pauses, as though the wind were gradually subsiding. This is akin to the *perdendosi* effect admired by Kastner. Throughout the cadenza the solo part contains many instances of slowly rising or falling thirds, sometimes also doubled in thirds: features reminiscent of Ex. 4.3(ii).

The location of an Aeolian harp imitation in a cadenza is apt. Not only do many stylistic traits of the post-Classical concerto cadenza fit comfortably with the harp's typical music – unpredictable and unmeasured bursts of melodic fragments or arpeggios interspersed with sustained chords and long pauses – but the harp's literary connection with imagination also finds a resonance. The Classical cadenza owed much to the eighteenth-century improvisatory 'fantasy' principle, which in part reflected the working of the imagination as understood in eighteenth-century empiricist philosophy. Seemingly unconnected styles and moods were juxtaposed in defiance of conventional rules of musical 'association'. Elgar's cadenza certainly contains many 'flights of fancy' in this sense. But at the same time as it evokes 'nature' conceived as freedom and spontaneity, the cadenza also reveals the 'inner' world familiar from Chapter 2 as opposed to the everyday 'present reality' represented by the finale overall. Here the violin can dwell on recollections from the concerto's 'past'. Ernest Newman called the cadenza 'an interlude of serious and profound contemplation, as it were the soul retiring into itself and seeking its strength inwardly, in the midst of the swirling life all around it'.[75] Once again, the imitation of natural sounds ultimately serves a deeper, and multifaceted, concept of nature, which fruitfully links literary connotations on the one hand and the form of the concerto on the other.[76]

NATURE AND FORM

A scene from David Pownall's BBC Radio play *Elgar's Third* (1994) stands as a warning against a too-literal interpretation of Elgar's stories about nature. In 1934 the dying and drugged-up Elgar is taken out by none other than the former Prime Minister Stanley Baldwin for one last look at the Worcestershire countryside.

ELGAR [*thinking to himself*]: In those woods, by those waters, I applied myself deciduously. On the sky there were bar-lines drawn by birds. Notes floated by in the shape of twigs and, on one occasion, a dead sheep. All I ever did was copy it down, dumb. Even the instruments allocated themselves. The dark flutes, the bright trombones. There was never any other way of doing it for me. No human mind taught me music. I heard what was being played on the world's strings, winds and skins, and dutifully, obediently, entered it on paper. Where is there need to be penitent? What is my sin, unless this is all a lie and I created it in pride and rivalry? The wind in the reeds is the wind in an oboe. The mouth, the lip, the lung, is not mine. Not mine. I did no blowing, nor was the spittle that dribbled from the pipe any human saliva.[77]

Pownall's Elgar looks back on his career in anxiety, trying to justify his life's work by erasing himself as an author and insisting that his music came from some higher source. It was not driven by 'pride and rivalry'. The belief that the artist is a mere vessel through which inspiration flows is a standard Romantic myth, exemplified by the figure of the Aeolian harp for the poetic imagination. Elgar himself gave voice to this myth – albeit not in quite the absurd manner of his fictional alter ego – when he observed that there was music in the air and 'you – simply . . . take as much as you require'. The myth has been perpetuated in writings on Elgar that claim to hear the landscape of Worcestershire in his notes.

In reality, Elgar's music was mediated by a host of factors, not least the music that he learned in the decidedly non-rural environments of his father's music shop and the back desks of orchestral violin sections. The technical knowledge he acquired there and elsewhere facilitated the carefully contrived impression of immediacy that characterises many passages in his compositions. But, as this chapter has argued, Romantic conceit and pastoral legend can still offer productive contexts for understanding Elgar's music, as long as the focus is shifted from the music's alleged content to its form. Just as Elgar's verbal utterances borrow their forms from literary conventions, so the meaning of 'nature' in his music is not limited to the imitation of Pan's piping, the rushing of the wind, or the harmonics of an Aeolian harp, but includes the positioning of those sounds within larger contexts. The impression of freshness or vitality that the imitations convey depends partly on the existence of some overall 'mundane' context from which the freshness can emerge or with which it can be contrasted. There is a common effect in Elgar's music whereby 'reality' – determined by some relatively familiar formal process that takes place within a movement – gives way, in a sudden moment of transformation, to a magical inner world of simplicity or innocence. Such transformative moments ('threshold' is the word used by the Angel in *Gerontius*) – are usually the places where the imitation of natural sounds is heard. This opens various possibilities for nature on the formal level. Nature music may, for instance, occupy the central section in a ternary form, or appear during interruptions or paren-thetical interludes in larger movements.

In some respects, then, 'nature' in Elgar's practice resembles 'memory' as the latter was understood in Chapter 2, and indeed there is considerable overlap in his compositions. Most obviously, the 'haze' that usually intro-duces thematic reminiscences may coincide with the rustling effects that have been explored in this chapter. In both cases Elgar plays with a distinction between artful 'music' and sheer 'sound'. Furthermore, the dualism implied by his treatment of thematic reminiscence finds a parallel in the differentiation of enchanted and mundane worlds considered here. Thus the moment in the *Introduction and Allegro* identified by W. H. Reed as an Aeolian harp imitation (Ex. 4.4(ii)) is at the same time a kind of thematic reminiscence (compare with Ex. 2.2 and discussion). The signifi-cance of memory for the cadenza of the Violin Concerto, including the passages which imitate an Aeolian harp, has been discussed in detail in Chapters 1 and 2. The 'rustling' arpeggios in the finale of the Piano Quintet (Ex. 2.6(i)) make a transition between outer and inner worlds and prepare for the recollection of thematic material associated with an eerie corner of the Sussex countryside. Variation XIII of the 'Enigma' Variations, dis-cussed in Chapter 2 as a form of memory, may also contain an Aeolian harp imitation.[78]

On the other hand, there are some notable differences between nature and memory in Elgar. Nature tends to lack any overt suggestion either of irony or of the uncanny. Aside from the Violin Concerto, nature is seldom to be found at the 'penultimate position' in a movement or work; it is more commonly located at a 'centre'. The 'river music' in the First Symphony's second movement, for instance, occupies what amounts roughly to a trio position within a scherzo. At the parallel stage in the third movement of the Second Symphony (fig. 106) there is a 'piping' tune on clarinets and flutes which alternately stands out from, and mingles with, background orches-tral rustling. The first movement of the First Symphony contains nature at its very heart: after a dramatic climax at the centre of the development section, rustling arpeggios on the harp herald a sudden transition to a delicate pastoral interlude (fig. 29: 5). The arpeggios in the Piano Quintet's finale lead to an interlude which substitutes for a development section in a sonata form. The Aeolian harp imitation in the *Introduction and Allegro* occurs approximately halfway through the work, while that in the Violin

Sonata marks a point of relaxation within an otherwise stormy movement. Elgar told Alfred Littleton that the return of the motto at the centre of the Second Symphony's first movement (fig. 30) – a moment when the energy of that movement has reached its lowest ebb – conveyed 'real (remote) peace'.[79] Although the point should not be pushed too far, it would seem that Elgar's symphonic movements often embark on restless journeys before encountering something remote and enchanted near their mid-point. That new thing may emerge suddenly and spontaneously, like an unpredictable gust of wind across the strings of an Aeolian harp. But it soon fades, and the journey is resumed.

The inevitable fading helps to clarify the sense in which nature in Elgar is a mode of nostalgia. For although Elgar borrows a Romantic theme, he seldom follows through its implications in the way the English Romantic poets did. Most of their wind poetry was written in the years following the failure of the French Revolution, a movement on which they had pinned fervent hopes. It had briefly made sense to believe in a spontaneous popular uprising that would replace the existing political order and establish an ideal society grounded in nature. This would be, as Abrams puts it, 'an imminent, abrupt, and total turn to perfection'.[80] When those hopes were dashed, the Romantics did not discard their revolutionary forms of utterance; rather, they internalised them. Their interest now concerned the revival of the imagination and the possibility of enduring subjective epiphany. By contrast, the quickening effect of 'nature' in Elgar is local; it seldom alters the overall course of an instrumental movement. Had Elgar followed the Romantics faithfully, he would have tended to align nature with the symphonic technique that musicologists today know as 'breakthrough'.[81] Instead, after borrowing ideas from generally 'open' literary forms, he mapped them onto 'closed' musical forms. As a result, the hopes attendant on the music of nature are glimpsed, but cannot harden into certainty or faith.

CHAPTER 5

Childhood

'When Elgar was a boy, he spent hours on his own, riding on his father's pony along the ridges of the Malvern Hills.' So begins the narration to Ken Russell's BBC Monitor film *Elgar* (1962). The film achieved impressive popularity at the time of its early broadcasts, and became a cornerstone of the Elgar revival of the 1960s. Its skilful juxtaposition of Elgar's music with images of the Worcestershire countryside helped to cement the popular association of his music with nature. The BBC withheld the film from video release for many years, permitting only the occasional public viewing, and it acquired something of a cult status. In that time, the single most abiding image – the one that stuck in the minds of people who only dimly recalled the rest – was the opening sequence showing a boy on a white pony riding towards the Malvern Hills and then galloping up the central ridge to the summit, to the strains of one of the most energetic passages in Elgar's *Introduction and Allegro* (Fig. 5.1). Along with the other actors in the film, the boy is silent – at that time the BBC did not permit dialogue in factual films. Yet there is no one to talk to in any case, for the camera largely avoids signs of human habitation, the only other living creatures to be seen being sheep and rabbits. As the boy reins in the pony and turns to gaze across the Worcestershire countryside, the music reaches its climax: a serene restatement of the theme from the opening bars of the Introduction, now transposed from G minor to D major, but quickly dying away, all passion spent (see Ex. 2.2). The whole episode is so evocative that it seems too good to be true – and it almost certainly is. There is no evidence that the young Edward made equestrian excursions, let alone of the distance implied by the film (it is eight miles from Worcester to the Malvern Hills). After all, for William Henry Elgar the use of a horse was an aspect of his business, taking him on his piano-tuning rounds to the homes of the rural Worcestershire gentry. It would have been foolish of him to allow his son to put the beast through its paces merely for pleasure, as if he were the aristocratic owner of a stable. So, despite Russell's otherwise sterling efforts

Fig. 5.1 'Elgar as a Boy on Pony' from Ken Russell's film *Elgar* (1962)

to draw attention to Elgar's true social background, his invention of this picturesque tale, with snow-white steed and pristine landscape, disguises the practical economic realities faced by a Victorian 'tradesman'. There is plentiful ammunition here for the anti-nostalgia critic.[1]

In fact the subject of Elgar and childhood induces curious lapses and moments of critical indulgence among even the most scrupulous of his admirers. The prime case is the two *Wand of Youth* suites (1907), which the composer designated Op. 1A and 1B and claimed to be based on music composed for a play devised by himself and his brother and sisters, and to date from around 1870 when Edward would have been in his early teens. Although never performed, the play was meant to illustrate the imaginative gulf between the children and their parents, and the consequent misunderstandings on the part of the latter. Elgar maintained that the music had been left essentially unchanged apart from orchestration: 'occasionally an obviously commonplace phrase has been polished but on the whole the little pieces remains [*sic*] as originally planned.'[2]

This version of events is attractive but, on close examination, not wholly credible. For a start, the music contrives to sound utterly spontaneous and innocent (Elgar himself called it 'naïf'), childlike yet never childish – a sign of considerable compositional sophistication. And the scenario of the play is suspiciously reminiscent of Kenneth Grahame's *The Golden Age* (1895) – a runaway bestseller in the early years of the twentieth century – right down to the pejorative epithets for the adults ('the Olympians' / 'The Old People'). Yet it was not until Christopher Grogan's commentary in volume 25 of the Elgar Complete Edition (2001) that Elgar's account of the suites' genesis was challenged.[3] Grogan admits that a childhood play probably existed and that music was composed for it, but questions how much of that music is to be found in *The Wand of Youth*. Elgar was inconsistent as to the exact date of the play, and in any case no manuscript evidence survives from the period. On the other hand, music from several of the pieces is found in sketchbooks dating from 1878–81 when he was in his early twenties and working as a composer and music director at the Worcester County Lunatic Asylum at Powick. To be sure, there is a melody labelled '1867' in a sketchbook of 1901, yet the piece that later absorbed it, 'Fairies and Giants', has no discernible function in the play as the adult Elgar described it, and the tune may not originally have been used at all. In other cases, fragmentary early drafts suggest that in 1907 a good deal of composition rather than transcription was taking place. Furthermore, Grogan shows that the sources from 1907 start to refer to the concept of a play only halfway through the process of composition – the pieces previously having been called simply 'children's music' – and points out that Elgar settled on the descriptive titles rather late in the day, despite the very specific dramatic significance he eventually assigned to some of the movements. Indeed, the information Elgar disclosed about the play was provided only in answer to eager requests for information from others, and his most detailed account dates from as late as 1929. Grogan concludes that the heterogeneous 'children's music' and the memory of the play had gradually merged in the composer's mind, and that 'Elgar's imagination, coloured by intense nostalgia' gave the project a new reality.[4] This version of events was elaborated in Elgar's writings and later became inscribed in the secondary literature.

Of course, in the final count, Grogan's judicious analysis of the sources does not constitute proof positive that Elgar's statements about the play were inaccurate – it merely shows that, on balance, the available evidence tells against them. Indeed it is always possible that in the future new evidence might surface to back Elgar up – the matter would then be settled.[5] The point raised by Grogan's work is not that Elgar scholars intentionally promoted a fantasy that they knew to be false, but rather that they collectively glossed over the issue, happy to take Elgar's rather unlikely story at face value despite the uncertain evidence. Why did it take so long to reach a sober assessment of the matter?

This chapter argues that what is ultimately at stake is the figure known to literary theory as the 'Romantic child', a cluster of ideas which took shape around the turn of the nineteenth century and was eagerly adopted and celebrated by the later Victorians and the Edwardians. Several of these ideas have recently been discussed in connection with Elgar by Michael Allis and J. P. E. Harper-Scott.[6] The Romantic child is conspicuous in Elgar's statements about his own childhood, which evoke it just as they do Romantic nature imagery, sometimes at the same time. But it also finds its way into Elgar scholarship, its fullest expression being Jerrold Northrop Moore's account of Elgar's childhood and his emphasis on adult retrospection in his biography *Edward Elgar: A Creative Life* (1984). As will become clear, Moore is drawn into an elaboration of Elgar's own myths. Yet that is not to deny the presence of a child-like impulse in Elgar's music that deserves serious attention. It is the argument of this chapter that as a composer he was capable of laying bare the truth about the Romantic child – that it does not ultimately revolve around children at all, literal or metaphorical, but is concerned with the staging of adult desires and dissatisfactions. In particular, as a musician Elgar seems inclined to illustrate the feelings of an adult who, far from successfully recovering or preserving an inner child-self, can summon that vision only fleetingly in moments of reverie which, like his encounters with enchanted nature, soon fade. Again this nostalgia is reflective rather than restorative. Finally, the chapter considers the continuing grip of the Romantic child complex on Elgar's music in the guise of the youthful solo performer of Elgar.

THE ROMANTIC CHILD

Although the attitude to childhood in literary Romanticism resists easy definition, a nexus of child-centred images can nevertheless be identified which come together with some cogency in early nineteenth-century England, which were accorded prestige by the Victorians, and which even today quietly inform some of our attitudes to childhood.[7] The Romantic perspective celebrates childhood as a special and uniquely important phase of life, one quite different from adulthood and a potential source of salutary lessons for the adult. Rousseau's *Emile* (1762) is a model in this regard, with its passionate argument against burdening children with book learning or rational culture of any kind until a late stage of adolescence, and its insistence that the child be allowed to develop first and foremost as a child, closely attuned to nature. The Romantics endowed their literary children with enviable clarity of perception – sometimes even visionary abilities.

The consciousness of the child is unified and autonomous, uncompromised by adult ties to particular historical and social conditions. Like the figure of the 'genius' – a comparable favourite of the Romantics – the child possesses a keen imaginative faculty and a special affinity with nature. 'Thou best Philosopher ... haunted forever by the eternal mind, / Mighty Prophet! Seer blest!' exclaimed Wordsworth in his *Ode: Intimations of Immortality from Recollections of Early Childhood* (1807), a poem that exercised wide influence in the Victorian age. The corollary to this impulse to set up childhood as a separate sphere was the desire of adults to recapture that lost Eden in place of their own 'postlapsarian guilt and gloom',[8] a tendency which has been extensively chronicled. To quote some representative Victorian doggerel: 'Backward, turn backward, O time in your flight, / Make me a child again just for tonight.' 'I'd give all wealth that years have piled / The slow result of life's decay / To be once more a little child / For one bright summer day.'[9] Alternatively, the child could be figured as an angel or messenger of God, bearing with it a glimpse of heaven. 'Trailing clouds of glory do we come / From God, who is our home: / Heaven lies about us in our infancy!' as the *Immortality* ode's most often repeated lines have it. In this sense the child may acquire nothing less than a redemptive function. 'Infancy', observed Emerson, 'is the perpetual Messiah, which comes into the arms of fallen men and pleads with them to return to paradise.'[10] Thomas Cooper Gotch's painting *The Child Enthroned* (1894) draws on the iconography of 'Christ in majesty', portraying a seated girl, richly clothed, with an unmistakable halo around her head. Towards the end of the nineteenth century the internalisation of this idea became especially popular, so that the recovery of an individual's own child-self could be said to hold the key to future happiness or creativity.

A generation ago, many critics would have been inclined to read the history of the Romantic child during Elgar's formative years – the late nineteenth century – as a gradual falling away from the Romantics' (supposedly) genuine psychological insights. For Peter Coveney in 1967, the Romantics attempted to reconnect childhood with adult consciousness, using the child figure to say something relevant to all human experience, whereas later acolytes such as Lewis Carroll and J. M. Barrie indulged in an irresponsible, regressive escape that testifies to nothing more than their maladjustment. 'Their interest in childhood serves not to integrate childhood and adult experience, but to create a barrier of nostalgia and regret between childhood and the potential responses of adult life.'[11] By contrast, recent literary criticism has witnessed new historiographies of childhood which view traditional canonic hierarchies with suspicion and read all idealising accounts of childhood, whether Romantic or post-Romantic, with an eye to their ideological content. It is pointed out, for instance, that the circumscribing of the childhood sphere, physically, psychologically and economically, is a relatively recent phenomenon which can be linked to the mentality of the confident middle classes of eighteenth-century Europe. The Romantic child can be seen as a bourgeois, adult, male preoccupation, coming to stand in the Victorian period – alongside the figure of the wife and mother – as an icon of a domestic realm that offered the husband a precious refuge from the cut and thrust of the competitive world of work. (Men, of course, were spared the day-to-day nuisances of child-rearing, and could afford to idealise.) The image of the child has also been identified with what Jerome McGann in 1983 called 'the Romantic ideology': the construction of an autonomous, ahistorical mode of consciousness adrift from the social and material worlds. Moreover, the practice of virtual child-worship in the later nineteenth century can be viewed as the transference of religious impulses following the mid-century crisis of faith. In particular, Victorians of an Evangelical upbringing preferred to jettison the idea of childhood as laden with original sin and instead project the story of Genesis onto their own lives, regarding the transition to adulthood as a personal Fall.[12] Such approaches to the topic take the literature of Elgar's late Victorian contemporaries no more or less seriously than they do the discourse of the Romantics. From this perspective, merely to dismiss the former out of hand as a morbid cult is to miss the point.

It is not hard to situate Elgar's own utterances on childhood within the framework established by the Romantics. Assuming that we are wary of a literal interpretation of his claims, cited in Chapter 4, to be on some level a *puer aeternus* ('still at heart' the dreamy child and perceiving 'nothing between that infancy and now') they read as an effort to figure the artist's creative imagination as a child within. The boy sitting in the reeds by the Severn has many ancestors in Romantic poetry, which abounds in solitary, silent children in unpeopled landscapes. In an episode from Wordsworth's *The Prelude* and also in Coleridge's 'To the River Otter', the poet imagines his child-self by a riverbank. The young Elgar's attempts to catch the elusive music confirm Thomas De Quincey's estimation of the child's 'special power of listening for the tones of truth'.[13] Often the Romantic child alone in a landscape is a musician – generally a singer or piper. In Wordsworth's 'The Danish Boy', 'Lucy Gray' and 'Ruth' from *Lyrical Ballads* (1798), the music uttered by the child is strange and unsettling, reflecting an inner loneliness as well as the wildness of the external nature that is described in each poem. At the same time, Elgar's story about the boy at the riverbank reflects common patterns of post-Romantic retrospective self-representation. In portraying his child-self at home in a pleasant rural setting and yet doomed to suffer neglect and rejection, Elgar's confession to Colvin fits a pattern of vacillation between two opposite, contending impulses which can be detected again and again in Victorian autobiographical writings. Although childhood is portrayed as a privileged time of blissful innocence, there is also a desire to make clear that the author was not 'spoiled' (a dread word in the Victorian child-rearing vocabulary). The child has to suffer hardships before finally winning through to success as an adult.[14] This gives reminiscences such as Elgar's a characteristic pathos: the former self was acutely alive – hard-pressed but happy.

MOORE'S 'BETTER LAND'

Jerrold Northrop Moore is the author and editor of a series of monuments of Elgar scholarship, including *Edward Elgar: A Creative Life* (1984), by far the most weighty biographical tome to be devoted to the composer, and one which painstakingly documents Elgar's activities almost day by day. Despite this achievement, however, Moore's biographical writings weave some simple myths around Elgar's life and music, most notably as regards the composer's childhood and its significance. The story Moore tells has influenced writers on Elgar at the popular end of the spectrum,[15] and is worth examining in some detail. For Moore, at the heart of this 'creative life' stands a kind of nostalgia. 'Music and biography share the expression of time remembered' begins Chapter 1, while the book's closing lines come full circle, claiming that Elgar's response to the rapid changes witnessed in the course of his lifetime was 'to seek the illumination of time remembered. For all those of his generation and the future who would feel the insight of retrospection, he had made of that evanescence his music.'[16] This is a realisation of implications arising from the first of the book's four main parts, entitled, predictably enough, 'The Wand of Youth'. Its three constituent chapters, 'The Better Land', 'Divisions' and 'Ensembles', map the tripartite structure of Quest Romance onto Elgar's childhood: a primal unity is followed by a catastrophic division and a search for the original unity, which is then achieved in a higher form. The mature composer plays out the quest on an epic scale.

Moore's principal point of reference is the birthplace cottage at Broadheath. The Elgar family rented it for just three years and left when Edward was only 2 years old. According to his elder sister Lucy – whose

intensely nostalgic recollections, penned over fifty years after the events
they describe, Moore cites at length – the initial move from Worcester was
at their mother's behest; she wanted to raise her children in the midst of
nature. The eventual move back to the city (on account of William Henry
Elgar's business), is remembered by Lucy as traumatic. Life at the cottage,
by contrast, she portrays as a virtually uninterrupted idyll presided over by
a dominant maternal presence. The children were taught to love the
countryside and perceive their Creator in every blade of grass. Lucy
recounts Edward's arrival in this arcadia with the traditional literary signal
for the auspicious birth: rejoicing nature. 'How well I remember the day
he was born! The air was sweet with the perfume of flowers, bees
were humming, and all the earth was lovely.'[17] While admitting that
Broadheath later became 'really a state of mind' for the Elgar children,
Moore joins Lucy in her rhetoric of Eden and impending Fall. Their
mother had given them 'a base of the firmest security on which to build
their lives – as long as they should remain in the countryside'.[18]

The role of music in this environment is defined by its characteristic
division of time by means of pulse, rhythm and cyclic repetition. Moore
claims that a baby first becomes sensitive to these parameters about halfway
through pregnancy.

Before birth, in the dark womb, the baby's first consciousness of any experience
comes in the mother's heart beat, her breathing and walking, and the sound of her
voice. So pulse and rhythm, movement and sound – all manifesting themselves
through time – appear on the *tabula rasa* before there is anything to see.[19]

Later, the natural cycles of the days and seasons would be noticed by the
infant. Ann Elgar's reciting of a favourite poem, 'The Better Land', and
William Henry Elgar's regular musical soirées furnished further sources of
repetition and return – in the latter case reinforced by the very structure of
the songs and arias that were performed. Such patterns laid the foundation
of Edward's musical sensibility.

It is the sense of pulse – the source of life itself – that gives music its first and
fundamental appeal. Even the most complex rhythm draws its power ultimately
from some hint of simple pulse repetition – some pattern of events moving
steadily, regularly forward in time. What is the repeating pulse of music if not a
precise miniature of those larger pulses of nature, the cycles of hours and seasons
returning? Music offers a means for venturing out from the babyhood of primal
dark physical feeling toward the great world outside.[20]

The pleasures of Broadheath would not, however, find a permanent
place in Elgar's conscious memory. This is because, according to Moore,

during infancy there is no frame of reference through which to select or reject information. 'The operation of any memory must signify some rough structure of values.'[21] On the other hand, early infancy is precisely the time when the frame of reference itself is being formed. The retention of memories is a sign that a rudimentary kind of individuality is already in place.

For the two-year-old Edward that earliest experience had been at Broadheath. Though no conscious memory might ever reveal it to him, he would carry it with him always and everywhere: it was, together with what was in him of his parents, an aspect of himself.[22]

For Moore, then, Broadheath lies even deeper than memory, for it structures memory, and thus helps to shape Elgar's whole experience of the world.

The second chapter, 'Divisions', explores the world of Worcester in the 1860s to which the Elgars returned. This is where Edward's conscious memories are said to begin. Yet, with his psyche moulded by the stability and wholeness of Broadheath, Moore's Elgar inevitably finds many of the new stimuli to his dissatisfaction. The family's lower-middle-class status and Catholic affiliation make him aware of social and religious divisions. His skill at music separates him from other children. Above all, the river Severn running along the western edge of the city divides town from country, and Edward's present from 'the Better Land of his past'.[23] For Moore, the boy's inklings of disillusion are the context for the 'dreamy child' letter, and he links it also to a verse of Arthur O'Shaughnessy's ode *The Music Makers* (1874) – much later to be set by Elgar – which begins: 'Great hail! We cry to the corners / From the dazzling unknown shore; / Bring us hither your sun and summers, / and renew our world as of yore.'

In the reeds by Severn side, the dreamy child who faced the intimate, unknown country across the river might feel only the need to reunite his father's world of music with his mother's world of nature and the spirit. But the uniting this time should be permanent. The child had brought a sheet of paper to try to write it down.[24]

In other words, the child tries to heal his alienation by turning to something mysterious and enchanted, distant yet familiar. The music seems to emanate indirectly from the countryside of the opposite bank as well as from the reeds about him. Yet that impulse is at the same time a backward glance, an attempt to grasp a piece of the boy's essential self that has never been fully available to his consciousness.

The third chapter, 'Ensembles', attempts to pin down the musical symptoms of this yearning by examining Elgar's early efforts at composition. In 1867 he returned to the hamlet of Broadheath to spend a summer holiday

Ex. 5.1 'Tune from Broadheath' as cited by Moore (*Creative Life*, 33–4)

with friends of the family. This was the date he later assigned to the opening
melody of 'Fairies and Giants', labelled in the 1901 sketchbook 'Humoreske a
tune from Broadheath 1867'.[25] Although not explicitly committing himself
to Elgar's claim, Moore maintains that 'this return to the Better Land of his
own beginning brought about the real entry to what he had longed for in the
reeds on the city side of the Severn'.[26] Referring to the version in the
sketchbook (Ex. 5.1), Moore draws attention to the blank upper staff –
strictly speaking, unnecessary to the notation of the tune. 'The blank staves
seemed to invite other voices to join in a rising ensemble – like the ensemble
of voices that rose when the wind went through the reeds.'[27] Perhaps the two
staves imply a duet between Elgar and (as yet silent) nature.

According to Moore the tune anticipates numerous aspects of Elgar's
mature style. The most obvious are repetition and sequence: the former on
the level of the four-bar phrase, the latter in the treatment of the falling fifth
motif. The descending direction of the sequence is in itself a characteristic
Elgar trait. Since the repeated notes can be brought off better on the
indicated cellos and basses than on a piano, and the descending fifths
and rising fourths are easily accomplished through string crossing, Moore
detects Elgar already thinking without reference to the piano, a practice
the composer later claimed to be essential to his compositional process.
Finally, Moore notes the tonal relationship implied by the 'F♯ minor jape'

indicated at the end of the tune. In the *Wand of Youth* suite, this modulation introduces a new section in F♯ major, and Moore observes that the
juxtaposition of keys related by semitone step became 'another favourite
device of his maturity'.[28] Yet, at the same time as they point ahead to the
adult, these features – above all the varied repetitions – embed the music in
the landscape of Elgar's infancy:

Sequence-writing repeats a single shape in changing positions. Of all melodic
devices, then, it most resembles and suggests the patterns of nature in the countryside round Broadheath: gentle undulations of field and hedgerow, copse and dell –
fruit trees planted in rows to make an orchard – the linked chain of the Malvern
Hills rising up suddenly out of the Severn Valley – and flowing through all that
landscape, the curving and re-curving river.[29]

Moore even hears each of the falling fifths in the tune as a temporary
'arrival', mirroring Edward's summer visit to Broadheath.

If, according to Moore, the 'tune from Broadheath' adumbrates Elgar's
later style, then the music for the children's play points forward to some
further aspects of his adult psychology and compositional practice. The
play's scenery included a forest stream dividing the world of the Old People
from the children's fairyland; the grown-ups were to be lured across it for
their enlightenment. For Moore this repeats the Severn's division of
Worcestershire into city and countryside, the symbol of the young Elgar's
nascent dissatisfaction (albeit with the children now happily ensconced in
their Better Land). Still more significantly, the Broadheath tune had supposedly been composed several years before the play, and must therefore
have been consciously reused, just as the adult Elgar would regularly raid old
sketchbooks from the distant past – above all (as Moore sees it) for the *Wand
of Youth* music. As the work of an early teenager, the play's music thus
'hovered between childhood and maturity, looking uneasily forward, looking fondly back'. At this moment 'the nostalgia that was to shape much of his
mature style began to make itself felt'.[30] By recycling his material, the young
composer had already embarked upon the quest that would later preoccupy
the adult: the search for wholeness through the retrieval of the past.

An idea, once entered in a sketchbook, might ripen toward a maturity of its own.
Then it could give its hint of the Better Land beyond the stream of time, where old
ideas might be 'transfigured' – where the Older Person scrutinising the notes of his
former self might find those impulses transfigured through the Fairies and Giants,
the Moths and Butterflies of his own recollecting.[31]

Alternatively, the very act of engaging with old material might release
an otherwise latent source of creativity. Moore, like several other Elgar

commentators, connects the long-postponed symphonic breakthrough that Elgar achieved in 1908 with the experience of composing the *Wand of Youth* music in the second half of 1907. In fact, he regards that experience as having assisted Elgar in overcoming a crisis in his creative life, precipitated by his fiftieth birthday in June 1907.[32]

For evocative power, Moore's mythic narrative surpasses many of the semi-fictional novels and films that have been inspired by Elgar's life and music. Its basic concept is simple yet rich in ramifications. Moore is familiar with the topography of Elgarian longing – the reeds, the hills and the birthplace – and deftly draws them into the story. The Better Land stretched out beyond the far, western bank of the Severn recalls the Promised Land of the Israelites located on the far, western bank of the Jordan. Moore's use of the blank staff in Elgar's sketch as a figure for the reeds' music shows an intuitive grasp of the ancient trope they refer to; like Kenneth Grahame he suggests a music that lies just beyond the realm of perception. And although he is evidently working within a Romantic paradigm, he complicates the picture in various ways. There is little time for happy innocence between the idyllic but unremembered infancy at Broadheath and the incipient disillusion of the Worcester years. The 'Shades of the prison-house' that, according to Wordsworth, 'begin to close / Upon the growing Boy' do so early for Elgar. The music for the play is not just an innocent game but anticipates the adult composer's quest for synthesis. Indeed, the trauma of the departure from Broadheath leaves the adult Elgar deeply dissatisfied, perhaps even unconsciously scarred and resentful of his father: a Freudian rather than Romantic touch.

If read as straight biography, though, Moore's account of Elgar's childhood is dubious in its arguments, reductive in its excessive emphasis on retrospect as the force driving Elgar's creativity, and uncritical of the relevant sources. Moore is unwilling to admit that, as David Cannadine puts it in his review of *A Creative Life*, 'Elgar was not only a music maker, but a myth-maker as well, whose words about himself were often as deceptive as his photographs'.[33] Even supposing Elgar's dating of the 'tune from Broadheath' to be accurate and his sketch of thirty-five years later to have left it entirely unaltered, that frail snatch of melody can hardly withstand the projection onto it of so much of his mature idiom, with the contours of the Worcestershire landscape added for good measure. The idea that writing the *Wand of Youth* resolved Elgar's mid-life crisis and unlocked his creative energies for the composition of a symphony is also disputable: Elgar was a man of many creative crises, and they continued through the winter of 1907–8, well after the suites had been completed and before the symphony was seriously under way. Two decades after *A Creative Life*, Moore published another biographical study, entitled *Elgar: Child of Dreams* (2004), which narrows its focus still further, pursuing the same ideas about nature, childhood and retrospection with oppressive monotony. The topic is in urgent need of new perspectives.

STARLIGHT AND RECOLLECTION

The drawbacks of Moore's approach suggest that in tackling the problem of childhood in Elgar it would be better to eschew speculation about his early life and compositions and also to leave aside questions about general qualities of his mature style. Similarly, the idea that retrospection was the key to his creative process should be treated warily. Instead attention could fruitfully be focused on the true subject of the discourse of the Romantic child – the adult – and the manner in which Elgar articulates adult longing in the medium of music.

The music for *The Starlight Express* serves as a better case study in this regard than the *Wand of Youth* suites, since the substantial numbers in the score are sung by a nostalgic adult character ('The Organ Grinder'). Although the play is sometimes derided as an escapist fantasy for wartime with an incomprehensible scenario, it is in fact a reworking of an ancient cosmic mythology which puts special emphasis on the act of recollection. The play was adapted from Algernon Blackwood's novel *A Prisoner in Fairyland* (1913) by Blackwood and Violet A. Pearn, and was produced by Lena Ashwell at the Kingsway Theatre, London, over the Christmas period 1915–16. Elgar was a late collaborator, having been approached to compose incidental music only in the second week of November. Nevertheless he put heart and soul into the project and eventually composed over fifty numbers. He evidently sensed a kindred spirit in Blackwood, whose novels about distracted adults finding redemption and imaginative inspiration through the magical influence of children draw on the same turn-of-the-century literary sources as the *Wand of Youth* story. Despite last-minute frictions over the costumes and sets, *The Starlight Express* enjoyed a reasonable run. The critics admired the music but were puzzled by the story, and a full-scale revival has never been – and surely never will be – attempted.[34]

A Prisoner in Fairyland explores a set of relationships which preoccupied Blackwood and which he examined further in two other novels: *The Education of Uncle Paul* (1909) and *The Extra Day* (1915). In each case an uncle intrudes upon a family unit that comprises one or two parents and three children (two girls and a boy). The uncle is the only adult fully sensitive to the imaginative world of the children. He helps to give form to their dreamy visions; on the other hand, his initiation into their fantastic worlds enables him to achieve for himself and for others a kind of spiritual reawakening. The books therefore fit squarely into the tradition of the 'redemptive child'. In *A Prisoner in Fairyland*, Henry Rogers is a 40-year-old London businessman who retires with a fortune and vague plans for philanthropy. He is suddenly reminded of the country village of his youth, and on an impulse pays it his first visit since he left school. As he stands in the garden where he used to play, he suddenly feels the visceral presence of the ideas and characters that peopled his imagination. In his daydream, they all pile into an old third-class railway carriage standing in the garden – the 'Starlight Express' – which was a present from his father and the site of thrilling childhood adventures. The characters are known as the 'Sprites' and include a tramp, a lamplighter, a sweep, a gypsy, 'the laughter', a head gardener and a dustman. The Starlight Express leaps into the sky and Henry directs it to the village of Bourcelles in the Swiss Jura, where his cousin lives. He then awakens from the reverie and decides to pay a real visit to the cousin and his family. Upon his arrival he finds the adult community 'wumbled' – discontented, muddled, out of touch. In particular, his cousin, a writer, is groping towards a philosophy of life but cannot get his ideas down in coherent form. After befriending the children, Henry accompanies them on a series of nocturnal dream-adventures to a cave in the mountains where starlight collects in great quantities as dust. They see the Starlight Express draw up at the Star Cave and the Sprites alight and enter, before emerging laden with stardust. The Sprites will take the dust around the world and scatter it over people, bringing harmony and understanding – 'sympathy'. This must be done before the 'interfering sun' has time to rise. Henry and the children do likewise, secretly scattering the dust over their family and friends. Finally they manage to entice the children's parents into the Star Cave itself. The weariness and tensions of the adults are gradually healed, the father finds inspiration, and Henry decides to abandon a half-baked charitable scheme in favour of a more active, personal mode of philanthropy.

The central idea of the novel is the power and reality of thought, which Blackwood, who had a keen interest in the occult and was a novice in the Hermetic Order of the Golden Dawn, believed could spread instantaneously across the universe, reaching all minds properly attuned to it.[35] The Starlight Express is 'a train of thought'; the stardust that its passengers carry is fine and sticky, making people metaphorically adhere to one another and bringing sympathy and insight. When people are touched by starlight or sprinkled with stardust they translate their dreaming into action: they try to help others. Children are the conduits that keep human beings in touch with the stars. The story's principal concern is thus the minds of adults, especially those, like Henry, who retain a spark of their childhood vision. The familiar Victorian ingredients are there: the world of commerce stifles the imagination; the countryside provides a haven from city life; both women and children are said to occupy an enchanted space 'close to the sources of life';[36] and the goal of the story is the achievement of a type of Christian virtue with an emphasis on good works.

The most obvious literary reference for Blackwood's concepts is once again the *Immortality* ode, which deals in metaphors of light and darkness, celebrates 'the primal sympathy', and holds that 'Our birth is but a sleep and a forgetting: / The Soul that rises with us, our life's Star, / Hath had elsewhere its setting, / And cometh from afar'. Wordsworth in turn drew on the Platonic doctrine of *anamnesis*, according to which human beings, prior to their birth, dwelt in a celestial home and partook of divine understanding. As they forget their origin upon their arrival on earth, the acquisition of earthly knowledge is nothing but a process of recollection – or, more literally, 'unforgetting'.[37] The conceit of the ode is that newborn babies have in some sense forgotten less than their elders.

Nevertheless, *A Prisoner in Fairyland* and *The Starlight Express* point to an independent tradition of thought, though similarly indebted to Plato, which Blackwood probably knew from his Hermetic studies. The Gnostic writings of the Manichaeans (followers of the third-century Babylonian prophet Mani) developed an elaborate cosmogony, intended as a kind of meta-religion, with the problem of *anamnesis* at its heart.[38] They posited two equal, opposite and eternal principles, Light and Darkness, which originally occupied quite different realms, the one ethereal, the other material. There was however a calamitous disruption of this equilibrium when the forces of Darkness invaded the realm of Light. The 'Father' of the Light engendered a 'primal man' to fight them off, but he fell unconscious in the battle, and sparks of Light became trapped in the world of matter. The Father then created a deity called the 'living spirit', who issued an awakening call to the primal man. The present universe came into existence as a kind of machine for refining and releasing the particles of light that were dispersed and imprisoned in matter and for returning them to their divine home. It plays out a struggle between the two contending forces, with religious prophets repeating the living spirit's call in an effort to stimulate the Light's dormant desires by reminding it of its true being.

Redemption is conceived as 're-collection' in two senses: remembering one's origin and gathering up the scattered particles to build a 'body of light'. These themes are evident throughout Blackwood and Pearn's play. The importance of *anamnesis* is confirmed by Henry's cousin's complaint that 'the earth has forgotten it's a star' and by the character of Miss Waghorn, a testy old lady who has lost her memory. The division between the material and the spiritual is symbolised by the children's desire to get out of their bodies at night and to find a way through the narrow opening at the mouth of the Star Cave – you have to be thin (like children) to get through, although luckily 'everybody's thin somewhere'.[39]

The Manichaean doctrine holds an obvious appeal for the nostalgic imagination: it is contemptuous of the present world and looks back to a distant moment of unity. Yet its eschatological vision precludes a modern conception of linear time and denies the finality of death (unredeemed Light is simply reincarnated in the world of material). Practical religion is understood as a forward-looking strategy of awakening and escape from the cycle. This aspect of the mythology is emphasised in Blackwood and Pearn's play, but it is one that has worn poorly with the years. Today the three-stage narrative that it invokes – another instance of Quest Romance – seems impossibly facile for 1915. And, given Elgar's bleak coupling of death and retrospection in *Falstaff* two years earlier, *The Starlight Express* seems a regression for him – discomforting because of its offer of comfort.

On the other hand, Elgar does not always have to articulate the philosophy of the play in his music. When he has the opportunity to diverge from it or to explore the reflective aspects of childhood nostalgia, the music is at its finest.[40] This is the case with the few full numbers he had to compose: the individual songs for the Organ Grinder that precede each act (most of the rest of the score is necessarily fragmentary in structure). The character of the Organ Grinder is absent from *A Prisoner in Fairyland* – it was added for the stage play. He behaves sometimes as a Sprite, sometimes as a kind of Greek chorus, observing and commenting on the action, and sometimes as the embodiment of a general adult longing for a return to childhood, independent of the rest of the story. The sound of his organ (based on consecutive, 'empty' fifths) is a point of reference throughout the incidental music and proves useful as a framing device – in fact it opens and closes the whole score. In the songs, though, it supplies the frame not for dramatic actions but for a specific type of musical process, helping to focus attention on the juxtaposition of and transitions between incompatible worlds.

The song that precedes Act I, 'O Children, Open Your Arms', begins with the barrel-organ music but soon breaks into a lively polonaise as a group of children dance around the player. The pace slows and the singer implores – with a frank eroticism which would presumably have been tolerated in its day – 'O children, open your arms to me, / Let your hair fall over my eyes'.[41] In answer to this call for enchantment Elgar introduces one of several quotations from the *Wand of Youth* to be found in the score. This one is from the piece called 'Little Bells'. It becomes a touchstone for the work – a leitmotiv associated with starlight and magic. The words do not fit especially well – Elgar has to adjust them as best he can, sometimes resulting in a rather aimless vocal line – but the choice is nevertheless apt. This is partly because of the diatonic augmented fourths and diminished fifths in the chords in the second half of the first three bars (see Ex. 5.2(i), first three bars of duple metre). In Chapter 3 Elgar's liking for these intervals was identified as a factor that inclined his noble idiom towards melancholy. In this song, of course, diatonicism is used to signify innocence rather than nobility, so these harmonies serve instead to mitigate any sense of an unclouded idyll. Most significantly, though, the choice of 'Little Bells' works well because the original tune includes a sequential repetition of its opening bars a minor third higher. Elgar contrives to have a new harmonic sonority arrive just as the singer falls into a dream. 'Let me sleep a moment and then awake [B♭ minor chord] in your garden of sweet surprise!' The effect is enhanced by the passing of the melody from violins to clarinet for the critical bar. 'Surprise' also receives a telling harmonic twist. Departing from the model of 'Little Bells' by denying a cadential preparation in D♭ major, Elgar pauses on a first-inversion B♭ minor chord – the overall tonic minor, but in its context a 'cold' sound. The spell is now due to be broken. A reminder of the harsh world of the grown-ups is set to a theme later to be associated with the 'interfering sun' and accompanied by detached chords for horns and trombones (fig. 6). Finally the polonaise returns to frame the whole dream-episode.

There follows a strophic setting of the next two verses of the poem, never straying far from the home tonic, B♭ major. Although the sentiments are similar ('O children, open your hearts to me, / and tell me your wonderful thoughts. / Who lives in the palace inside your brain? / Who plays in its outer courts?'), the music functions as a respite after the intensity of the first verse and as a means of re-stabilising the tonic. The fourth verse, however, returns to the enchantment of 'Little Bells', but dips even further and more swiftly than before into flat-key areas (Ex. 5.2(ii)). The first phrase begins in the same fashion as the first verse, but falls stepwise to a low D♭ (in accordance with the words: 'O children, I pray you, sing low to me') and the music settles on a B♭ minor chord much sooner than in the first verse

(i) fig. 4: 6–fig. 6: 2
Ex. 5.2 'To the Children' (*The Starlight Express*) BL Add. MS.52530A

(ii) fig. 14: 1–fig. 17: 1
Ex. 5.2 (cont.)

(at 'hands'). 'Little Bells' now enters a minor third higher than before, suggesting at its outset D♭ major, the flat mediant. Its sequential repetition, a minor third higher still, continues the flatward drift (five bars later). Again the context is an erotic induction into a dream world, with the line 'I'm lost in your Fairylands' deftly aligned with the tonal shift. A clarinet provides touches of variety in instrumental colour. The tonal path is partly retraced by an unambiguous cadential preparation in D♭ major just before fig. 17, the first striking modulation in a sharpward rather than flatward direction. An unwelcome reminder of the grown-ups' world (fig. 17) leads back to a final statement of the polonaise.

The song that precedes Act III, 'My old tunes are rather broken' is a lively setting of the Organ Grinder's reminiscences. The tunes 'come from far away, / bringing just a little token / of a long-forgotten day'. The first three of the five verses relate the events of an evening when he played for some children and the Sprites while they danced around the Starlight Express. In the last verse the old man reassures himself that his tunes are still wanted, since children, to whom they are 'ne'er forgotten', love to hear him in the street. Each verse uses similar music, beginning with two boisterous phrases – presumably one of the 'old tunes' – and concluding in a slower, more reflective vein as the Organ Grinder casts back his mind. A sprightly orchestral ritornello with allusions to the 'March' from the *Wand of Youth* separates the verses. The emotionally intense fourth verse, however, breaks this mould. The old tune is slowed and transformed into a tranquil hymn which reveals that the man's latter-day performances have been as a Sprite: 'Now I am a Constellation / Free from ev'ry earthly care'. This reflective mood is followed by a lyrical outburst – again with recourse to 'Little Bells' – as he insists that 'my tunes are still entrancing, / As that night in leafy June'. This time the theme begins in the subdominant, E♭ major (the tonic of this song is again B♭). There is a brief *fortissimo* tutti at the flatward turn of 'Little Bells'. The delicacy of the modulations in 'O children' is reserved for the sharpward return to E♭ major, which parallels the return to D♭ major in Ex. 5.2(ii). After a few soft bars of stable E♭ major, the ritornello returns and leads the music back to the tonic for the final verse.

Each of these episodes functions as a still centre within its respective song. Each withdraws from a musical 'present' or from a mundane world that is subsequently reasserted before the piece can end – techniques familiar from Chapters 2 and 4. They set up precisely the kind of opposition on which the imagery of the Romantic child thrives. Yet there is a twist to Elgar's musical rendering of the Romantic framework. Although the episodes are musical 'centres', they can hardly be said to portray centredness in a psychological sense. They rely on the establishment of incompatible worlds and the ensuing possibilities for contrast, rupture and displacement. To be precise, there are two types of frame-breaking manoeuvre at work here: those that suggest the gentle sliding into a dream, and those that denote a rude awakening. At the same time, there are two characteristic modulatory impulses: those that 'delve' flatward, as though deepening or enriching the subject's experience, and those that 'rise' sharpward with a freshening effect. The episodes share a basic tonal trajectory, each making a decisive move to flat-key regions followed by a partial return prior to the awakening. The character of these visions is unstable and abortive, telling of an alienated adult consciousness which can find only fleeting solace in its fanciful reveries. The story this music tells is more believable than Elgar's characterisation of himself as an eternal child or Blackwood and Pearn's message of harmony and love at the end of *The Starlight Express*.

The Organ Grinder's songs suggest a more general perspective on the theme of childhood in Elgar's music. There are many passages, some not explicitly linked to childhood subjects, that make their effect by pausing for a brief interlude in a flat-key region, by articulating 'boundaries' between the tonal areas, and by playing off the resulting 'mundane' and 'enchanted' spheres. In such cases, 'childhood' could refer simply to a certain structure of feeling along with a set of musical techniques for generating a sense of what might be termed 'wide-eyed wonder'. Contemporary literature that celebrated the cult of childhood used similar techniques: contrasting worlds (Wonderland, Neverland, and their respective mundane counterparts) and a focus on the thresholds between worlds (a looking-glass, the gate into a secret, walled garden, and, in Elgar's play, a forest stream). Blackwood's fictional works are especially rich in the latter – witness for instance the crack at the opening of the Star Cave.[42] Instances of 'childhood' can thus overlap with 'nature' in Elgar. Yet the overlap is only partial. 'Childhood' is not associated with onomatopoeic sounds in the way that is typically the case with 'nature'; instead the threshold is articulated by tonal means.

A good example of childhood in this sense is found in the exposition of the First Symphony's first movement: an episode in F major, with strings and a sinuous flute obbligato providing rustling (or perhaps babbling) sounds. Here childhood and nature certainly overlap. As with Elgar's episodes involving thematic reminiscences, the manner in which this interlude is entered and left is crucial to its effect. As the dynamics fall and the orchestral texture is pared down, a series of discrete tonal shifts take place (Ex. 5.3(i)). The stormy music first gives way to a lilting melody passed from violins to clarinet, accompanied by incipient rustling on the harp (fig. 11).

(i) fig. 10: 4–fig. 12
Ex. 5.3 Symphony No. 1, I

The change of orchestral colour and of metre coincides with a change from two flats to a 'white-key' tonal area – a decisively 'freshening' moment. Thenceforth the modulatory direction is flatwards, with a B♭ appearing five bars later, an A♭ two bars after that, and soon an E♭ too, although the last two are cancelled, leading to the single-flat area of F major for the interlude. The preparation for the return to the vigorous 'outer' music likewise entails dynamic reduction and recourse to a spare texture using just a few strings, but this time the flatward drift is even more marked (Ex. 5.3(ii)). After settling in the local tonic, F major, the music veers into B♭ minor, and still further flatward with the C♭s and F♭ two bars before fig. 14. The restless,

(ii) fig. 13: 8–18
Ex. 5.3 (cont.)

'two-flat' music finally returns (fig. 14), being reached via the enharmonic reinterpretation of a diminished seventh, and energetic material from the first-theme group of the exposition soon reappears in its chromatically tinged A minor. Although the main tonal regions of the exposition are not, on paper, at all distant from each other (A minor/D minor and F major), the perspective-lengthening tonal and textural shifts during the transitions to and from the F major interlude make it sound far removed from its surroundings.

Another example is found in the pastoral Scene III of *Caractacus*. The G major of the Woodland Interlude gives way to its subdominant, C major, for the soft chanting of British youths and maidens as they weave sacred garlands (fig. 5). Their song keeps slipping down a tone to settle on B♭ major harmony. On the second occasion the orchestra continues the stepwise sequence to A♭ major, with the theme now taken by clarinet (fig. 10). A diminished seventh reverses the music's flatward course, and the original G major of the Interlude is re-established for the entry of the soprano. These dreamy harmonic shifts help to capture a mood of fragile innocence that is to be destroyed by the Roman invaders.

The opening of Part II of *Gerontius* adumbrates many of the ideas found in the Organ Grinder's songs: sleep, awakening, dreaming, and a sense of refreshment coming to an old man. The hushed orchestral prelude, suggesting the suspension of earthly temporality, moves from the initial tonic, F major, to the subdominant, where a long B♭ bass pedal is sustained until a cadence is made on the submediant. When the soul of Gerontius enters with an A ('I went to sleep'), clarinets answer with the prelude's main motif, now transposed to the submediant major key of D. This move is balanced by a sudden tack flatward when strings take up the accompaniment at 'and now I am refreshed', suggesting an E♭ major area. A further step in the same direction is taken at 'A strange refreshment', as clarinets re-enter with a lilting tune in F minor (the overall tonic minor; fig. 5). After a cadence in A♭ major the mood and key of the prelude return, the soul wondering at the stillness of his surroundings and his inability to 'hear' even the beat of time. Following the pattern of the prelude there is now a modulation to the subdominant, but it is relatively undramatised in comparison with the preceding episode. It is not until the soul resumes its reflections on the effects of the new experiences upon its inner condition ('This silence pours a solitariness / Into the very essence of my soul') that the music moves decisively to a flat-key region, with the return of the F minor material (fig. 8). This time, though, there is no framing F major to return to – instead the soul starts to feel the presence of the Guardian Angel and is drawn out of its introspection altogether as new tonal areas and musical ideas are established. Elgar's 'childlike' tonal digressions tend to be associated with a pensive, inward gaze and with cyclical patterns of flatward modulation and return; they do not sit easily within musical structures that support exchange and dialogue.

THE ELGARIAN CHILD TRANSFORMED

When the cellist Jacqueline du Pré was awarded an honorary doctorate by the University of London, John Barron, Professor of Greek at King's College, delivered an oration which concluded with a recitation of the final verse of Wordsworth's poem, 'The Solitary Reaper':

> Whate'er the theme, the Maiden sang
> As if her song could have no ending:
> I saw her singing at her work,

And o'er the sickle bending; –
I listened, motionless and still;
And, as I mounted up the hill,
The music in my heart I bore,
Long after it was heard no more.[43]

The last two lines were a reminder that du Pré's career had been cut short in her late twenties by multiple sclerosis, while at the same time offering an assurance that the prodigious achievements of her early years would never be forgotten. Yet the professor's choice of poem has further and more potent significance, for he eulogises du Pré by identifying her with a Romantic child. The poem tells of a 'Highland Lass' who sings to herself in a deserted field as she reaps. Her song is beautiful and seemingly melancholy, but the poet cannot understand the words (in a note, Wordsworth explains that she is supposed to be singing in Gaelic). So she is enigmatic and elusive: in the end the poet can only walk on and leave her to her work. The transient, unearthly impression of the girl recalls audiences' responses to the youthful du Pré, whose appearance was sometimes likened to an angel and her exceptional talents praised as 'heaven-sent-gifts'. After her death at the age of 42, the combined efforts of the music, film and publishing industries ensured that for the public she took on a tragic, Peter Pan-like persona, the early recordings ensuring her reputation but confining her to the role of *puella aeterna*.

The fact that du Pré was closely linked with the Elgar Cello Concerto – indeed, was largely responsible for the revival of the work in the 1960s – was a most fruitful paradox. For the concerto, composed in 1919, carries strong overtones of melancholy and regret; today it is nothing less than a cliché to call it Elgar's farewell to the shattered ideals of the pre-war world. For du Pré's sister Hilary, 'Jackie's ability to portray the emotions of a man in the autumn of his life was one of her extraordinary and inexplicable capacities'. After her adult concert debut at the Royal Festival Hall at the age of 17, the *Daily Mail* critic Percy Cater wrote that 'to me it was affecting that this later Elgar work, with its hints of autumn, should be presented to us by a girl in her springtime'. The documentary film director Christopher Nupen reflected on her ability to capture Elgar's melancholy: 'I have always thought that in some strange way it was directly related to her youth; a curious combination of youthful sensitivity, uninhibited energy and musical honesty.'[44] The partnership with the elderly Sir John Barbirolli on her first recording of the concerto – a living link to the composer – reinforced the topos of age / youth. Occasionally her unrestrained rendering of the concerto met with critical resistance – at least in the early days. 'If her interpretation had a fault it was that it missed Elgar's characteristic vein of understatement; the work's autumnal ambiguities faded in the light of such uncompromising ardour.'[45] To this day, some Elgarians continue to find the expression on her recordings exaggerated. On the whole, however, critical opinion has extolled the du Pré/Elgar combination. Reviewing one of her last public performances in 1973, Neville Cardus felt that she had tempered the virtuosity of her earliest interpretations of the concerto, and now

went to the heart of the matter with a devotion remarkable in so young an artist, so that we did not seem to be hearing, as overhearing, music which has the sunset touch on it, telling of the end of an epoch in our island story and, also, telling of Elgar's acceptance of the end. The bright day is done, and he is for the dark. Towards the close of the concerto Elgar recalls a theme from the slow movement and the falling cadences are even self-pitying. Jacqueline du Pré got the wounding juice out of this self-revealing passage: her tone came from her sensitively quivering fingers.[46]

The binary oppositions that clustered around du Pré's Elgar – age/youth, male composer/female performer, autumn/spring, restraint/abandon – thus worked to the long-term advantage of both cellist and concerto.

Yet the case of the Cello Concerto is a strange one. It is not to detract from du Pré's formative role in the 1960s Elgar revival to observe that in some respects the work had been waiting for her to come along. This is more than a matter of pointing out the obvious precedent of the Elgar/Yehudi Menuhin partnership that had famously recorded the Violin Concerto in 1932. For something in the Cello Concerto had already suggested to J. B. Priestley a potent matrix of ideas about youth, age and renewal, which he had worked through in his play *The Linden Tree* (1948), anticipating du Pré's debut with the work by fourteen years. In the play, a professor of history is nearing the end of his career at a university in the fictional town of Burmanley, a supposedly undistinguished place to which he moved from Oxford many years previously (possibly out of a sense of idealism, and much to his wife's chagrin). He is now seen as outmoded by the university authorities, who are pressuring him to retire. He has four children, three of whom have left home and become cynical or disillusioned with the world of post-war Britain. Only the 18-year-old Dinah, who plays the cello, is still innocent and open-minded. As Mrs Cotton, the housekeeper, tells the Professor, '18. But she still lives in the land o'childhood, where you an' me's forgotten'.[47] The Professor retains a special affection for his youngest daughter, since, unlike the other adults in his family, he is not yet wholly given over to disenchantment.

Nevertheless, when he overhears her practising the Elgar concerto he perceives in the music:

a kind of long farewell. An elderly man remembers his world before the war of 1914, some of it years and years before perhaps – being a boy at Worcester – or Germany in the nineties – long days on the Malvern Hills – smiling Edwardian afternoons – Maclaren and Ranji batting at Lords, then Richter or Nikisch at the Queen's Hall – all gone, lost for ever – and so he distils his tenderness and regret, drop by drop, and seals the sweet melancholy in a Concerto for cello. And he goes, too, where all the old green sunny days and the twinkling nights went – gone, gone. But then what happens? Why, a little miracle . . . Young Dinah Linden, all youth, all eagerness, saying hello and not farewell to anything, who knows and cares nothing about Bavaria in the nineties or the secure and golden Edwardian afternoons, here in Burmanley, this very afternoon . . . unseals for us the precious distillation, uncovers the tenderness and regret, which are ours now as well as his, and our lives and Elgar's, Burmanley to-day and the Malvern Hills in a lost sunlight, are all magically intertwined.[48]

Dinah is playing the 'second subject' of the first movement (Priestley probably means the music starting at fig. 7 in the score), and the Professor warms to his subject:

But that theme, you know – (hums it a moment) you can tell at once it's a farewell to a long-lost summer afternoon. It's got a deep drowsy summerishness that belongs to everybody's youth – it's telling you quite plainly that now there aren't any such afternoons – the sun's never as hot, the grass as thick, the shade as deep and drowsy – and where are the bumble bees?[49]

Later he and Dinah listen to part of the recording by Pablo Casals. They reach the moment near the end of the finale when a theme from the slow movement is recalled and then the cello takes up the bold opening gesture of the whole work one last time (a passage discussed in Chapter 2, and mentioned by Neville Cardus in the review of a du Pré performance quoted above). Dinah thinks Elgar is 'saying goodbye' to the earlier themes. The Professor agrees: 'Wandering through the darkening house of life – touching all the things he loved – crying farewell – forever – forever – '.[50] At the end of the play, the Professor's friend, the University Secretary, arrives to tell him he has been sidelined by the Vice-Chancellor. The two reflect on a favourite theme of Priestley's: the darkening prospect of human life in a modern age of machines, whether educational, bureaucratic, capitalist or trade unionist. 'Here in Burmanley', hopes the Professor, 'with Dinah and her kind – and a few friends and allies – I can still blow a little – brighten an ember or two.' The secretary tells him that 'the young and the old are the best now, Robert. There's a lot of rotten stuff in the middle'. That has always been the case, answers the Professor. 'Nearer the door in and the door out, and with more spirit to spare. The world's too much with middles, who are busy looking for promotion and a seat on the Board.'[51] The curtain falls with the Professor and his daughter alone on the stage, he reading aloud from the manuscript of his latest book.

One way to end this chapter would be to point out the continuing popularity of the Elgar Cello Concerto among today's audiences and today's young British cellists, who find success by following in the footsteps of du Pré. This would provide an opportunity to celebrate the absorption of the work into the mainstream repertory as a triumph of the Elgar revival. But there is a disadvantage to that route, for it risks again investing in a Romantic discourse of reinvigoration and renewal through youth. A bleaker angle on the topic may be appropriate. After all, the continual use of the concerto for the debuts of young performers at major festivals and as a vehicle at competition finals could be seen as, at best, a static ritual, at worst a safe commercial pitch that guarantees an audience and trades on the fame and tragedy of du Pré. From this perspective it seems more likely that, at the start of the twenty-first century, the latter-day transformation of the Romantic child into a post-pubescent performer has already run its course as a means of freshly imagining Elgar's music. The 1995 Channel 4 television film *Elgar's Tenth Muse*, directed by Paul Yule, for instance, engages the subject at length but has nothing new to offer. James Fox (who over-acts along with the rest of the cast) plays the post-war Elgar of 1919 as an upper-class dimwit who stumbles around his Sussex retreat with furrowed brow, looking mournful and confused. Elgar's sorrows over the war, his dying wife and his absent muse are ameliorated by an encounter with the vivacious young Hungarian violinist Jelly d'Aranyi, who plays his Violin Sonata at a private soirée. The historical fact of their meeting provides the starting point for the film's fictional scenario. Elgar takes a fancy to d'Aranyi, and their relationship, though abortive, briefly revives his old spirit. The theme of youth and age is announced as early as the opening credits, which are set against a modern performance of the Adagio of the Cello Concerto in a London church by the BBC Symphony Orchestra and the then BBC Young Musician of the Year, Natalie Clein (who had won the competition playing the work). Elgar himself haunts the proceedings from the gallery, already looking sorrowful, and, in a close-up shot, closing his eyes in anguish as the orchestra takes up the cello's sighing phrase (the third beat of fig. 37). Just to make sure the message gets home, the slogan on the cover of the subsequently released video plunges the Romantic child into a final bathos: *'because every end is also a new beginning*'.[52] In fact the slogan is true in an unfortunately literal sense, since the very idea used at the beginning of this film had already appeared near the end of two stage plays. David Pownall's *Elgar's Rondo* concludes with Elgar observing a female cellist in modern dress playing the concerto, and the echo of the later stages of *The Linden Tree* is obvious too. Today any renewal promised by the Romantic child in relation to Elgar's music seems increasingly stale.

CHAPTER 6

Identity

Previous chapters have been much concerned with so-called 'inner' and 'outer' layers in Elgar's music, the effect of their juxtaposition in the course of a work and their links to literary and other contexts. To understand Elgar in terms of subjective dualism is hardly new. In the inter-war period, a dichotomy between contrasted personae in Elgar's music was mooted, although at that stage it was seen as an almost schizophrenic trait, signifying at best compositional unevenness, at worst erratic fluctuation in taste. By contrast, since the 1960s a similar approach has opened the way for an effective defensive manoeuvre in the now burgeoning sphere of Elgarian apologetics. In this scenario the outer Elgar is implicitly denigrated, or, at the very least, set up as an obvious 'default' Elgar that the inquisitive critic will try to scrape beneath. Just as latter-day biography has aimed to look beyond the country squire, the over-dressed courtier and the Edwardian gentleman, making much instead of the nature-lover, the religious mystic and the childlike dreamer, so sympathetic Elgar criticism has usually deemed the musical inner persona – in whatever guise it appears in a work – the more attractive and authentic. This chapter addresses both the compositional and the verbal rhetorics associated with that critical approach. Along the way, it takes special heed of the social and political implications. One of the reasons for Elgar's enduring appeal in contemporary Britain is that concepts that frame questions about his personal identity seem also to lend themselves conveniently to the discussion of a national identity: 'Englishness'. The political tone of that discussion is often unexpectedly progressive.

In the 1920s, the delineation of dual personalities became a popular strategy for dealing with eminent figures of previous generations who had, for various reasons, become faintly embarrassing. When Cecil Gray applied the idea to Elgar, he cited Harold Nicolson's distinction between Tennyson the public bard and Tennyson the melancholy mystic, and quoted one of Bernard Shaw's characters on the 'eastern' Kipling ('a writer of merit') versus the 'western' Kipling ('an amusing barbarian').[1] Gray similarly distinguished between the composer of the symphonies and 'the self-appointed Musician Laureate of the British Empire, always ready to hymn rapturously the glories of our blood and state at the slightest provocation'. However, even the serious Elgar emerges damaged from the essay, partly because of Gray's overall knockabout tone, partly because in his opinion the imperialist tone intrudes upon all the works, exerting 'a pernicious and subtly contaminating influence'.[2] An article by Frank Howes entitled 'The Two Elgars', penned just one year after the composer's death, likewise makes reference to Harold Nicolson, this time on the subject of Lord Curzon, who possessed 'a certain simplicity and understanding of fundamentals persisting behind a façade of elaborate splendour and pride in vainglorious inessentials'.[3] Howes thought there were virtually two different people struggling inside Elgar, who correspond roughly to 'the Elgar who writes for strings and the Elgar who writes for brass'. The two often inhabit the same work, resulting in 'a vein of tinsel among a rich vein of gold'.[4] Howes does not search for a critical perspective that would accommodate both; like Gray, he deems the intrusion of one upon the other to be problematic.

It was not until the era of the Mahler revival in Britain, when the idea of a single work assuming several different, perhaps even contradictory, 'voices' became a topic of particular interest, that a position of accommodation was persuasively advanced. Anthony Payne, protesting in 1962 against the negative image of Elgar as a complacent imperialist, declared that 'Elgar never conceived a confident vision in his life. Gestures of apparent confidence there may be, but it is not difficult to see these outbursts for what they really are, the moments of unreal extroversion that characterise the nervous inward personality. The signs are plain to see in the tonal fluctuations and the tendency to withdraw on to some distant poetic plane.'[5] The picture Payne went on to draw of a nervy Elgar creating unstable symphonic processes was taken up by Kennedy. 'The outbursts of extrovert grandiloquence in the symphonies are always followed by withdrawn, cloistered passages of tender lyricism, the general effect, as in Mahler, emphasising the instability of the full conception.'[6] Kennedy contrasts the 'laureate' with the 'mystic' Elgar, the 'London pride' with the 'windflower' Elgar. This view acknowledges both Elgars, though it betrays a preference for what Kennedy calls Elgar's 'withdrawn style', the moments when, as Vaughan Williams put it, 'he seems to have withdrawn into the solitude of his own sanctuary'.[7]

When, in non-pejorative versions of the 'two Elgars' concept, this or a similar preference is uttered explicitly, the usual corollary is to urge the critic or the listener to engage in a search 'beyond' or 'beneath' the 'super-ficial' level. Thus A. E. Sheldon speaks of 'stripping away' the populist Elgar to leave 'a composer of visionary imaginings'. Ernest Newman aims 'to cut away some of the dead wood that has accumulated, with the passage of the years, at the roots of the great tree of Elgar's best music'.[8] Kennedy advises: 'If we want to understand his music, we should forget its external trappings and accretions and remember only his descriptions of the Cello Concerto and the Second Symphony: "a man's attitude to life" and "the passionate pilgrimage of a soul".' Elsewhere he insists: 'What we owe him is the effort of stripping away from [the marches] the political accretions and listening to them simply as music.'[9] Kennedy's embarrassment at the political associations of Elgar's music is palpable, and the insistence that it expresses uncontaminated personal subjectivity is a recurrent theme in his writings. Jerrold Northrop Moore's interpretation of the First Symphony's finale pushes this line of argument to a tendentious extreme. 'The Symphony's understanding is something like a final rejection of "the soldier instinct in me" – in favour of an acknowledgement of the truest inspiration in the wind of nature, rising through the aeolian harp in the composer's study window. This grand singing of the pastoral ideal through lengthening motto music [the E♭ minor episode] entirely overshadows the little Allegro recapitulation that follows.' Moore concludes that 'his truest inspiration lies in this language of private pastoral, and not finally in any public "marching", however compelling'.[10]

Today, the updated version of the 'two Elgars' idea structures much discourse on the composer by his admirers. Its advocates tend to mix special pleading with some measure of insight. The music certainly seems to invite this kind of treatment on many occasions; the techniques already outlined in this book – thematic reminiscence, frame-breaking gestures, the delineation of enchanted spheres, the articulation of thresholds – confirm as much.[11] The present chapter examines the internalisation of nostalgia through the construction of Elgarian – and by extension national – identities through the use of inner/outer oppositions, both in Elgar's musical practice and in his reception. Such oppositions are doubly inter-esting because, although they map with ease onto sympathetic conceptions of Englishness, they tend to be conservative with only a lower-case 'c'.[12] Elgar's Left-leaning admirers are powerfully attracted to the inner/outer model; it is they, after all, who are most embarrassed by the tub-thumping Elgar. The linkage of Elgar and national identity under examination here, then, is not the one that is enjoyed in the boxes at the Last Night of the Proms. There is no reason why that audience should not feel the tug of the present version from time to time, but it is not they who advocate it persistently and persuasively.

The following discussion is far from a comprehensive survey of contributions to the 'two Elgars' question, still less an examination of the numerous ways in which commentators have tried (and generally failed) to locate an intrinsic Englishness in the music. Instead it seeks, by means of three case studies, to mark out the coordinates of the debate and show what is at stake. The first of these concerns the writings of J. B. Priestley, the most eloquent advocate of the sympathetic critical position that emerged in the 1960s. A progressive social critic as well as a man of letters, Priestley relished the intimate side of Elgar, which for him represented the true Englishness of 'the people', free from any establishment posturing. The second case study arises from dissatisfaction with arguments like Priestley's, which attribute to the music some fixed, 'deep' identity. In the choral works of the late 1890s, Elgar stages two encounters between different aspects of the contested notions of Englishness that were under discussion in late Victorian society. Here, even more clearly than in the later symphonic works, he plays off two personae against one another for dramatic effect. The final section of the chapter discusses David Rudkin's television play *Penda's Fen* (1974), which takes a radical view of the questions of nation and identity, rejecting the idea that 'Englishness' can or should be understood as coherent or stable. Even in this scenario, however, Elgar has something significant to contribute: Rudkin's modern-day protagonist sees past the conventional English gentleman to a visionary artist who illuminates the truth, as the playwright sees it, about the layered, conflicted nature of all human identity.

THE FEMININE ELEMENT INSIDE

J. B. Priestley (1894–1984), social critic, novelist, playwright and essayist, eloquent wartime broadcaster, 'founding father of the social democratic era',[13] and long-time expositor on British society and character, had a rare understanding of the expressive profile of Elgar's music and a gift for responding to it with engaging prose. As shown in Chapters 2 and 5, he worked the music into his fictional writings, where it helped to illuminate characters' feelings or relationships. Sometimes this meant simply an appeal to the music's mood, as with the Cello Concerto – a work to which he had frequent recourse when lamenting a vanished, better world. But he also had a keen ear for Elgar's techniques of frame-breaking and reminiscence, as evinced by Dinah Linden's reflections on the finale of the Cello

Concerto and by the epiphany experienced by Laura Casey as the distant tones of the 'Welsh tune' drift to her ears. Priestley, whose affinity for Elgar may owe something to his affectionate memories of his Edwardian childhood in Bradford, made much of the music during the 1940s and 1950s, the very time when Elgar's reputation was suffering an eclipse.[14] When, in the 1970s, he formalised his long-held ideas about English national character and about the Edwardian era in two popular histories, *The Edwardians* (1970) and *The English* (1973), he mounted a robust defence of Elgar, insisting that listeners should delve beneath the 'persona', as he called it, to discover a visionary poet of tender, melancholy 'Englishness'. Like Elgar's scholarly and artistic defenders of the 1960s, he answered the irony of the composer's inter-war critics by appropriating the 'two Elgars' model and turning it to his advantage. Indeed, from a literary point of view Priestley represents the culmination of that strategy, for he brought to bear on Elgar a nostalgia of unmatched lyricism.

Priestley's reputation as a Left-wing social commentator was established with his *English Journey* (1934), which recounted a tour of the country and contained a candid account of depressed northern districts which came as a shock to much of his middle-class readership. In that book Priestley distinguishes three Englands. First there is 'Old England': rural, pre-industrial, implicitly southern, epitomised by the Cotswolds. Then comes industrial England: a nineteenth-century urban landscape of the Midlands and the North, often unkind to its inhabitants, and always ugly and polluting. Finally Priestley identifies a modern, post-war England, which in his view is an extension of America, and is characterised by arterial roads, filling stations, cafés, suburban bungalows and Woolworths. Modern England's egalitarianism is welcome in so far as it makes commodities affordable to all, but it is demoralising in its appeal to people's most commonplace aspirations.[15] Priestley is beguiled by Old England, although he recognises that a return to medieval society is hardly desirable.

England's rural landscape nevertheless yields an important insight into the national character, an idea Priestley's writings advanced persistently. On account of the climate, the countryside is almost always misty and hazy so that nothing stands out too sharply and the topographical features seem to merge softly into one another. Similarly, the English mind – unlike its continental counterpart – tends to blur matters of intellect and intuition. Priestley spoke of 'a haze, rubbing away the hard edges of ideas, softening and blending the hues of passion. Reason is there, but not all conquering.'[16] Forty years after *English Journey*, in *The English*, he elevated this principle of mingling intellect and intuition, conscious and unconscious thought, to the single secret, the clue, to the English character, and pursued it through the whole book.[17] From this perspective the hazy countryside of Old England is enduringly relevant to modern England, even though in practice the nation is poised somewhere between the nineteenth- and twentieth-century modes of civilisation.

Priestley became ever more anxious about the survival of this underlying Englishness. Like many social critics of his generation, he believed that an influx of American commercial values and productions into modern England posed a threat to the national character and way of life. In the 1930s he completed several novels that address the corrupting influence of mass culture on the English working class, and for the rest of his life he periodically railed against its corrosive effects.[18] The English, he felt, were in danger of auctioning their birthright. By the 1970s he was gloomy about the future: 'Englishness is not as strong as it was ... It needs to be nurtured.'[19]

Priestley's personal sense of loss can be partly traced to his memories of his Bradford childhood before the First World War. He drew on them creatively in the inter-war years, especially in his novel *The Good Companions* (1929), and referred to them tenderly in later non-fiction. In Priestley's account of his own past, he grew up among 'the people', in touch with their ethos and aspirations, relishing their culture of regional pride, their colourful characters, and their exciting popular entertainments such as music halls, clubs and holiday outings. For Priestley, this was an innocent, pre-lapsarian world that was changed for ever by the war and then gradually undermined still further by the insidious spread of mass culture.[20] His Bradford thus stood for all of England. In the 1960s, when he had been living in the south for decades, Priestley explained that 'Part of me is still in Bradford, though when I return there now I wander about half lost, a melancholy stranger'.[21] Despite his frequent recourse to rural pan-egyric, then, Priestley would hardly have concurred with Stanley Baldwin that 'England is the country'. His longing was directed at an urban community of industrial England – albeit a community that had to make the best of a distinctly unpromising environment.

In reality Priestley belonged to the lower middle class. His father was a Sabbatarian schoolteacher and an ethical socialist, and he inherited some of these values. 'My politics are based entirely on compassion,' he explained. He was impatient with Marxist doctrine and vocabulary, eschewing any systematic development of notions of class and always appealing instead to 'the people'. Moreover, his outlook rested on a rejection of materialism, whether of a socialist or a capitalist description. Priestley can best be understood as one of the last representatives of an insular tradition of nineteenth-century English popular radicalism which urged the inhabitants of the provincial, industrial regions to wrest back the nation from the control of privileged elites.[22] An unabashed 'Little Englander' who disapproved of the empire and harangued the English about overlooked social problems at home, Priestley was by the same token no internationalist. Indeed his impassioned treatment of nation and Englishness as essential qualities reflects his peculiar version of socialism with its disavowal of class analysis. In his later writings, a conventional anti-capitalist, mass-culture critique is brought together with an urgent plea to save the integrity of a single national identity.

Given the obvious historical multiplicity of behaviours, motives, aptitudes and aspects presented by actual English people, it is necessary for Priestley to argue that the English are rather easily lured and detached from their basic identity; other, inauthentic selves can step in and take its place, at least to all appearances. On one level, therefore, Englishness is a protean quality, although in his more self-assured moments Priestley believes that 'these differences, obvious enough above ground, don't go down and strike at the roots'.[23] As regards his writings on Elgar, the most important of the replacement identities are those associated with the ruling class of the nineteenth century. He decries the stoic, repressed products of the public schools as misguided imitations of the Duke of Wellington (who, having been born in Ireland, he conveniently classifies as not really English at all). On their account the English have acquired an undeserved reputation as 'chilly, reptilian creatures, incapable of feeling' – whereas the underlying reality is the reverse.[24] Priestley dislikes even more the 'Big Englanders', the unthinking imperialists, 'red-faced, staring, loud-voiced fellows, wanting to go and boss everybody about all over the world'.[25] One of the central goals of *The English*, with its enquiry into English intuition at the expense of the 'despotic intellect', is to allow for 'a cast and habit of mind that are feminine, not belonging to the robustly masculine image that Englishmen have projected down the centuries'. 'It is possible', Priestley explains, 'to be aggressively over-masculine outside, if only to hide or simply to protect the feminine element inside.'[26]

When writing about Elgar, Priestley is always careful to dispel misconceptions (as he sees them) by exposing for what it is the 'retired-colonel-off-to-the-races *persona*', the 'carapace to the sensitive quivering artist'. 'Too much has been made of him as a complacent Edwardian Imperialist. This belongs to his persona, not to the personality discovered in his serious music.'[27] Priestley deploys this defensive move as part of a rhetoric that identifies and extols the resulting 'true' Elgar behind the mask. In *The English*, having dismissed the label 'typically Edwardian' as a 'shallow comment on his *persona*', he explains that the 'serious music' 'goes against the spirit of his age and is filled with sudden anger – the brass suddenly raging against the strings and woodwind – and dubieties and bewilderment and regrets and a nostalgia not for youth and the Malvern hills but for some world we have all lost'.[28] Earlier he had rejected the idea that the English are an unmusical people – in fact they are well suited to composition, for it demands a blending of conscious and unconscious elements. 'Technical mastery and a calculation of effect' cannot alone produce great music. 'Irrational elements, emerging from the unconscious, must be fused into such music.'[29] This helps him to account for the peculiar appeal of Elgar to his countrymen. 'Here his Englishness, so open to the unconscious, so defiant of rationality, calls to our Englishness.' The point extends even to conductors. Boult and Barbirolli are successful interpreters, but foreigners 'when at last they do decide to include some Elgar, seem to be baffled by his characteristic rhythms and cadences and often miss the whole shape and flow of him'.[30]

In a popular volume entitled *Particular Pleasures* (1975) Priestley singles out the First Symphony for special praise. This time he explains that his American acquaintances are especially prone to misunderstand the composer. He puts it down to Elgar's Englishness once again, not what he regards as the superficial variety of Englishness – folk tunes and 'hey nonney, etc.' – but a deep one. 'No, Elgar was never in his work superficially English, but both as a composer and as a man he was Deeply English, something not easily understood in New York, Chicago, Los Angeles.' The term 'deep England' was adopted in the 1980s by cultural critics and detractors of the British heritage industry to belittle what they saw as a reactionary streak of countryside-worship inherited by contemporary Britain from the 1930s.[31] But here Priestley uses the 'superficial' / 'deep' polarity, along with prepositions such as 'behind' and 'below', to make a forceful point about Elgar:

What is this deep Englishness that enchants fellow countrymen like myself? It is easy for us to recognise and enjoy but hard to explain. We are at heart an imaginative people – it is our dramatist-poets and actors who have conquered the world, not our shopkeepers – and we applaud bold dramatic statements that challenge the imagination, like those of Churchill in 1940; but behind them we welcome a brooding tenderness, and behind or below that still a dreamy melancholy. (Foreign visitors in the seventeenth and eighteenth centuries noted this, before the Industrial Revolution and the Empire buried it a little deeper.) All Elgar's more important music reflects and expresses, boldly or exquisitely, these characteristics.[32]

His favourite movement from the First Symphony is the third, 'one of the great adagios of all time. I don't know how often I have listened to it, either in a concert hall or through recordings, but its dying fall – with those muted trombones a stroke of genius – still clutches at my heart.' His response to the work is to draw on his rural metaphor for English identity, the indefinite, hazy landscape. Having sidelined Elgar's native countryside as an interpretative tool in *The English*, he now lets it come into its own, echoing the rhapsodies of Professor Linden, but in a less doleful vein:

My American friends can like it or lump it, but I find in this work the bold dramatic statements, the brooding tenderness, the underlying dreamy melancholy, of deep Englishness in all its varying moods. Out of this music, to me who know them well, the Malvern Hills rise in sunlight, in mist and dusk, in starry silence, in full sunlight again, in the vanishing days and nights of a lost summertime. And from the blaring brass down to muted strings, this is what the inspired Elgar is telling me.[33]

Still, Priestley's finest writing on Elgar is found in *The Edwardians*, for in that book he brings his most felicitous prose and his rhetoric of authentic and inauthentic identities to bear on the very structure of the music. He now deems Elgar 'essentially Edwardian'. This does not quite contradict his position in *The English* because, as he explains, he does not mean Edwardian in the sense of the *Pomp and Circumstance* marches. Rather, 'there is in him and his music all the rich confusion of this age, the deepening doubt, the melancholy whispers from the unconscious, as well as all that hope and glory. He is very English in this, just as he is in his characteristic rhythms and cadences.' In this way Priestley can make a perceptive point about Elgar's 'withdrawal' techniques:

Over and above his inventiveness and magnificent orchestration, and more important than they are, is something that never fails even now to ravish my ear and catch at my heart. It is the kind of passage, for ever recurring, when strings are quietened and the jagged thunder of his brass has gone, and like a purple-and-sepia sunset suddenly revealing patches of purest cerulean or fading apple-green, it is all different, strangely beautiful as music and catching at the heart because the man himself, no longer masterful, seems to be staring at us out of a sorrowing bewilderment. These moments when the *persona* is dropped are to me the secret of Elgar's lasting enchantment.[34]

The structure of this paragraph skilfully reflects its content: in the final sentence the elaborate similes and involved syntax are gone; the utterance is succinct and direct; and the insertion of 'to me' strikes the vital personal note.

So J. B. Priestley's experience of Elgar conjures up a deep, authentic, shared identity which reaches behind what he sees as the superficial versions of Englishness promoted by the establishment. The true Elgar is gentle, melancholy, brooding, tender – perhaps even 'feminine'. Despite its lyrical tone, Priestley's prose serves a nostalgia of protest, a nostalgia that purports, at least, to come 'from below'. Or perhaps better, 'from outside', for the glorification of Elgar's Worcestershire countryside is part of a celebration of the provincial in contrast to the political, cultural and economic 'centre'. In Elgar's processes of symphonic withdrawal Priestley glimpses an alternative centre – albeit one that is on the point of extinction.

If Priestley's contribution to Elgarian discourse is impressive as rhetoric – its eloquent language dispelling prejudices and reminding the reader of Elgar's most heartfelt passages – then as philosophy it is rather more flawed. Today we have learned to be suspicious of essentialising accounts of national identity, which are always potentially hegemonic in some way or other – even when in the hands of a compassionate social critic such as Priestley. The particular version of Englishness that he chooses as the true, essential one reflects a certain taste in English history and culture, with the various traits of which he disapproves being conveniently downgraded as false Englishness. (One of the consequences of this move is that his position is unchallengeable by counterexamples.) Moreover, like many of his fellow apologists, Priestley runs the risk of selling Elgar short in certain ways. By deploying the 'outer' Elgar always as a foil – a pose to be dismissed before turning to more important matters – he neglects the possibility that it might be regarded as a rhetorical weapon in Elgar's own armoury. It now seems appropriate to explore that possibility further. Some of the best places to do so are the choral works of the late 1890s, for there Elgar allows the contrasted idioms that would later underpin the moments of withdrawal in the symphonic works to stand explicitly for dramatic characters representing opposing spiritual and political values.

IMPERIALIST NOSTALGIA

The topic of Elgar and empire stands behind many of the inner/outer dichotomies that have developed in his reception. The familiar association need not be rehearsed in detail here. It is well known that the librettos of *Caractacus* (1898) and the *Coronation Ode* (1902) at times advance imperialist, even expansionist, sentiments. Some of Elgar's orchestral marches accompanied British imperial pageantry, and indeed were formative in its very construction at the turn of the twentieth century.[35] It is also widely understood that, while the link with imperialism may have helped Elgar's career, it dealt a serious blow to his posthumous reputation. The fierce reaction of intellectuals after the Great War against the imperialism of the previous generation hastened the waning of Elgar's star in the eyes of musical opinion-formers. More recently the annual Last Night of the Proms and its offshoots have ensured that the issue remains etched in the public consciousness. Elgar's defenders in the 1960s revival naturally played down the association. The pieces that overtly expressed imperialist sentiments were usually deemed minor works or potboilers to which Elgar the artist was never truly committed or which he came to renounce.[36] According to Kennedy, writing as late as 1990, Elgar the Edwardian and Elgar the imperialist 'for a long time ... obscured the real Elgar, who was someone very different'. Again he calls for a deeper kind of listening to overcome this concealment: 'The real Elgar is always there, of course. He is in *The Banner of St. George* and all the marches. But it takes attuned ears to hear him, or it did until quite recently.'[37] J. B. Priestley would have agreed.

Today Elgar's period of unfashionableness has receded sufficiently to allow for reassessment of his imperialism. Indeed it is currently the 1960s view of Elgar (rather than that of the 1920s) that serves as the 'default' position against which writers measure their thoughts.[38] Jeffrey Richards's chapter on Elgar in his book *Imperialism and Music* (2001) is a bold attempt to trump both Elgar's accusers and defenders by deconstructing the inner/ outer opposition itself. Richards is happy to acknowledge Elgar's imperialism and is unembarrassed by it; Elgar's vision of empire embraces justice, peace, freedom and equality, with the colonies destined for eventual independence. (The question of whether that vision is not simply propaganda that justifies commercially driven conquest – what the historian Peter Gay would call an 'alibi for aggression' – is passed over.)[39] The melancholy and mysticism that are usually said to be part of the inner Elgar are in fact characteristic of his imperialism too, just as they were with Kipling, Buchan, Rider Haggard and other contemporaries. 'Melancholy was part of the imperial religion, the necessary melancholy that the mission calls for so much sacrifice and many casualties.' According to Richards, then, the 'true and secret' Elgar was just as inspired by imperialism as the overtly patriotic Elgar.[40]

As a largely sympathetic account of Elgar's ideology, Richards's argument has its drawbacks: in the end Elgar's melancholy sounds very much like the melancholy of 'the White Man's burden'. But he is right to look for the interdependence of the 'two Elgars', and this section will do the same, albeit in a different way. The focus will be the two cantatas of the late 1890s,

Scenes from the Saga of King Olaf (1896) and *Caractacus* (1898), written in
the years when Elgar's ceremonial and pastoral idioms were both being
formed. These works stage scenarios of colonial encounter and conquest,
taking place in medieval Norway and ancient Britain respectively. They are
at times disturbing, on account of their easy accommodation with comfortable Victorian assumptions about the benevolence of imperial power.
Yet the cloak of antiquity means that Elgar does not have to eliminate all
complexity from the relationships between colonisers and colonised; unlike
in later items of near-propaganda such as the *Coronation Ode* (1902) and
the masque *The Crown of India* (1912), it is not a prerequisite here that the
expansionist power should be eulogised without qualification. The colonised party may be given a chance to speak. In this way, competing concepts
of national identity in the late-Victorian period are personified and made
to interact in a drama. Melancholy is once again the mediating factor
between the two, but instead of the melancholy of duty and sacrifice
evoked by Richards, it is an altogether more atavistic affair.

The anthropologist Renato Rosaldo has coined the term 'imperialist
nostalgia' for a moment of mourning felt by agents of modern colonialism
for the traditional state of a culture that they themselves have permanently
altered or even eliminated. Rosaldo regards this nostalgia as the counterpart to the sense of mission that impelled many imperialists in Western,
industrialised nations to try to modernise static, 'primitive' cultures. Once
progress becomes a virtue in itself, a psychological space is opened within
'advanced' societies that accommodates a longing for a stable, unchanging
refuge. Rosaldo points to examples among American colonial officials
and evangelical missionaries in the Philippines, who came to regret the
passing of the 'backward' customs that they had helped to stamp out.
Furthermore, imperialist nostalgia is often entwined with criteria of nature
and culture, especially when a modern culture degrades its environment
and then elevates nature to a sacred concept. An example is the emergence
of the category of 'Appalachia' in the United States and the romanticisation
of Native Americans at the very moment that the frontier was closing
and racism being fashioned into doctrine. The relevance of this concept
to the pastoral impulse in late nineteenth-century, industrial England is
also clear.[41]

Rosaldo's verdict on imperialist nostalgia is harsh: 'In any of its versions ... [it] uses a pose of "innocent yearning" both to capture people's
imaginations and to conceal its complicity with often brutal domination.'[42] In the case of Elgar, though, the issue is in one sense turned on
its head, potentially to the composer's advantage. The patriotic element in

his output is the obvious pose, whereas the imperialist nostalgia is an unexpected corollary of fleeting duration, which promises to add a dimension to his alleged complacency. Moreover, in Elgar's historical displacements of the colonial relationship, the distinction between self and other is blurred. In these cantatas, it is likely that, as the drama unfolded, a late-Victorian audience could quite easily have identified now with one side, now with the other.

King Olaf was composed against the background of the Victorian surge of interest in the 'old north', as witnessed by countless treatises, translations, novels, poems and pictures, which familiarised the British with the term 'Viking' and added depth and sympathy to the picture of violent, barbarian raiders that had been the dominant image of the Norsemen for previous generations. A sense of kinship stood behind much of this cultural phenomenon – a feeling that the Vikings embodied what was best about the contemporary English national character. It was a favourite habit of nineteenth-century nationalists throughout Europe to interpret the actions and conflicts of ancient tribes and peoples in terms of contemporary mores; after all, in the genealogical thinking of the day, ancient peoples, living in discrete groups, had 'purer' blood than their descendants, having suffered less 'mixing'. They therefore personified certain basic impulses of modern nations which had been disguised or watered down in the interim. Enthusiasts of Norse culture and institutions were certain that the English had greatly benefited from the settlement of those peoples in the old Danelaw region in the north and east of the country. For instance, Samuel Laing – a formative influence on Victorian attitudes on account of his translation of Snorri Sturluson's *Heimskringla* – celebrated the vitality and raw energy of the early seafarers, whose freedom from feudalism gave them a critical advantage over the more 'slavish' nations of Europe that languished under tyranny. As a land of granite, even Norway's geology resisted the erection of feudal castles, while government was conducted by constitutional monarchy informed by participatory democracy in the local open-air assembly or 'Thing'. Laing was hostile to Catholicism and to the political systems of Germany, both of which he saw as enduringly repressive and productive of servile passivity among the populations. It was no wonder that in medieval England the Catholic Anglo-Saxons – whom Laing regarded as 'German' in descent – had been overrun by the Norsemen. On account of a basic mentality they lacked resolve in fighting, and unlike the invaders they had little property or freedom that would have encouraged them to defend their way of life. For Laing, modern British democracy, empire, stable society, security and freedom could be traced to the Viking contribution.[43] Although his enthusiasm did not pass unchallenged, its influence can be discerned in many later aspects of the Victorian revival of the old north, sometimes taken to extremes. Charles Kingsley imagined the 'male' Vikings impregnating the 'female' Anglo-Saxons and providing a much-needed injection of manliness.[44] William and Mary Howitt opened the introduction to their book *The Literature and Romance of Northern Europe* (1852) with a paean to British power, prestige, enterprise, commerce, stability and conquest. In their view, this triumph owed little to the Anglo-Saxon element in British ancestry, for that people was slothful and weak and had 'degenerated' by the time the Danes arrived on English shores. The Howitts were unperturbed by the aggression of their heroes; like later Social Darwinists, they applauded the triumph of a strong, vigorous people over a tired, passive one.[45]

Olaf Tryggvason's Saga from the *Heimskringla* describes an exemplary Viking warrior who, for the Victorians, had the added attraction of observing the right religion. Olaf is heir to the throne of Norway, but his father is murdered and his mother flees while still pregnant. After enduring a childhood of slavery in Estonia, Olaf embarks on a series of adventures on the high seas, is converted to Christianity in the Orkneys, and returns to Norway to convert and claim his homeland. There he defeats the rulers and tears down the symbols of pagan religion. It is no wonder that the story of this king appealed to the hero-worshipping Thomas Carlyle, who thoroughly approved of his methods and described him as 'the wildly beautifulest man, in body and in soul, that one has ever heard of in the North'. (Robert Leighton's adventure novel for schoolboys *Olaf the Glorious* (1895), published the year before Elgar's setting, sustains the swashbuckling theme.)[46] Elgar based his cantata on the version of the story found in Longfellow's *Tales of a Wayside Inn* (1863–73), which follows Laing's translation but stresses Olaf's efforts for the conversion of Norway, his attempts to find a wife and his death in a battle at sea. (Extra lines were added by Elgar's Malvern neighbour H. A. Acworth.) The final libretto legitimises Olaf's assault by painting the pagan religion as black as possible: near the beginning Thor lays down a challenge to Christ, claiming that, in the North, 'Force rules the world still, / Has ruled it, shall rule it; / Meekness is weakness, / Strength is triumphant'. Olaf, by contrast, serves the 'God of peace'. This evasion clearly irritated Ernest Newman, for one, who complained that 'a quarrelsome, high-spirited, land-grabbing, bad-mannered, courageous viking – a real creature of his day – is made to figure as a saint'. 'It is a mistake for a modern composer to wrap this raw being in religious music and make him pose as a kind of bulwark of the faith.'[47]

Still, Elgar and Acworth were not blind to the few hints left by Longfellow as to the king's shortcomings. (His high-handed snubbing of Queen Sigrid of Svithiod, for instance, who refuses to marry him if the price is her religious conversion, eventually leads to his demise.) And if Olaf stands on one level for a progressive, modernising imperialism, it is notable that Elgar eschews the most obvious means available to him to characterise that idea – he does not give Olaf any music in his grand, processional idiom. The triumphant close of the conversion scene avoids any truly expansive melody. Amongst the numerous quasi-Wagnerian leitmotivs that help to bind together the loosely connected scenes, those associated with Christianity are relatively compact (Ex. 6.1). It is not until the middle of the central scene, 'The Wraith of Odin', that Elgar at last unleashes his grand style. And it is here that the imperialist nostalgia is felt, for the gesture celebrates not the conqueror but his vanquished foe.

In this scene, Olaf is feasting in the hall at Augvaldsness, with his skalds (bards) singing and the guests making merry. Suddenly the doors swing open and a one-eyed stranger with a grey beard is revealed. The king welcomes him and gives him a seat at the royal table. The old man tells tales of distant lands and transfixes Olaf and the guests with a recitation

(i) fig. Y: 1–8 (orchestral parts only)

(ii) fig. W: 1–2

Ex. 6.1 'The Conversion' (*Scenes from the Saga of King Olaf*): two motifs associated with Christianity

from the 'Havamal' – the part of the Poetic Edda traditionally attributed to Odin himself. Olaf sleeps, but when morning breaks the mysterious stranger is nowhere to be found, even though no one has seen him leave, the doors are barred, and there are no footprints. Olaf realises this was the wraith of Odin, who perished upon the conversion of Norway. He draws the conclusion that the Faith is secure.

Looking back almost thirty years later, Elgar confessed that he had 'never done anything like' the music for this scene before or since.[48] His judgement was sound – it is the undoubted high point of the score. The choice of leitmotivs is apt, the music captures the weird atmosphere of the tale, the choral writing is brilliant, and the quick march to the refrain 'Dead rides Sir Morten of Fogelsang' is suitably hair-raising.[49] As with all the scenes in the cantata, the action is prefaced by a brief solo for a voice personifying a skald. At the words 'How the wraith of Odin old', the orchestra plays Odin's motif with its unusual harmonies and chromatic steps. The next line, 'Song and tale and saga told', is accompanied by the theme which begins the Introduction to the whole cantata ('There is a wondrous book of legends in the old Norse tongue'), in its original key – Elgar's key of mystery, G minor. Elgar thought of the Introduction to the work as a gathering of skalds resolving to tell the succession of tales that make up the saga. Its music returns to close the work and the G minor theme thus functions on each of its appearances both as a referent for the concept 'saga' and as a framing device indicating an induction into the enchanted world of the *Heimskringla*. The central climax of 'The Wraith of Odin' uses the same technique; this time, however, a second 'saga' theme from the Introduction is employed – a theme which until this point has not been reprised in the course of the work. Having sounded faintly trite on its initial appearances in the Introduction, the tune is now allowed to unfold in the utmost grandeur (Ex. 6.2). As the god recites his own words ('Then from his lips in music rolled / The Havamal of Odin old, / With sounds mysterious as the roar / Of billows on a distant shore'), Elgar summons the most expansive sound from his orchestra, augmented by the organ. The texture is composed of Elgar's favoured three parts in 'open' spacing with the bass marching downwards. The tempo slackens for this section and the basic pulse is changed from crochet to minim, ensuring a stately tread. (The tempo subsequently picks up again for the next statement of the refrain and the rest of the story.) The subsequent use of Olaf's solemn chorale tune (Ex. 6.1(i)) for the words 'I know that Odin the Great is dead; / Sure is the triumph of our Faith' cannot match the sublimity of the preceding interlude. Indeed it seems almost puny in comparison, as

Ex. 6.2 'The Wraith of Odin' (*Scenes from the Saga of King Olaf*), fig. I: 1–16

the king appears to admit with his epithet for the defeated deity. 'Never was I so enthralled / Either by Saga-man or Scald' he confesses. Elgar omitted those lines of Longfellow's, but his music perfectly conveys their sentiment.

This dynamic of enchantment is the key to the scene. In a variant on Elgar's usual frame-breaking techniques, one of the defining components of the frame itself – the second 'saga' motif – returns as something framed, an interlude set apart from the rest of the movement. Olaf, having started the cantata inside the narrative frame, has now, as it were, broken through to join the audience, no less entranced than they by the grandeur and exoticism of the ancient poems. Such feelings have become available to him because he has become a force of modernity: goal-directed, Christianising, politically unifying. In Odin's performance he hears an echo of his own former self: as the skald says before the chorus, 'Sing ye now and with the strain / Ancient mem'ries wake again'.

In *King Olaf*, the musical rendering of imperialist nostalgia does not draw on the familiar opposition of musical idioms that would later define the outer and the inner Elgars respectively – confident expansiveness and withdrawn wistfulness. Instead it is the enchanted, inner self that is figured as something grand and noble. The emergence of the better-known stylistic matrix can be traced to *Caractacus*, composed two years later. The intervening period had witnessed the first blossoming of Elgar's patriotic idiom in the works he composed for the Diamond Jubilee celebrations of 1897: the *Imperial March* and the cantata *The Banner of St. George*. This style was pressed into service for the 'Triumphal March' for the Roman legions in *Caractacus*. At the same time, most of the story is set in the Worcestershire countryside, leaving Elgar plenty of scope to indulge his new vein of pastoral lyricism. Like *King Olaf,* the work stages an encounter between two facets of a single identity – in this case more obviously modern British identity. But here the relationship between the two is even more conflicted.

Caractacus relates the story of the British chieftain's last stand against the Roman invader, including his preparations on the Malvern Hills, his consultation with local druids, an idyllic pastoral scene, his defeat by the Roman army, his captivity in Rome, his audience with the Emperor Claudius and his successful appeal for clemency for his fellow captives and his people. Today the work is best remembered for its jingoistic final chorus, which assures the audience that, despite their defeat, the British will take up the Roman mantle and build an even greater empire, one based on the 'order, law and liberty' that Caractacus urges the emperor to teach his people. The final lines read

> And when at last they find it,
> The nations all shall stand
> And hymn the praise of Britain,
> Like brothers, hand in hand.

When Jaeger voiced reservations, Elgar explained that it was he who had suggested a patriotic finale to the librettist (again H. A. Acworth). Although he claimed that he had not bargained for the brazenness of the eventual result, he defended it.[50] Subsequent reaction to the final chorus from Elgar's advocates has ranged from embarrassment to derision. Ernest Newman, for instance, complained that the work ends in 'a sputter of bathos and rant'.[51] Most commentators agree that, regardless of the political message, the sentiments are contrived, given that the rest of *Caractacus* revolves around a fateful defeat. In the context of the present argument, however, the illogicality of the chorus is highly suggestive. It reads like a token effort to paper over the cracks that the work comes dangerously close to exposing in the contested ground of late nineteenth-century 'Englishness', assuring the audience that a happy synthesis of ancient Roman and British values will eventually triumph. (There was a special imperative to avoid an ambivalent ending given that Elgar hoped to dedicate the work to Queen Victoria – and eventually did so.) It is thus worth examining the historical conventions of the representation of these respective peoples, to reveal the peculiarities of Elgar's version of the *Caractacus* story and to characterise the crucial tensions in the work.

By the late nineteenth century, the celebration of ancient warriors who resisted the Roman legions had become a Europe-wide phenomenon, with imposing monuments erected to Vercingetorix in France, Boadicea in England and Arminius (Hermann) in Germany, amongst others. The advantage of these northern pagan heroes as figureheads was that they were unattached to any particular religion, class or political party and could serve as a rallying point for a whole nation. In the case of Caractacus, the era of his greatest popularity as a subject for art and literature – the decades around the turn of the nineteenth century – came well before the Victorian advances in the fields of geology and archaeology that revolutionised the understanding of the distant past. Reliable historical information about ancient figures – and their respective civilisations – was often scanty at that time and their image in the public mind was largely the construction of modern people who projected their own desires or fears onto these shadowy ancestors. The British picture of Caractacus was partly informed by the biblical and classical texts that were the main sources of accepted information about antiquity, and which seemed to imply that a single aboriginal people with a single culture had inhabited the British Isles before the Roman (and later the Saxon) invasions. These 'ancient Britons' or 'Celts' were thought to have practised druidic religion, built ancient monuments such as Stonehenge and been present practically since the beginning of human history – or post-diluvian history, at any rate.[52]

The late eighteenth century, perhaps under the influence of Rousseau's primitivism, was especially sympathetic to the ancient Britons, portraying them as noble savages, simple in dress, thought and desire, with a fierce love of their homeland and their freedom. In this guise they were celebrated in numerous poems, plays and paintings, such as the verse dramas *Boadicea* (1753) by Richard Glover and *Caractacus* (1759) by William Mason. Yet, for all their primal innocence, the Britons were not regarded as inhabitants of an idyllic, Arcadian landscape. Rather, when portrayed in paintings, they were shown in harsh, gloomy, or barren surroundings. Druids – seen as guardians of a community's collective memory and readers of the auguries of sacrifice – inhabited dense oak thickets and stern, megalithic temples. In one popular pictorial genre, a bard is shown hurling defiance at encroaching Roman legions from the top of a craggy outcrop above a river, a gale tugging at his long hair and beard. In the language of Edmund Burke's famous contemporaneous essay, the settings for the ancient Britons are 'sublime' rather than 'beautiful', calculated to inspire awe and even terror. The urbane Romans have come face to face with nature untamed.[53]

Fig. 6.1 Charles Grignion, *Noble Behaviour of Caractacus*, after Francis Hayman,
n.d. Engraving. 41.9 × 39.2 cm

Despite these unwelcoming environs, eighteenth-century admirers of
ancient Celtic Britain were convinced of the nobility of their ancestors,
especially as regards their fierce love of liberty and independence which
inspired their resistance to Roman rule. Since one of the few attested facts
concerning Caractacus was his capture and confinement as an honoured
prisoner in the emperor's household, painters of British history liked to
imagine the first encounter between the two men, at which Caractacus,
in chains, pleads with Claudius to be merciful to his people. Francis
Hayman's *The Noble Behaviour of Caractacus, Before the Emperor Claudius*
(1751) initiated an iconographic tradition which continued until at least the
1840s (Fig. 6.1).[54]

Elgar's *Caractacus* clearly draws on this tradition, although in many ways
it represents a deliberate revival rather than a continuation. The Victorian
period witnessed the gradual eclipse of 'Celtic' Britain as a source of
national myth and a growing preference for peoples who seemed less easily
vanquished, such as the Vikings, and, to some extent, the Saxons. The

Celtic inhabitants of the British Isles had been pushed out of the fertile lowlands by a succession of Germanic invaders who were perceived as more vigorous and hard working. When it came to heroes of national liberation, then, the Victorians preferred Alfred to Caractacus. In the predominant view, modern-day Celts could boast picturesque traditions and a penchant for dreamy artistic visions, but they were not made, as were the English, for commercial and military expansion, technological innovation and world leadership. Anxieties over Catholic Irish immigration only compounded the stereotype. Still, if Elgar's choice of subject represents a revival of an eighteenth-century tradition, his setting goes some way towards making the story more palatable to his contemporaries. The elements of nobility, independence and valour on the side of the ancient Britons are emphasised, while the pagan druids are made into villains. The Woodland Interlude and Scene III present the Britons in a true pastoral Arcadia that owes little to eighteenth-century representations and much to the rural impulse in late Victorian culture. This impression is if anything reinforced by the fact that the idyll is not unclouded. Caractacus's daughter Eigen and her lover Orbin, who meet in the forest, know that invasion is imminent, and a series of diatonic augmented fourths and diminished fifths in the thematic material, carefully articulated through dynamics, adds pathos to the musical expression of their rustic wandering and courting (Ex. 6.3). There is an

(i) fig. I: 1–2

(ii) fig. II: 2–3
Ex. 6.3 *Caractacus*, Scene III, inflected diatonicism

obvious parallel with the use of 'Little Bells' in the Organ Grinder's songs from *The Starlight Express* (Ex. 5.2).

Nevertheless, it still cannot be taken for granted that a late-Victorian audience would have unreservedly identified with Caractacus's side in the conflict, Britons or no. After all, this was an uncultured tribe fighting imperial forces on the frontiers of empire. Ever since Disraeli had persuaded Parliament in 1876 to confer the title Empress of India on Queen Victoria, Britain had become consciously imperialist, and naturally looked to ancient Rome as an example, both in attitude and language. The terms 'colony', 'dominion', 'empire' itself and much of the vocabulary for talking about annexed territories were originally coined during Rome's imperial phase.[55] But Rome stood as both a model and a warning. Its engineering achievements and efficient colonial rule had great appeal, yet its subjugation of conquered peoples, its (initial) paganism, the absolute power wielded by its emperors, and above all the decline and decadence described so vividly by Edward Gibbon, made the Victorians decidedly uncomfortable. To cap it all, there was the troubling association with post-revolutionary France, since both Napoleon I and III had consciously sought to recapture the glories of ancient Rome, the latter albeit shambolically. So, for the Victorians, 'Rome could be seen simultaneously as colonising oppressor and model of colonial administration, intermittently resented imperial power and prototype of future empires and monarchies'.[56] The hero of G. A. Henty's novel *Beric the Briton: A Story of the Roman Invasion* (1893) – like *Olaf the Glorious* an exciting tale for Victorian male youth – admires Roman society and defends it to his undiscriminating peers, while yearning for freedom and hating the colonisers' contempt for their subject peoples. 'Though I would exult in seeing the last Roman driven from our land, I should like after their departure to see us adopt what is good and orderly and decent in their customs and laws.'[57]

Beric's call for synthesis might provide a rationale for taking the final chorus of *Caractacus* at face value. Yet the latent tensions in the work are not so easily resolved. After all, by the end of the 1890s, a similar confrontation between a rustic people and an advanced empire was being played out in South Africa, with disturbing consequences. Although the Boer War did not begin until a year after the premiere of *Caractacus*, opinion regarding the British interest in South Africa and the image of Britain's antagonists there was already being formed in the wake of the debacle of the Jameson Raid in 1895. The outbreak of war led to an almost unprecedented upsurge in public displays of patriotism, yet there was a diverse coalition of opposition voices which, though initially scorned by the popular press as 'Pro-Boers', grew in confidence as the conflict dragged on into its guerrilla phase. In some strands of this opposition, English ruralist radicalism joined with anti-imperialism and continental anti-capitalism to paint a picture of the Boers as preserving the true values of England, with the forces of imperialism – representing England's animus, as it were – ineluctably closing in upon them.[58] In the eyes of the Pro-Boers, the Dutch and French settlers could boast many of the same virtues that Elgar's cantata attributes to the ancient Britons: independence, fortitude, simplicity of living, a love of home and liberty, an obstinate resistance to outside interference, a small-community ethos and, above all, ties to the land. For the MP Leonard Courtney, 'they are like our ancestors of many years ago'.[59] By contrast, the modern-day British, having forgotten their true identity in the rush for progress and development, were ruthlessly attempting to wrest control of the gold and diamond mines of the Transvaal, egged on by powerful financiers. Johannesburg was a pit of depravity to match anything described by Gibbon, crawling with specula-tors, gamblers, prostitutes and every urban vice. ('Monte Carlo super-imposed on Sodom and Gomorrah' was one verdict.)[60] According to the Labour leader Keir Hardie, 'As a pastoral people the Boers doubtless have all the failings of the fine qualities which pertain to that mode of life; but whatever these failings might have been they are as virtues compared to the turbid pollution and refined cruelty which is inseparable from the oper-ation of capitalism.'[61] The socialist Edward Carpenter wrote, 'If ever a people on earth made good their right to their land these people did. They loved it passionately – it was the Promised Land of their wanderings – and they love it still. (Perhaps our people who have no land, cannot understand that!) *And they will fight for it to the end.*'[62] In reality, of course, the British Pro-Boers' view of the settlers was somewhat idealised. As Stewart Weaver explains, 'The Boer who beguiled them ... was a Boer of their own making, an artful blend of historical fact and pastoral fancy whose brief it was to recall the English to a sense of their own agrarian roots and diminish if not defeat their imperial resolve.'[63]

There is no evidence that Elgar himself felt the tug of the Boer idyll, and in any case he would never have publicly aligned himself with political radicals or even Liberals. But the sympathisers' discourse shows clearly how at the turn of the century an imperialist venture could be appropriated as the stage for a conceptual confrontation between two aspects of Englishness. In *Caractacus*, that confrontation is played out directly in the final scene, for there the defeated British king is thrust into the midst of cosmopolitan, imperial Rome. Claudius commands him to speak, and

Ex. 6.4 *Caractacus*, Scene VI (Caractacus's nostalgia), fig. 28: 1–fig. 29: 1

Elgar translates into music the iconographic tradition of the noble king's plea with the help of some techniques of his 'chivalrous rhetoric' (fig. 25). After a statement of the weary 'captives' motif, Caractacus continues 'We liv'd in peace, was that a crime to thee, / That thy fierce eagle stoop'd upon our nest?' The orchestra takes up the 'woodland' music from the earlier Interlude, as he sings 'A freeborn chieftain, and a people free, / We dwelt among our woodlands, and were blest' (Ex. 6.4). When Elgar told A. J. Jaeger 'the trees are singing my music – or have I sung theirs?', he cited this very music (in its initial version; see Ex. 6.3(i); compare Ex. 6.4 fig. 28: 1 and 4). Earlier he had confessed to Jaeger: 'I made old Caractacus stop as if broken down … & choke & say "woodlands" again because I'm so madly devoted to my woods.'[64] (He was at the time enjoying a summer of sylvan pleasures near his rented cottage, Birchwood, on the Malvern Hills.) As Ex. 6.4 makes clear, it is the trees' music with its diatonic augmented fourth that precipitates the king's nostalgia; he himself sings the interval on 'we dwelt among our woodlands'. Caractacus's speech, with its combination of stern defiance and poignant memories of home, marks the definitive emergence of Elgar's characteristic strain of heroic melancholy or noble resignation that was examined in Chapter 3 – its alternately 'innocent' and 'regal' diatonicism enriched by the yearning instability of the augmented fourth.

After the king's speech, his daughter Eigen and her lover Orbin continue his lament for their lost countryside, again recalling material from Scene III. The chorus, personifying the Roman crowd, bays for their blood in a manner familiar from Bach's Passions. The emperor at first claims that the gods speak their will through the people, but, after the impressive plea, pities the noble sorrow of the Britons and decides to spare them. His music gains a reciprocal strain of nobility when he declares 'We grant you grace'. Claudius, then, has succumbed to imperialist nostalgia. It is no wonder that the illogical final chorus of *Caractacus* is so loudly insistent: the final scene leaves plenty of unresolved complexities to cover over.

A DEMON FOR COUNTERPOINT

The uneasy ambiguities of Elgarian inner/outer identity, so clearly evident in *King Olaf* and *Caractacus*, are seldom highlighted by critics or artists. A notable exception is David Rudkin's *Penda's Fen*, a BBC television 'Play for Today' from 1974 (directed by Alan Clarke). This is one of the boldest attempts to work Elgar into an independent creative venture, for although set in the familiar Worcestershire countryside, with the Malvern Hills and Elgar's music figuring centrally, the play is a work of radical social criticism which condemns conventional English morality and religion as violent, morbid and repressive. Like much of Rudkin's drama, it explores an individual's search for personal identity in the face of inhibiting social norms and boundaries.[65] The story is a coming-of-age narrative about a troubled contemporary teenager, Stephen Franklin. At the outset Stephen's adolescent longings reveal an outlook of extreme Conservatism: he prizes racial purity, doctrinal Christianity, 'family values', the school cadet corps – but also the music of Elgar. The latter is the only component to survive a personal crisis precipitated by a succession of urgent dreams and visions involving angels and demons, homoerotic feelings for his schoolmates, a horrific mutilation ritual, a revelatory meeting with the ghost of Elgar himself, a glimpse of the crucified Christ, and finally an encounter on the Malvern Hills with King Penda of Mercia, England's last pagan ruler.

Stephen learns to embrace a new, heterogeneous identity, rejecting the strict disciplines that had enraptured him at first. In this way Rudkin can play the 'two Elgars' problem to advantage. In Stephen's vision Elgar appears outwardly as a crusty old gentleman, yet beneath the exterior he is vulnerable – brought low by age, disease and sorrow – while his music asks searching questions by means of harmonic dissonance and driving counterpoint.

The play opens with images of rural Worcestershire and the distant Malvern Hills (the latter are a constant motif – one of several echoes of Ken Russell's *Elgar*). On the soundtrack is the soft singing of the chorus of assistants from Part II of *The Dream of Gerontius* – the moment of calm just before the soul goes before its Judge ('Lord be merciful, Lord deliver him'). Stephen's voice is heard: 'Oh my country. I say over and over: I *am* one of your sons, it is true; I am, I *am*. Yet how shall I show my love?'[66] The Angel enters with her triumphant song that the soul is saved. But, as the tempo broadens, her cry of 'Alleluia' is suspended on the third syllable – the climactic top A (Ex. 6.5).[67] The note turns into the screech of a siren; barbed wire is superimposed on the landscape. A scorched hand and arm reach up from the ground, vainly trying to break free from captivity.

When the nightmare fades the music continues. Stephen is listening to *Gerontius* in his room in the Worcestershire rectory of his father, the Revd Franklin. He follows the score intently. The ominous chords that outline the 'judgement' theme as the soul is about to meet the divine gaze build their crescendo. But just as the music reaches the dreadful, dissonant chord that marks the climax of the entire work, Stephen's mother enters the room and dislodges the needle of the record player. Later, that chord, as yet denied him, will help Stephen to acknowledge the dissonance in his own identity. After his mother leaves, he reads what he has written about *Gerontius* in his school exercise book. 'I think the greatest visionary work in English music is "The Dream of Gerontius" by Sir Edward Elgar. It poses the most important question: what is to happen to my soul?' He describes Gerontius's death and judgement, the angels and demons he encounters, and the great chord itself: 'the Moment of the Glance of God ... Surely the most shattering moment in all of music'. He gazes out of the window at the sunset on the distant Malvern Hills. 'To hear in your head – such sounds ... Have Heaven and Hell between your ears ... And walk on those hills: and hear the Angel and the Demon ... The Judgement: on those hills.'[68]

Later scenes reveal Stephen to be a conscientious – indeed priggish – student at his traditionalist, rugby-playing boys' school. He is innocent for

Ex. 6.5 *The Dream of Gerontius*, Part II, fig. 116: 3–fig. 117: 7, as adapted in *Penda's Fen* (reduction as in vocal score)

his age, failing to recognise his own sexual attraction to the local milkboy. At a school debate he speaks passionately in favour of the motion 'This House believes that the Media are a Source of Evil to Society', extolling British liberties as conventionally understood but approving an injunction that has been recently upheld by the courts banning a TV documentary called 'Who was Jesus?' – a programme Stephen dubs 'atheistic and subversive trash'. When his father chairs an 'Any Questions?' meeting at the local parish hall, Stephen is scandalised by the radical tirade of a local playwright, William Arne (possibly a self-parody by the author), who defends the striking workers in their dispute with the government of the day. Arne conjures up a sinister picture of 'the manipulators and fixers and psychopaths who hold the real power in the land'. Stephen is especially discomforted when Arne speaks about the local countryside, 'an ancient fen' where, although the ground feels firm today, it is in fact hollow. 'Somewhere beneath, is being constructed, something – We're not sup-posed to know. A Top Secret.'[69] Arne thinks that a nuclear bunker or a defence installation is being built. Later he tells the Revd Franklin that all over the world governments are choosing to site their sinister scientific experiments in remote places that were considered sacred by the ancient inhabitants, 'as though thereby to bottle the primal genie of the earth; and to pervert him'. One of those earth spirits – a true *genius loci* – is Penda, who will preside over Stephen's eventual revolt against establish-ment values.

Stephen reports a dream in which he sees a black demon perched on top of the spire of his father's church. He finds that he can turn it into an angel and back at will (shades perhaps of Blake's *Marriage of Heaven and Hell*, especially since 'Jerusalem' has just been sung at school with Stephen playing the organ). The following night Stephen dreams that a gigantic golden angel appears from behind the Malvern Hills. The script reads 'He stands titanic upon the hills, his face towards us. He resembles the Epstein Lucifer: male and at the same time female [Stephen had earlier commented on the androgyny of the Guardian Angel in *Gerontius*]; a power of dark-ness, yet radiant with light.'[70] The dream moves to Stephen's classroom. The Sixth Form boys are engaged in a muddy, heaving rugby scrum; Stephen alone is dressed in school uniform, standing apart from the rest, 'his eyes bleak with carnal guilt'. At the same time the angel is seen advancing down the hill. Stephen, his jacket now removed, tries to prevent drops of mud from spattering him. The face of one of his schoolmates appears – the blond-haired, blue-eyed, future School Captain. Stephen's hand reaches out to touch his neck, moves down his body to his waist, and

(i) 'angular' motif

(ii) 'yearning' motif
Ex. 6.6 *Introduction and Allegro*, fugue

then down to a 'flaming torch' which appears below. This sequence is accompanied by the fugue from Elgar's *Introduction and Allegro*, which, as Rudkin points out, the composer referred to as a 'devil of a fugue'. The fugue subject is an 'angular dancing tune' whose phrases 'dart, swoop and whirl away like sparks'.[71] One of the countersubjects, familiar from earlier in the Allegro, is a 'yearning' melody, which the author connects with the scrum and the spattering. The counterpoint thus sets two aspects of Stephen's desire against one another (Ex. 6.6).

The music fades and the dream turns into a paralysing nightmare. Stephen wakes to find a grinning demon's face inches from his own. When he manages to turn on a light, the demon remains crouched on his chest in the incubus position. Stephen tries to recoil from it but cannot move. At last he manages to reach towards it instead. But despite this acknowledgement, his sexuality is as yet only a source of shame for Stephen: 'unnatural' he whispers in horror.

Stephen's next two visions occur in pastoral scenes rich with Elgarian resonance. He passes a barrier in a road blocking the way to a village called Pinvin (originally 'Pendefen', meaning 'Penda's fen'). Sitting amongst the reeds by the bank of a river, he reflects on his discovery in 'agony and rejoicing'. The angel of his dream appears behind him, now of human dimensions, 'tender and terrible, remorseless, kind'. 'The reeds and grasses dip and nudge him, as though urging him into onehood with the things that move and grow.'[72] He overcomes his fear of being 'unnatural', perceiving a 'new darker self'. In a second pastoral episode, Stephen cycles through the countryside in casual clothes, as though liberated, with the Malvern Hills closer than before. In a reference to Ken Russell's *Elgar* film, the music is the *Introduction and Allegro* once again, this time the reprise of the second subject material (Russell had used the same music to accompany Elgar himself cycling up the hills). Stephen whistles the tune to himself, travelling faster and faster. But suddenly, as the violins leap to a high note (fig. 29), the face of the dream-demon flashes before him, the music abruptly ceases and Stephen falls unconscious by the roadside. Again in a dream, he picks himself up and passes the barrier on the way to Pinvin. Here he encounters a gruesome spectacle. Approaching a half-timbered manor house surrounded by immaculate hedges and clipped topiary bushes, he hears a sound of chopping. A group of people are sitting in a circle on the lawn, dressed in yellow and white, apparently healthy, happy and relaxed. They wait expectantly, 'eyes bright on the brink of some redemption'. In the middle of the lawn is a tree stump where the people take turns to place their hands ready to be severed by a smartly dressed man wielding an axe. They seem to regard this as a joyful privilege. Stephen sees the couple who had brought the injunction against the 'Jesus' documentary – he had held up their photograph to show the class during his speech and called them 'a father and mother of England'. They approach him, beckoning, and he is paralysed with horror. His unconscious is telling him that conventional English society mutilates its willingly cooperative people.

In the next vision Stephen shelters from the rain in a dark, derelict military building in a quiet corner of the countryside. An elderly man in a wheelchair is cowering there too. It is the ghost of Elgar, who is grief-stricken over his lost past and ready to confide. The once 'imperious countenance' is today a 'shrunken wisp', echoing the sorry state of the military surroundings. Elgar eagerly relates his memories, though their sequence is disconnected and they are separated by silences (in this regard they resemble the thematic reminiscences in the Violin Concerto cadenza or *Falstaff*). He reveals that he plucked a certain 'sublime' moment from *Gerontius* not 'from the angels' or 'from the air', but from the whine of a dog for a bone.[73] He recalls an operation on his stomach performed without full anaesthetic; he watched the surgeon disembowelling him. 'My vitals; my sustaining blood. Is all that . . . *Elgar*? Very interesting.' Then he asks whether anyone has 'solved' the Enigma – in other words, identified the tune that supposedly runs in counterpoint against the theme of the *Variations*, Op. 36. Stephen explains that all the attempted solutions are unsatisfactory. 'The tune that fits', observes Elgar in frustration, 'is under all their noses. They will never spot it . . . because they have no demon for counterpoint!' He whispers the solution to Stephen, whose amused reaction suggests that it is unlikely or commonplace. Elgar invites him to fit the themes together, singing the 'Enigma' tune while Stephen silently imagines the countersubject. Elgar vanishes, but Stephen feels 'an overflowing inner triumph, exaltation . . . The music swirls up in him, welling and delirious in thrilling tumult.' The camera rushes out of the shelter towards the light. The accompanying music is the 'squall-like crescendo' following the 'Roman Armies' episode from *In the South*, which Rudkin calls 'one of the most demonically exciting upsurges ever composed' (at fig. 26). Stephen has realised that Elgar's music is not the repository of a pure, undefiled English identity, but, like him, is a mixture – sometimes noble, but sometimes earthy or vulgar. The counterpoint of contradictory impulses within him has perhaps even helped him to perceive in his mind's ear an Elgarian counterpoint that others have missed.

Meanwhile, Stephen's future is uncertain. He is sent before his Headmaster to answer for abandoning the cadet corps; later the other boys overpower him and tie up his hair like a girl's. On his eighteenth birthday, his parents reveal that he was adopted; he is of mixed race, and neither parent was English. He also discovers that his adoptive father, the rector, is the author of a radical theological dissertation called 'The Buried Jesus', which claims that the Gospel was tampered with. 'To the reader who shouts Blasphemy!', it reads, 'I say "Blasphemy worse, that the Name of this life-enhancing revolutionary Jesus should now be dangled like a halo above a sick culture centred on authority and death".'[74] But later, as they walk home one evening through a glowing pastoral scene, the Revd Franklin offers Stephen hope for the future by evoking England's far-distant past. In Jesus, 'the Legislator and the Demon fuse', yet he has been posthumously perverted by 'the doctrine men'. 'We crucify him over and over.'[75] The concept of the pagan – meaning 'of the village' – offers sanity in the midst of the evils of the twentieth century. 'The village is sneered at, as something petty. Petty it can be, yet it works . . . Man may yet in the nick of time revolt and save himself: revolt from the monolith, come back to the village.' The Revd Franklin remembers the pagan King Penda, 'fighting his last battle, against the *new* machine'.

Stephen enters his father's church alone, and sits down at the organ. As he plays music from *Gerontius* a jagged crack appears in the floor of the aisle. Stephen turns to the climax of Part II that was heard (abortively) at the beginning of the film; when he reaches the great, dissonant chord he lands on it with all his force (Ex. 6.7, fig. 120). The crack in the aisle widens to an abyss; yet somehow 'it is not enough'. With his hands and feet he presses down every note he can and holds them. In the organ mirror he glimpses a pair of feet pierced by a nail, 'like detail from Grünwald

Ex. 6.7 *The Dream of Gerontius*, Part II, the moment of judgement, as adapted in *Penda's Fen*
(reduction as in vocal score)

Crucifixion', according to the script. A voice whispers 'Stephen Franklin . . .
Unbury me . . . Free me from this tree.'[76]

In the final scene the Malvern Hills themselves are reached at last.
Stephen sits motionless in the sunset, as though waiting. Now comes the
play's crisis: he encounters the 'mother and father of England' for a second
time. They are still in an unnervingly joyful mood and claim him as their
own. Satan-like, on the hilltop, they promise him power and inheritance –
at a price. 'You have to come with us. You are our Child of Light, You have
to be born in us. Then you become Pure Light.'[77] Stephen finally finds his
voice and cries 'No! No! I am nothing pure! . . . My race is mixed, my sex is
mixed, I am woman and man, and light with darkness, mixed, *mixed*!' He
runs from them, and his organ dissonance sounds again. The couple try to
destroy him, but he calls to Penda, whereupon the king materialises on a
throne and saves him. 'There you have seen your true dark enemies of
England,' he tells Stephen. 'Sick Father and Mother, who would have us
children for ever.' Stephen, by contrast, has been 'marked down' to cherish
the 'deep dark flame' that still flickers in the fen, the 'sacred demon of
ungovernableness'. The king bestows his blessing: 'Stephen be secret, child
be strange: dark, true, impure and dissonant. Cherish our flame. Our dawn
shall come.' As Stephen walks down the hill in darkness, there is no music –
only birdsong and distant, everyday sounds from the town below.

Like J. B. Priestley, Rudkin refuses to concede the pastoral ground (in an
almost literal sense), attempting to claim it for what might be called the
'Elgarian Left'. Yet his view of human identity as multifaceted and contradictory is more believable than Priestley's essentialised Englishness. To be
sure, criticisms could be raised against *Penda's Fen*. Rudkin's interest in
village life, earth spirits and the material qualities of the land occasionally
recalls the 'blood and soil' ideology of early twentieth-century Fascism. Yet

the impression is misleading, for he insists on the impurity of 'blood'. A more substantial objection concerns the portrayal of the English village as liberal and progressive at heart. In 1974 people like the Franklins and Arnes – who discuss issues such as homosexual adoption with sympathy and without embarrassment – were surely not altogether representative of the rural population. (A glance at the Pinvin village website in April 2003 revealed its main preoccupation to be a campaign against a proposed nearby accommodation centre for asylum seekers.)[78] But the improbability of some of the events in the play is not decisive; after all, it is a polemic, and parades its mysticism overtly.

As regards Elgar's music, Rudkin's main focus is not the symphonic techniques of climax and withdrawal that so much concerned Elgar commentators at the time of the play: he is more interested in the Elgar of ingenious counterpoint, searing dissonance and religious vision. In this way, Elgar's music can be the thread that ties the old and the new Stephen. At the outset it is the single aspect of the boy's culture that nudges him towards questioning and wonder rather than complacency; by the end it helps him make sense of his new self. It ensures that his new identity does not seem like a creation *ex nihilo*. The 'two Elgars' are present all along, but when Stephen meets the composer his rigid, establishment side is associated with death and decay, right down to the choice of location in the deserted army building. Rudkin's intuition that the Angel in *Gerontius* has some link with androgyny and the subversion of heterosexual norms strikingly anticipates the recent writings of the Elgar scholar Byron Adams, who has situated the work in relation to the aesthetics of *fin-de-siècle* decadence.[79] Still, Rudkin has to engage in a selective reading of the theology: there can be no place for Newman's conception of the 'purifying' flame that burns away the stain of sin. It is significant that none of the music of *Gerontius* that comes after the great dissonance is heard or even referred to – music which, in pointing forward to purgatory, in some sense resolves both the chord and the tensions developed in the composition. Stephen's spiritual quest – figured as a journey across the Worcestershire landscape towards the hills – is to make sense of the dissonance alone, even to become it.

David Rudkin fashions a radical nostalgia that condemns the authoritarian and technocratic aspects of modernity and echoes William Cobbett, William Blake and William Morris. He looks back to a supposedly tolerant, peaceful, ancient England and forward to the individual's prospects for personal transformation. King Penda represents the last concrete manifestation of an Englishness deeper than all others, rooted in the earth itself – a fundamental obstinacy and resistance to imposed authority. Penda's spirit is now weak – witness all the rulers, laws and establishment doctrines that have been imposed on the people since his day, such as the spread of Christianity, the Norman Conquest and even Stephen's militaristic school drill – yet it is still alive, and can potentially be cultivated. It gives a faint glimpse of an England that might have been and might, in the distant future, yet be. Rudkin's work reminds us again that there is no direct path from nostalgia, or from Elgar's music, to the political Right. The music sets the terms for a debate on identity, but it does not point ineluctably to any single outcome.

CHAPTER 7

Waters

Memories and ghosts, fading nobility, enchanted nature, lost youth, authentic identity: the foregoing chapters have sketched the main themes of Elgarian nostalgia. With this framework in place, the present chapter is a kind of epilogue, presenting three case studies in Elgar reception. It examines some of the most thought-provoking artistic works that feature Elgar, two literary and one pictorial: C. Day Lewis's poem *Edward Elgar 1857–1934* (1962), Norman Perryman's watercolour triptych *Elgar's Dream* (1996) and James Hamilton-Paterson's novel *Gerontius* (1989). The three works draw together the themes discussed in this book under the prevailing image of moving waters. That image provides an effective means to explore various types of Elgarian longing and their ramifications. It functions, as it were, as a point of confluence of certain facts of biography, stories told as semi-autobiographical anecdote, aspects of specific compositions, and potent myths and habits of mind that informed Elgar's art and subsequent reactions to it. Thus each of these works is able to present a multi-dimensional picture of nostalgia and of other Elgarian topics.

Fluvial imagery features prominently in the memories that Elgar recounted to others and in statements of his that are frequently rehearsed by biographers. The story of the child by the Severn 'longing for something very great' has already been discussed at length in Chapters 4 and 5. In 1916 Elgar told Percy Scholes about the 'atmosphere of music' in which he was brought up: 'A stream of music flowed through our house and the shop, and I was all the time bathing in it.'[1] The interview took place in 'Severn House', the name Elgar gave to the property in Hampstead where he lived between 1912 and 1922; although the location was far from Worcestershire, he perhaps still hoped to gain inspiration from the memory of his native waters. The imagery is brought full circle by Elgar's deathbed request to be cremated and have his ashes scattered at the confluence of the rivers Severn and Teme just south of Worcester.

The first commentator to link Elgar's music with moving waters was Ernest Newman, whose remarkable early review of the Second Symphony suggests that in the finale 'the chain of sequences – as long, indeed, as the movement itself – rolls on to its beautiful end like a winding and broken river that at last gathers all its waters together and finds the sea'.[2] Michael Kennedy ends several of his writings on Elgar by reflecting on waters. 'We are back to the river theme again', he concludes in one essay. The valedictory 'Coda' to *Portrait of Elgar* states that 'always, through his life and music, there runs this motif of the river'. Elgar's work, Kennedy continues, 'gathers personal associations which become poignant with the passage of time, and when the poignancy seems almost unbearable, the music becomes a renewing stream of solace'.[3] Daniel Grimley and Julian Rushton invoke Newman's metaphor and echo Kennedy's rhetoric in the final paragraph of their Introduction to the recent *Cambridge Companion to Elgar*.[4] Finally, as noted in Chapter 5, another biographer, Jerrold Northrop Moore, makes much of the dividing function that rivers may have played in Elgar's imagination – the stream in his childhood play and the Severn at the edge of the city of Worcester.

It is unsurprising that Elgar's connections with rivers should have been seized upon and expanded in these ways, for they are especially suitable for the expression of nostalgia. The usefulness of the image of the river lies principally in its paradoxical association in the Western imagination with the characteristics of two different concepts of time: cyclical and linear.[5] On the one hand, the existence of a hydrological cycle linking rivers and oceans in a single everlasting process – a fact which has been recognised since antiquity – means that rivers can stand as emblems of eternal recurrence and return. The example of the Nile – the 'river of rivers' for both Classical and post-Renaissance Europeans – with its almost miraculous fertility and the regular pattern of flooding that made possible the existence of civilisation in Egypt – means that rivers participate centrally in Western religious and mythical interpretations of seasonal renewal. Examples include the legends of Isis and Osiris and of Hercules, Acheloüs and the *cornucopia*. For Christians, submersion in the purifying waters of the Jordan signifies spiritual rebirth.

On the other hand, rivers are also powerful signifiers of irreversible change. For the observer at any given location on the bank, a river's flow is unmistakably linear and unidirectional. Rivers are marked by transience and mutability, their entire contents flowing irreversibly to a final dissolution of identity in the all-encompassing oneness of the ocean. Their progress mirrors that of the individual life, and they can stand for modern, dynamic, goal-directed consciousness. Rivers may be perceived to chart the progress of civilisations and empires from their source to their maturity – a point the Romans understood in relation to the Tiber. Under these circumstances, the upstream direction can become a focus for longing. According to the historian of the fluvial imagination Wyman H. Herendeen, 'In its movement downstream society, becoming more and more civilized, also attempts to return to its source, to affirm its links with the past, and measure, as it were, its progress.'[6] In short, although hydrological necessity dictates that some waters will eventually return to the source, from the linear perspective that source seems wholly irrecoverable, a fact that acquires added poignancy from the knowledge that the flow now passing the downstream viewer had once been at that 'earlier' place. Thus the source can stand for a lost past, youth or innocence. In the Bible, for instance, four of the world's great rivers flow out of Eden. Alternatively the source can signify enchantment, mystery and the irrational. The source of the Nile has tantalised visitors to Africa from Caesar to the Victorian explorers. It has always seemed just out of reach, a metaphor for the inexplicable, exotic allure of the 'orient', eluding the grasp of Western technology and empire.

Another aspect of the usefulness of rivers in nostalgic discourse arises from a perspective orthogonal to the direction of flow. In this respect rivers are liminal phenomena that can function as boundaries between political regions or as conceptual thresholds between spiritual states. The Jordan, the Rubicon and the (mythical) Styx are obvious instances; closer to home the Severn was historically a front line for beleaguered native British tribes in the face of invading forces, such as the Romans and Saxons. The stream in the Elgar children's play divided the grown-ups' world from fairyland. The imagery of rivers can replicate contrasts between mundane and enchanted spheres and the dividing lines between them – topics that are central to Elgarian nostalgia.

Rivers may suggest musical enchantment in other ways too. Like music itself, the flow of waters is bound to the temporal dimension. The babbling of a brook, the rushing of a stream, the crashing of waves, just like the rustling of wind in foliage, are conventional poetic devices for suggesting an elusive music unavailable to notation, and appealed especially to the Romantics. When the soul of Gerontius hears a 'grand mysterious harmony' issuing from the House of Judgement around him, the effect is like 'the deep and solemn sound of many waters'. When the wraith of Odin recites the words of the Havamal, King Olaf hears 'sounds mysterious as the roar / Of billows on a distant shore'.

By the nineteenth century, then, the imagery of moving waters presented a potent matrix of ideas. An instructive case study in the use of this imagery to articulate modern nostalgia can be found in the poetry of Matthew Arnold, a writer whose anguished response to modernity anticipated (and perhaps even shaped) Elgar's in striking ways. Arnold's poetic persona is continually disturbed by a seemingly impersonal and fragmented modern world from which God has withdrawn, and longs for earlier epochs in which objective nature was, supposedly, replete with meaning. Arnold has frequent recourse to characteristic imagery involving a river flowing through three distinct landscapes. Its source is in high, wooded mountains, a sylvan *locus amoenus* that resides in a dimly remembered past and can be recaptured at best in fleeting glimpses. As the river matures, it passes through a separating gorge to the landscape of the present and of the poet's alienated predicament. This is the 'dusty' or 'darkening' plain and may feature human cities. Sometimes the poet passes through the plain while floating on the river itself; sometimes the river is a deep, subterranean flow (as in the poem 'The Buried Life') that is revealed to consciousness only in moments of precious insight and that hints at an underlying purpose to existence after all. Finally the river reaches the 'wide-glimmering sea', which promises final release and equanimity.[7] It is easy to detect parallels with familiar processes in Elgar's music. His pastoral interludes would correspond to the remembered and desired source (the story of the child by the riverbank also has an 'upstream' feel to it), while the turbulent material that often surrounds those interludes (in, say, the First Symphony's first or second movements) would match the spiritual unease of the arid plain. Moments of thematic reminiscence within a sonata movement that point outside the present frame of consciousness to some other world (as in the First Symphony or the *Introduction and Allegro*) parallel Arnold's sudden glimpses of the purposeful 'buried life' flowing beneath the normal level of consciousness. And, to return to Ernest Newman's metaphor, the final issue of this musical river might be heard towards the end of the Second Symphony.

A FLOWING-AWAYNESS

Edward Elgar 1857–1934

I

A boy among the reeds on Severn shore
Sound-bathing: a ghost humming his 'cello tune

Upon the Malvern hills: and in between,
Mostly enigma. Who shall read this score?

The stiff, shy, blinking man in a norfolk suit:
The martinet: the gentle-minded squire:
The piano-tuner's son from Worcestershire:
The Edwardian grandee: how did they consort

In such luxuriant themes? Not privilege
Nor talent's cute, obsequious ear attuned
His soul to the striding rhythms, the unimpugned
Melancholy of a vulgar, vivid age.

Genius alone can move by singular ways
Yet home to the heart of all, the common chord;
Beat to its own time, timelessly make heard
A long-breathed statement or a hesitant phrase.

For me, beyond the marches of his pride,
Through the dark airs and rose-imperial themes,
A far West-country summer glares and glooms,
A boy calls from the reeds on Severn side.

2

Orchards are in it – the vale of Evesham blooming:
Rainshine of orchards blowing out of the past.
The sadness of remembering orchards that never bore,
Never for us bore fruit: year after year they fruited,
But all, all was premature –
We were not ripe to gather the full beauty.
And now when I hear 'orchards' I think of loss, recall
White tears of blossom streaming away downwind,
And wish the flower could have stayed to be one
    with the fruit it formed.
Oh, coolness at the core of early summers,
Woodwind haunting those green expectant alleys,
Our blossom falling, falling.

Hills are in it – the Malverns, Bredon, Cotswold.
A meadowsweetness of high summer days:
Clovering bees, time-honeyed bells, the lark's top C.
Hills where each sound, like larksong, passes into light,
And light is music all but seen.
Dawn's silvery tone and evening's crimson adagio;
Noonday on the full strings of sunshine simmering, dreaming,
No past, no future, the pulse of time unnoticed:
Cloud-shadows sweeping in arpeggios up the hillsides;
Grey, muted light which, brooding on stone, tree, clover

And cornfield, makes their colours sing most clear –
All moods and themes of light.

And a river – call it the Severn – a flowing-awayness.
Bray of moonlight on water; brassy flamelets
Of marigold, buttercup, flag-iris in water-meadows;
Kingfishers, mayflies, mills, regattas: the ever-rolling
Controlled percussion of thunderous weirs.
Rivers are passionate gods: they flood, they drown,
Roar themselves hoarse, ripple to gaiety, lull the land
With slow movements of tender meditation.
And in it too, in his music, I hear the famous river –
Always and never the same, carrying far
Beyond our view, reach after noble reach –
That bears its sons away.[8]

The example of C. Day Lewis (1904–72, Poet Laureate 1968) seems to
confirm the tendency, illustrated in Chapter 6, for Elgar's most interesting
interpreters to stand on the Left of the political spectrum. Day Lewis was a
member of the Communist Party in the 1930s, and, along with
W. H. Auden and several others of their generation, sought to achieve a
socially aware poetry with rhythms rooted in semi-colloquial modern speech.
By the same token he eschewed the recondite language of literary high
modernism. By the time of his verses on Elgar, published in his penultimate
volume of original poems *The Gate* (1962), Day Lewis's early political
idealism had softened and he espoused the democratic socialism of the
British Labour Party. His poetic voice had altered too; chastened by the
political events of the 1940s, it took an inward turn, searching for the sources
and roots of human life far from the modern 'machine' and the clash of
rival empires. He became especially concerned with what he called the
'lyric impulse' (the title of his Norton lectures at Harvard in 1964–5),
which he believed had been neglected by modernist poetry. He was also
interested in pastoral imagery inspired by Virgil and Thomas Hardy which
linked rural labour, landscape and the seasons in an eternal, ordered cycle.
At the same time, Day Lewis's personal rural past – however faintly
remembered – began to haunt his writing as he reflected on his forgotten
roots (his autobiographical account of his early years was entitled 'The
Buried Day'). His Anglo-Irish family had lived initially in County Laois
(then Queen's County), but moved to Malvern in Worcestershire during
his second year (auspicious from an Elgarian perspective, though as an
adult he could recall very little of his time there), and thence to London. By
the 1960s he had settled permanently in Greenwich. In this light, 'Edward

Elgar' can be seen to weave together a striking variety of personal, collective and literary longings.[9]

Day Lewis's Norton lectures, published as *The Lyric Impulse* (1965), represent a significant context for the poem. They trace in detail the history of the 'singing line' in English poetry. The lyric mode is defined as poetry in its purest and simplest form, the seemingly spontaneous presentation of a single feeling or state of mind. This mode points back to a historical moment when poetry was not yet fully separate from music: an echo of the primal unity of those arts. The recent history of poetry is in large part a story of increasing suppression of the lyric impulse as poets develop ever more radical or rarefied techniques. But, according to Day Lewis, even the modern poet feels – or ought to feel – a need to submit to the impulse, to communicate directly with poetry's 'primal source' rather than the many historical traditions through which it has been 'channelled'. This is a search for 'remote ancestors', for a 'primary, instinctual self', since, despite the divergence from music, the poetic sensibility is still 'haunted by the ghost of a tune, a dancing rhythm, the felt presence of that universal melody – however faint it may be today – through which primitive man expressed communion with his fellows and the joy of living'.[10] (One of Day Lewis's favourite lyric poets was Tom Moore, whose verses, he felt, were perfect for musical setting. In 'Avoca, Co. Wicklow' he portrays the merging of Moore's words with music as a confluence of rivers: 'His words came alive / But to music's flow / Like weeds in water . . . Words and tune met, flowed together in one / Melodious river. I drift calmly / Between its banks.')[11] In answer to the charge that a surrender to the lyric impulse is irresponsible – an escape from the complexity of the modern world – Day Lewis defends it as 'serious play' which helps to reunite the divided self, remind the subject of its 'roots' and satisfy the 'perpetual need for wholeness'.[12]

This longing for the musical in poetry finds echoes in the contemporaneous poem 'Edward Elgar', but does not map onto it in a straightforward way. Either of the poem's contrasted parts could, in their different ways, be claimed to uncover an elusive 'singing line'. Part 1 is symmetrical, strophic, rhymed, and cast roughly in iambic pentameter. It hints at what musicians would regard as ternary form through its first and last stanzas, especially the very first and last lines. On the other hand it is discursive and reflective, unlike Part 2. The latter, despite its irregularities and prose-like rhythms, is more lyrical in the sense that it emphasises the recounting of immediate impressions. Moreover it projects first-person subjectivity. Aside from matters of form, both parts of the poem echo the preoccupations of *The Lyric Impulse* in their opening of temporal and geographical spaces of longing and their identification of the distant objects of desire both with a lost simplicity and with music.

Part 1 begins by invoking three of Elgar's well-known utterances: the one about the 'dreamy child' in the reeds by the Severn; his account of bathing in the 'stream of music' flowing through his father's nearby establishment on Worcester High Street; and his deathbed remark to a friend that if in future he should hear a theme from the Cello Concerto floating across the Malvern Hills, 'don't be alarmed, it's only me'. (The latter may even have suggested the image in *The Lyric Impulse* of the poet 'haunted by the ghost of a tune'.) The enigma that lies 'in between' these chronological poles is Elgar's life and creative work. The second stanza supplies a list – the first of many in the poem. The use of dividing colons ensures that any sense of a bald enumeration of characteristics is avoided; the passage reads instead like a series of paradoxical oppositions. Of all the alternative personae, 'the piano-tuner's son from Worcestershire' stands out as the most sympathetic, partly because of its anticipation in the poem's first line, partly because of its positioning between the martinet, the squire and the grandee. The mention of several alternative 'outer' personae but only a single 'inner' one adds to the sense that the latter is special. The fourth stanza reveals the clue to the enigma to be the mediating power of Elgar's genius, which wins popularity while remaining true to the artist's temperament. Yet that power seems to be principally invested in the child, who, in the final stanza of Part 1, is identified as the secret essence of the composer. Like Day Lewis's own 'buried' self, the child is conceptually westward of the poet's current location, which may be London (the westward direction was a theme of Georgian and other poetry under the influence of A. E. Housman's 'blue remembered hills'). The marches and 'rose-imperial' themes seem 'closer' to the percipient, yet function as typical Elgarian disguises that conceal a deeper kernel. The riverside child is located 'beyond', 'through' and 'far', but issues a call to the 'me' that has made its first appearance in the first line of the stanza (compare J. B. Priestley's use of a similar phrase – 'to me' – cited in Chapter 6, p. 151).

The close focus on personal subjectivity in the final lines of Part 1 helps to soften an otherwise puzzling disjunction at the beginning of Part 2. The freer metre and new verse structure are combined with a change of topic and an impassioned elegiac tone. The 'it' in the first line likewise throws the reader. This pronoun appears also at the start of the second stanza; only towards the end of the third is it explained as referring to Elgar's music. The first person is used more liberally in Part 2 – in both singular and plural – and contributes to the impression of intense subjective experience.

In the course of Part 2 the relation between the parts is clarified gradually. The distant landscape and the secret, inner identity disclosed by Part 1 are endowed in Part 2 with a unique personal meaning and significance, with the speaking subject adopting the position of the 'me' in the final stanza of Part 1 and responding to the child's call. Despite similarities in form and subject matter, each of the three stanzas of Part 2 has a distinctive function. The first, elegiac, stanza laments the impossibility of combining the self-consciousness of maturity with the innocent enjoyment of youth ('We were not ripe to gather the full beauty'). The second tells of an almost synaesthetic response to music in which personal memories pour through the sounds. The third returns to the theme of the river; not now the upstream scene of the child among the reeds but 'the famous river' flowing away to the sea. This final acceptance of the inevitability of loss and death – in short, of linear time – is combined with the cyclic return of the poem's opening theme (the river) to poignant effect.

Indeed the subject of time provides the poem's most basic theme. Elgar's genius can 'Beat to its own tune, timelessly make heard / A long-breathed statement or a hesitant phrase'. Albert Gelpi points to these and other passages in Day Lewis's poetry which suggest that 'The poetic offspring of the imagination's desire reconciles existence to mortality'.[13] Such lines imply that poetic images are conceived 'in the poetic measure that composes and thereby reconciles contingencies into its own artificial (or art-making) time, whose recorded movement is impervious to clock time ... only through metrical time is chronological time conquered'.[14] The sentiment is underscored by the regular metre of Part 1. Part 2's irregular structure, by contrast, reflects the chaotic and troubling succession of memories that come flooding back to the subject upon hearing Elgar's music, and which can be ordered only through lists. For the most part these are past impressions of rural life: 'Malverns, Bredon, Cotswold'; 'Clovering bees, time-honeyed bells, the lark's top C'; 'stone, tree, clover / And cornfield'; 'marigold, buttercup, flag-iris'; 'Kingfishers, mayflies, mills, regattas'. Certain words and phrases are repeated almost obsessively: 'orchards', 'never bore', 'fruit', 'year', 'falling'. These techniques suggest a desperate attempt by the subject to recapture a lost fullness (witness the recurrence of the word 'all') by piling memory upon memory and grasping at individual perceptions in however haphazard a fashion. The disordered succession of thematic reminiscences towards the end of Elgar's Violin Concerto and *Falstaff* come to mind. The subject tries to reconstruct an idyllic past experience during which the passing of time itself seemed to be suspended: 'No past, no future, the pulse of time unnoticed'. The third stanza of Part 2 continues to suggest this mode of memory but combines it with an acceptance of progressive temporality and the inevitable onset of the future. The river is 'a flowing-awayness' which extends 'far beyond our view'. The ambiguity of the river as a poetic image – its association both with an eternal process and with constant mutability – is summed up succinctly with 'Always and never the same'. For the subject of Part 2, then, the inability to reconstitute a past perceived as replete and Edenic, leads, perhaps via the metrical order of 'his music', to a placid acceptance of fate.

According to the critic Joseph N. Riddel, 'If the weakness of Day Lewis'[s] poetry is its nostalgia (an obsession with an earlier, buried self – that self which was whole, presumably), its strength is in its humility (its awareness that it is condemned finally to a present of change and a future of death).'[15] This verdict goes straight to the point, although, from the perspective adopted in this book, the nostalgia need not be considered *a priori* a weakness. Indeed, in 'Edward Elgar' the intensity of the longing is destabilising and can be managed only by turning to the future. The poem handles familiar Elgarian techniques and themes with dexterity, opening spaces for the imagination by invoking nature, landscape, youth and age, haunting memories, and contrasted 'inner' and 'outer' personae. Finally, in its overall form it makes oblique reference to a specific Elgar work – perhaps it might be said a particular Elgar paradigm: the Second Symphony. The resemblance can be attributed to at least three factors: the way the lists and repetitions echo the sequences that Ernest Newman heard flowing inexorably onwards in the symphony's finale; the timely reference to nobility at the end of the poem ('reach after noble reach'); and, most tellingly, the way a recurring 'motto' theme (the river), first stated at the opening, returns expansively at the end in a mood of calm resignation.[16] This deft coordination of elegiac form and content makes the poem one of the most eloquent literary tributes to Elgar and his work.

PENAL WATERS

Norman Perryman's (b.1933) watercolour triptych *Elgar's Dream* (1996; Fig. 7.1) is an ambitious response to Elgar's music, and not only on account of its size (203 × 158 cm). The painting hangs in Symphony Hall, Birmingham, the town of Perryman's birth, as part of a collection of his works. Perryman has exhibited across Europe and has taken part in several 'performances' in collaboration with musicians and dancers, including a 1993 BBC television documentary entitled 'Concerto for Paintbrush and Orchestra'. In the latter he was seen painting a visual interpretation of

Fig. 7.1 Norman Perryman, *Elgar's Dream* (1996). Triptych watercolour 203 × 158 cm

Musorgsky's *Pictures at an Exhibition* in synchronisation with a performance of the work by the City of Birmingham Symphony Orchestra and
Simon Rattle, the images projected onto a screen. Most of his paintings are
on musical themes, either in the sense of 'kinetic performance art' such as
the Musorgsky interpretation, or as semi-figurative images of performers
with abstract shapes and 'graphic rhythms' which attempt to convey a sense
of the music through colour and pattern. At first Perryman painted with
oils but later he decided that the more 'transparent' medium of watercolour
was preferable for cultivating the 'illusion of movement' and suggesting the
ephemeral nature of music. 'Music, movement and watercolour', he
believes, 'have something in common.'[17]

The success of these pieces is admittedly mixed. The images of 'great
performers' that form the majority of the Symphony Hall Perryman
Collection play along with the cult of personality promoted by Classical
music agents and sections of the recording industry. In fact they resonate
uncomfortably with a common marketing strategy employed in contemporary advertising, whereby spiky shapes and splashes of primary colours

are used in an attempt to alter public perceptions of Classical concerts as staid and stuffy. The abstract patterns around the musicians are usually brilliant, swirling vortices, suggesting publicity-blurb clichés such as 'energy' and 'dynamism'. The text with which Perryman accompanies these images on his commercial website gushes embarrassingly.[18] Luckily, not all of Perryman's work is entirely compromised. When he avoids celebrity performers he can approach a kind of abstract expressionism that is often thought-provoking, as for instance in *Missa Criolla* (1975), *Circles: Berio and e.e. cummings* (1978) and even *Kobayashi Conducting Bartók* (1983). These works tend to be held in private collections or art galleries rather than concert halls. Evidently Perryman has an experimental as well as a public, accessible vein.

Elgar's Dream is one of his better public pieces.[19] In Symphony Hall the painting is displayed on a vertical surface, with narrow gaps between the three panels. Its form mimics that of many medieval triptychs, in which each side panel shows a landscape vista, while the central panel is devoted to spiritual and/or figurative content.[20] Unlike its medieval models, however, *Elgar's Dream* appears to have been a single whole during painting – there are many instances of single brushstrokes which cross the divisions between the panels – and much of the work's interest lies in the fact that the spiritual and landscape imagery significantly overlaps. The right panel shows the famous view of Worcester Cathedral across the river Severn, with the Severn reedbeds in the foreground. At the bottom of this region the claws of demons protrude from the dark reedbeds; they also appear in the central panel, clutching at the central figure (the soul of Gerontius). On the left panel the Malvern Hills in the background balance the cathedral (Perryman's familiarity with Elgarian geography dates to his childhood in Worcestershire), while Elgar himself can be seen in the foreground. The image of the composer is modelled on a photograph taken by William Eller in August 1900 when Elgar was finishing the score of *Gerontius*, so the identity of the manuscript he is working on is in no doubt. Immediately behind Elgar stands his wife Alice, and behind her are several of the 'friends pictured within' the 'Enigma' Variations, their features less distinguishable. The central panel shows three figures from *Gerontius*: the soul, the Guardian Angel and the priest. The soul has the features of Elgar himself in old age; he raises one arm in supplication towards the priest while the other trails beneath, perilously close to the demons. He is supported by a pair of hands, perhaps referring to lines in Part II of *Gerontius*: 'Another marvel: someone has me fast / Within his ample palm'; or 'In my most loving arms I now enfold thee'. The Angel gleams with light, right arm raised, in a pose reminiscent of Turner's late painting *The Angel Standing in the Sun* (1846), which has a 'vortex' form similar to that of the central panel of *Elgar's Dream*. In the centre of the painting a shaft of white light from the heavens cuts through the swirling colours and illuminates the face of the soul. Otherwise the main colours are purple (merging into green in the side panels) and orange, a garish combination in theory – and in colour reproductions – but effective in the original.

Another point lost in reproduction is the fact that the work emphasises its own physicality by means of effects that are possible only with the watery medium. The transparency and immediacy of watercolour contribute to a sense of movement and suggest the ephemerality of a dream. The priest salutes; the arms enfold; the demons clutch. The notes that Elgar writes – formed from flicked drops which have been joined up with lines – detach themselves from the pages of his manuscript and flow into the central panel. They also appear at the bottom of the central panel and are hinted at in the top of the left and the bottom of the right panels. The corners of the painting are appropriate regions for them, since the unpremeditated status of the noteheads suits their origins: the sky and the reeds respectively. The act of joining up the notes with deliberate brush strokes corresponds to the Elgarian compositional act of incorporating supposedly 'natural' music into a work of art and compositional artifice. The notes at the top left allow several interpretations. They might refer to Elgar's claims that 'there is music in the air, music all around us' and 'music is written on the skies', or they might portray celestial music pouring out of an opening in the heavens – the music could be the final reference to the 'Praise to the Holiest' refrain as it is quoted at the very end of *Gerontius*.

The idea that the scene represents the closing bars of the work might seem strange given the presence of the priest, who appears only in Part I. However, the painting in fact condenses two moments – the moment of death and the moment following the soul's judgement – into one, a practice in line with Elgar's treatment of the poem. (His music uses thematic reminiscence and leitmotiv techniques to emphasise that the whole process of Judgement takes place in the split second of death.) In that case it would seem that the hands supporting the soul are lowering it into the undifferentiated mass of colour in the centre of the painting, narrowly avoiding the demons at the bottom of the picture. After all, the soul's destination is not hell but purgatory. In the Angel's words:

> . . . o'er the penal waters, as they roll,
> I poise thee, and I lower thee, and hold thee.

And carefully I dip thee in the lake,
And thou, without a sob or a resistance,
Dost thro' the flood thy rapid passage take,
Sinking deep, deeper, into the dim distance.

On the other hand, certain abstract elements of the painting – the direction of the brush strokes and overall the flow of colour – suggest an alternative interpretation. The eye is led diagonally across the canvas from Elgar's score and the notes leaving it, through the central panel, and on to the Severn passing Worcester Cathedral. Another flow begins in the top left corner, circles around the priest and joins the general left-to-right motion in the centre. Thus, it might be argued, music emerges out of landscape, turns into dream, and condenses back into landscape. The 'rolling' of the 'penal waters' becomes the flow of a real river. This conception agrees with the actual direction of flow of the Severn at Worcester (left to right in the painting's right panel), so it is not entirely fanciful to conclude that Gerontius's soul is headed for the sea.

The blurring of distinctions is key to *Elgar's Dream*: geographical and spiritual, figurative and abstract, physical medium and conceptual content, dream and reality. The choice of watercolour is especially suitable for this blurring, and well as being appropriate to Gerontius's liquid destiny, the washing away of his sins. Whether the painting can be said to capture something of the spirit of Elgar's music is another matter. Perryman suggests that 'one might also view this painting as an almost abstract composition of flowing forms and colours, which reflect the rhythm and atmosphere suggested to me by this dramatic score'.[21] In one respect, however, despite the abundance of Elgarian themes on display, the painting cuts against the grain of Elgarian nostalgia as described in this book. By dissolving boundaries, it reverses Elgar's typical formal practice – albeit a practice that developed fully only in the years following the composition of *Gerontius*. In an alternative Elgarian triptych, we might expect boundaries to be sharply etched, the gaps between panels to be reflected precisely in the content of the painting, the music of nature not to join the general 'flow of inspiration' with such ease, and, above all, the distinction between dream and reality to be rigorously upheld.

SEVERN AND AMAZON

Whereas Day Lewis's poem concisely frames the dilemmas of the downstream condition and Perryman's painting captures a single moment in time (albeit combining several moments in a story at once), James Hamilton-Paterson's novel *Gerontius* (1989) works through a variety of Elgarian desires and dissatisfactions at a more leisurely pace, while weaving a fictional narrative around the voyage up the Amazon that the composer is known to have made in 1923. The theme must have appealed to Hamilton-Paterson (b. 1941), an Englishman in self-imposed exile in various distant locations, much of whose writing deals with displacement and life on and with the sea. Many critics regard him as a leading British novelist of his generation, and *Gerontius*, which won the Whitbread award for a first novel in 1989, represents his greatest public success. Elgar's uncharacteristically distant venture to South America is almost undocumented, allowing plenty of scope for the author. In the novel, the journey upstream represents an attempted escape on the part of the 66-year-old, muse-forsaken composer and also an effort to come to terms with the confusing world of memories that he inhabits in his post-war compositional silence. For the reader it is at the same time a gradual exposure of his strategies of self-deception and the flaws in his character. The novel eschews any obvious denouement in the narrative when the furthest upstream point is reached. There is no grand narrative sweep to make a linear flow from source to issue or vice versa. The chance discovery of an important person from Elgar's past leads to further self-reflection, but not to a crisis or moment of self-discovery. Indeed the book as a whole is largely 'plotless'; it privileges meditation over action in both content and structure, alternating Elgar's personal encounters, journal entries, reflections, memories and dreams with interludes involving other characters. The reader senses that upon his return to England Elgar's compositional impasse will remain in place.

Elgar's character is for the most part accurately drawn. Hamilton-Paterson captures his alternation between faith and disillusion, his tendency to self-dramatisation and self-indulgence, his sense of the visionary child within, his rage at the unmusical English middle classes, the aimlessness of his post-war years, and the mask of abruptness and philistinism that he latterly assumed in order to fend off anyone who spoke to him too directly about music. To be sure, it is odd to read a detailed, self-revelatory journal kept by Elgar (he did nothing of the kind in real life), and at times he seems too much the gloomy existentialist philosopher.[22] Nevertheless Hamilton-Paterson is clearly immersed in the Elgar literature, and many observations and exchanges, although strictly fictional, are based on real statements by Elgar, episodes in his social intercourse or composites of several such episodes. Elgar administers an ungracious brush-off to a woman who sang in the chorus at the premiere of *The Apostles* in 1903 and who compliments him lavishly on the work. To the ship's captain he claims ignorance of music, insisting that it was only a 'trade' which served him poorly and which he has now abandoned. In his journal and his reflections Elgar constantly returns to his imagined child-self, listening for the music of nature in waters, wind or vegetation, though he seldom discusses this topic in public. Indeed, his outward behaviour strikes two of the other characters as childish in the worst sense of the term. They are both women who experienced the effects of the Great War at first hand, one as a military nurse, the other through the loss of a son, and both are prone to impatience with Elgar's presentation of his own sense of loss.[23]

When it comes to moods of introspection and retrospection, however, Hamilton-Paterson's Elgar presents a sympathetic aspect. His shifting moods offer the chance to test different forms of memory and desire, yet the author remains wary of any investment in naive or cheap sentiment. This rule is proved by its one and only exception: an occasion on which Elgar is possessed by casual homesickness – nostalgia at its most trite. As his ship crosses the equator – a symbolic threshold – and nears the South American continent, the composer toys with the idea of spending the rest of his life on cruises around the world, forgetting himself in exotic places among diverting strangers. But he then recoils at the idea:

And suddenly he realised how horrid the entire notion was; that he didn't in the least want any of those things, that he wished at this very minute more than anything else to be walking the lanes of Worcestershire or sitting beside the Severn or the Teme. Never mind that it was late November and probably wet and cold. He saw a thousand pictures of his rivers in all weathers and none was unfriendly, none without its pleasurable echo.[24]

A succession of seemingly disconnected memories flash through his mind, their only link being home: lanes, cottages, kites, dogs, a whistled tune, the smell of woodsmoke ('the incense of nostalgia'). Unlike the sequences of impressions in Day Lewis's poem, however, these are perfectly accessible – they await him on his return. The fact that he longs for an English November – of all months – compounds the sense of a bout of self-indulgence. However, it is notable that the mood passes and does not recur later in the novel. Indeed, Elgar is soon drawn into reflection on his career and quite suddenly reaches a robust and entirely unsentimental assessment of the pre-war era in England. Those years he deems 'wilfully misremembered', not only by those who decry the age and his music as 'Pompenstance', but even by the people who lived through them and now recall them as 'a lost antediluvian land of innocence and plenty'.[25] When the ship's captain murmurs 'Ah, those were the days, eh?', Elgar comes back with 'Oh no they weren't' and launches into a refutation of the conventional wisdom of the time, listing tariff reform, the rise of trade unions, socialism, the suffragette movement, Irish home rule and the decline of British manufacturing as evidence for the unsettled mood of the period. He dates the nation's industrial decline to the 1870s, and reflects that at the very time Britain was overtaken by Germany he would have been teaching the violin at the girls' school in Malvern. The whole of his public career, then, took place while Britain was ostensibly celebrating its power and prosperity while secretly suffering unease at its inexorable decline. Kipling's *Recessional*, thinks Elgar, caught the mood only relatively late in the day (1897). He wonders whether a similar falling-away of artistic confidence had occurred in his own 'private soul' even during his period of greatest public acclaim. This passage in the novel comes close to anachronism as regards the words that are put into Elgar's mouth – he sounds like a revisionist historian. Yet the episode as a whole illustrates the author's differentiation between sentimentality and a deeper vein of disillusion. The latter is conveyed through such Elgarian tropes as doomed grandeur and contrasting inner and outer personae. By thus playing off contradictory impulses in (the fictional) Elgar's character through descriptions of his mood swings, the novel gives a telling insight into his mental state.

Much of Elgar's retrospection is involuntary, leading to a series of 'hauntings'. Indeed, from Terry Castle's perspective (discussed in Chapter 2), Hamilton-Paterson's Elgar would be little less than the representative modern subject, reaping the consequences of Romantic solipsism. Near the beginning of the novel, while drifting in and out of sleep on the train to Liverpool to catch his boat, he imagines speaking to the ghost of his close friend Alfred Rodewald, the Liverpool industrialist and conductor whose death had deeply affected him twenty years previously.[26] Later, in a café in Pará, he suddenly has a sensation of being young that he has not experienced in decades and resents it bitterly: 'Ghosts of the past self had no business sliding back out of hiding after decades of absence, cheerfully untouched by the tolls and ravages of a lived life.'[27] Upon reaching Manaos (the voyage's furthest upstream destination), he receives a letter from his former lover Magdalena von Pussels (a creation of the author), who, entirely unbeknown to him, has been living in the city for decades. He reflects that 'Once one had reached a certain age there was evidently no place on earth whose neutrality was guaranteed. The entire planet was peopled with ghosts. Even the most alien of its terrains might exude them, the most preposterous place quicken thoughts and memories.'[28] He concludes that, for the old, travel can no longer be an adventure because 'the exterior globe was increasingly displaced by an interior lifetime'. It would be 'an act of great purity' to erase subjective memories from the landscape and force oneself to perceive only the objects themselves: 'just clouds, just a forest, just a great river'. Elgar now feels he will never be capable of that act; he will be permanently haunted.

The motion of waters accompanies all these ruminations. When Elgar feels that nature has lost its power of enchantment he angrily substitutes a linear for a cyclical image of the river. What he heard by the Severn and Teme, listening to the wind in the reeds and willows was 'the slow slide of arterial England which at the time I idiotically supposed to be everlasting'.[29] On the other hand, in South America a reversal of linear time seems almost possible. 'In Amazonas at any rate it's easy to believe Time's ever-rolling stream flows backwards.'[30] He finds that his own past comes back to him more easily there. The waters of the southern hemisphere likewise blur the sense of clear boundaries to which Elgar, as a European, is accustomed. 'Everything in this part of the world is intent on flowing into everything else.' On one occasion, he feels his life's work to be insignificant and can recall only his troubles. 'Not a note written but whole hinterlands of emotion drained, tributary joining tributary until there was the impression of the sound of many waters, of a general sliding, of being a perilous bystander on a quayside watching a great river in spate, the turgid yellow swirls mere inches beneath his feet.'[31] His memories of youthful music-making and inspiration in the English countryside likewise turn liquid. 'River, hill and lane: they ran like water through his mind and left behind on scattered sheets of manuscript crooked rivulets of notes which glittered like mud-flats draining in the sun.'[32]

Watery inspiration is the theme of one of the finest passages in the novel, a rare moment when Elgar's disillusion abates and he recaptures something of the old creative spark. One day, as the composer sits on deck watching the ocean, he thinks of the English and European rivers that had inspired him in the past, and holds a sheet of manuscript paper and a pencil. 'And there, as it often had, the sight and sound of water in motion began to produce its familiar effects.'[33] Even the sound of the ship's engines contributes. These stimuli do not at first yield a tune as such, but open a 'lively space' for a tune – the kind of space that (in the world of the novel) had often come to him in the past. 'An immanence of rhythm, a sense of paragraphs, blocks of feeling and a glimpse of a shape two blank pages ahead unmistakably in his hand but as yet unreadable. And ever since he could remember, a flow of water could also create this ache and expectancy.' Such a framework would precede not only the tune but also the title of the work, the dedication and the literary games which Elgar liked to weave around his compositions. This account of the creative process seems plausible enough, judging from what is known about Elgar's sources of inspiration (the prompting of noises or images, whether natural or otherwise).

Elgar makes a successful sketch, which sends him into another reverie, this one sparked by a punning phrase he had once coined in a letter to a friend about something that had taken him back to 'boyhood's daze'. Now he recalls that this daze 'had come to him as he lay on his stomach on a drifting punt, fingers trailing sunlit water, dreaming open-eyed as his directionless craft nudged the hoof-pocked shallows beneath the bank and slowly swung its other end out into the stream, setting him off again now facing the other way. Backwards or forwards, who knew?'[34] There follows a radiant, lyrical passage that echoes the second stanza of Part 2 of Day Lewis's poem, recalling the 'daze' of the Malvern Hills, the sky, the bees and their pollen, and finally the organ loft. The following day, however, Elgar sits on the deck in the same place at the same time and sees and hears the same impressions, but no continuation presents itself, and the sketch is set aside. The episode thus fits into the novel in much the same way as a pastoral interlude in one of Elgar's own symphonic works – even though the content owes as much to Kenneth Grahame as to Elgar himself.

This preoccupation with the sources of inspiration is present already at the opening of the novel, which recounts at length an exotic dream that comes to Elgar as he dozes on the train to Liverpool. Although scattered with references to *Gerontius* and *The Apostles*, its relation to the rest of the book is oblique, and Elgar later recalls only snatches of it. The protagonist, known as 'the dreamer', climbs a high column in the Syrian desert upon which an ascetic saint sits permanently, meditating and enduring extraordinary privations. When the dreamer reaches the top he forgets the question he wanted to ask, but holds a conversation with the saint, who is gentle but provocative. The summit magically expands in size and the dreamer notices a pavilion and a courtyard. He perceives something sweet borne on the wind from beyond the courtyard, yet cannot tell which sense it affects. This idea refers to the early stages of Part II of *Gerontius* and the text brings home the point with a paraphrase of the soul's words at that stage. The lines that follow are another paraphrase, but from a less obvious source: the passage from *The Wind in the Willows* that was quoted in Chapter 4 (compare p. 89):

'What is it?' he asks.
'What it is. Call it what you like. Music, why not?'

And at once it gathers in his ears and he perceives that it is, after all, music. But it is quite unlike anything he has ever heard before, so beautiful and strange and new. It arouses a longing in him that is akin to pain and nothing seems worthwhile but just to hear that sound and go on listening to it for ever.[35]

It later turns out that Hamilton-Paterson's Elgar has memorised much of the 'Piper at the Gates of Dawn' chapter and even quotes the sentence about lilting dance music (see p. 89).[36] The saint later explains that the drifting sensation is not itself music – the dreamer merely hears it as such. For another person it might be perceived differently. 'You need only to discover the gateway – but no-one can help you do that. We are unique.'[37]

This 'sense of inaudible music' runs through the novel,[38] and is usually connected to Elgar's memories of his childhood (or rather his attempted memories, for sometimes he is put in mind only of the other occasions on which he has tried to remember). Hamilton-Paterson's Elgar does not get away with much myth-making; indeed, his disillusion makes him doubt the very basis of the 'dreamy child' story. In his journal Elgar deconstructs his own myth. He records that he has come to hate his muse – the voice that says 'translate me' as he feels the wind or looks at the landscape.[39] Long ago its traces were definite. 'Such were the notes, & only those notes, made by the wind passing through the trees & by the trees as the wind passed through them. Anyone who couldn't hear it was deaf or had the soul of a stone. Alas for the years it took to see why I was wrong.'[40] It now seems a 'miserable deception'. Elgar realises that it is the mind that 'moves', and that the trees would sing a different song to other ears. Echoing the saint on the column, he reflects that there might be a single 'raw material' for all the arts, but this brings no comfort: Elgar is too haunted by recollections – or imaginings – of his own childhood vision to start again with a new artistic philosophy.

Elgar's former lover, Magdalena von Pussels, whom he meets in Manaos, is also uneasy with the child in Elgar, but for different reasons. She too is afflicted by 'ghosts' from the past, but finds Elgar annoyingly uninterested in laying them to rest, preferring animated discussion of male hobbies with her friend, an English chaplain. After leaving Elgar she sits down at the piano and reflects on his flawed character – a passage near the end of the novel, just before the boat turns for home, which appears to come close to an authorial judgement (on the man – not the music). 'You're a baby, Edward, you always were. A brilliant baby; a genius baby, but a baby in your clamour for attention, attention, attention.'[41] Elgar, she says, manufactured 'that classic myth of the romantic artist – the lonely dreamer of the reed-beds taking dictation from the wind, young Ted Elgar up from Worcester whose genius was for ever being snubbed and thwarted by some upper-crust musical establishment in Cambridge and London'.[42] The reason she stopped seeing him in the old days was because 'Quite simply, I didn't want to become your mother'.[43] Now Elgar can do nothing to help himself, and must return home to his own landscape – familiar but disenchanted – and to the memories that recall other acts of memory rather than events. *Nostos* may be achieved this time, but *algos* will remain.

If Magdalena von Pussels were a Freudian – and as ambivalent about Elgar's music as she is about his personality – she might have enlarged witheringly on the significance of rivers for Elgar's art and imagination. For rivers and their motions not only offer a means to draw together the main themes in nostalgic discourse on Elgar, they also present the most obvious of targets for the anti-nostalgia critic. Waters, so the argument would go, whatever their other imaginative associations, have always stood for a primitive state of both matter and existence – formless, undifferentiated, unconscious. As such they are the final symbol of psychological regression. A preoccupation with waters indicates a longing for a return to the womb, where subject and object, self and world, are one. From this perspective, the works by C. Day Lewis and Norman Perryman discussed in this chapter and many of Elgar's musings in Hamilton-Paterson's *Gerontius* do not constitute productive engagements with the difficulties of human existence. Rather, they evade them. In the poem, the subject's obsessively recounted memories, far from being confronted and expunged, are given pseudo-sublimation in the all-consuming sea; in the painting, all boundaries are dissolved because Gerontius's sins (themselves merely the product of an imagination possessed by unhealthy Catholic self-hatred) can be washed away only by self-abasement and willing obliteration. In Elgarian nostalgia, according to this view, the original sin of all human beings is to have been born in the first place.

So are C. Day Lewis and James Hamilton-Paterson, along with Elgar the musician as well as the man, nothing more than overgrown babies? Surely not – any more than J. B. Priestley, David Rudkin and Ken Russell are closet Fascists. At its best, Elgarian nostalgia – as manifested both in his music and in responses to it – dwells in the 'pain' rather than just glorifying the 'return home', and offers critique and commentary in relation to the present, not merely escape. Even the closing minutes of *Gerontius* – at first glance Elgar's most 'regressive' episode, in which the contralto Angel soothes and caresses the soul with maternal love – are far from simple wish fulfilment. On the contrary, they mark a difficult parting, a farewell. Whatever other associations, roles and functions Elgar's music acquired in twentieth-century Britain, its unstinting rehearsal of that parting accounts for much of its continuing power to move and to compel.

Notes

1: NOSTALGIA

1. There is plentiful literature on this particular Elgarian enigma. See, for instance, Michael Kennedy, 'The Soul Enshrined: Elgar and his Violin Concerto', in Raymond Monk, ed., *Edward Elgar: Music and Literature* (Aldershot: Scolar Press, 1993), 72–82.

2. See Jean Starobinski, 'The Idea of Nostalgia', *Diogenes* 54 (1966), 81–103; George Rosen, 'Nostalgia: A "Forgotten" Psychological Disorder', *Clio Medica* 10/1 (1975), 29–51. See also Fred Davis, *Yearning for Yesterday: A Sociology of Nostalgia* (London and New York: Macmillan, 1979), 1; Nicholas Dames, *Amnesiac Selves: Nostalgia, Forgetting and British Fiction, 1810–1870* (Oxford and New York: Oxford University Press, 2001), 28–33; David Lowenthal, *The Past is a Foreign Country* (Cambridge: Cambridge University Press, 1985), 4–13.

3. The relationship is explored by Christopher Lasch, *The True and Only Heaven: Progress and its Critics* (London and New York: Norton, 1991), esp. 14, 82–3.

4. Novalis, *Briefe und Werke*, 3 vols. (Berlin: L. Schneider, 1943), III, 172, quoted (in German) in M. H. Abrams, *Natural Supernaturalism: Tradition and Revolution in Romantic Literature* (New York and London: Norton, 1973), 195.

5. Lowenthal, *Foreign Country*, 96–105; Malcolm Chase and Christopher Shaw, 'The Dimensions of Nostalgia', in Malcolm Chase and Christopher Shaw, eds., *The Imagined Past: History and Nostalgia* (Manchester and New York: Manchester University Press, 1989), 1–17 (pp. 2–3).

6. Svetlana Boym, *The Future of Nostalgia* (New York: Basic Books, 2001), 7.

7. See, for instance, Ian B. McKellar, *The Edwardian Age: Complacency and Concern* (Glasgow: Blackie, 1980); J. F. C. Harrison, *Late Victorian Britain* (London: Routledge, 1991); Vyvyen Brendon, *The Edwardian Age: 1901–14* (London: Hodder & Stoughton, 1996); David Powell, *The Edwardian Crisis: Britain 1901–14* (Basingstoke: Macmillan, 1996).

8. Eric Hobsbawm and Terrence Ranger, eds., *The Invention of Tradition* (Cambridge: Cambridge University Press, 1983).

9. See the discussion of David Rudkin's *Penda's Fen* in Chapter 6.

10. Kevin Allen, *Elgar the Cyclist in Worcester and Hereford: A Creative Odyssey* (Malvern Wells: Kevin Allen, 1997).

11. Christopher Lasch, 'The Politics of Nostalgia', *Harper's* 269 (1984), 65–70 (p. 65).
12. David Lowenthal, 'Nostalgia Tells it Like it Wasn't', in Chase and Shaw, *The Imagined Past*, 18–32 (p. 27).
13. Susan Stewart, *On Longing: Narratives of the Miniature, the Gigantic, the Souvenir, the Collection* (Durham, N. C., and London: Duke University Press, 1993), 23; Charles Maier, cited in Boym, *The Future of Nostalgia*, p. xiv; Jay Anderson, cited in Lowenthal, *Foreign Country*, 11.
14. James Coombs, *The Reagan Range: The Nostalgia Myth in American Politics* (Bowling Green: Bowling Green State University Popular Press, 1993).
15. Janice Doane and Devon Hodges, 'Introduction', in Janice Doane and Devon Hodges, eds., *Nostalgia and Sexual Difference: The Resistance to Contemporary Feminism* (New York: Methuen, 1987), 3–14 (p. 3).
16. 'When the real is no longer what it was, nostalgia assumes its full meaning.' Jean Baudrillard, *Simulacra and Simulation*, trans. Sheila Faria Glaser (Ann Arbor: University of Michigan Press, 1994), 6. See also Frederic Jameson, *Postmodernism, Or, The Cultural Logic of Late Capitalism* (London and New York: Verso, 1991), 19–21; and the essays on nostalgia in Bryan S. Turner, ed., *Theories of Modernity and Postmodernity* (London, Newbury Park and New Dehli: SAGE Publications, 1990), 'Part Two: Nostalgia and Memory', 31–87.
17. Bryan S. Turner, 'A Note on Nostalgia', *Theory, Culture and Society* 4/1 (1987), 147–56 (p. 153).
18. Robert Hewison, *The Heritage Industry: Britain in a Climate of Decline* (London: Methuen, 1987), 9, 47, 134.
19. Michael Kammen, cited in Boym, *The Future of Nostalgia*, p. xiv.
20. David Cannadine, *The Pleasures of the Past* (London: Collins, 1989), 259 (from the chapter 'Nostalgia', pp. 256–71). See also Patrick Wright, *On Living in an Old Country: The National Past in Contemporary Britain* (London: Verso, 1985).
21. *The Sunday Times*, 5 April 1998; quoted in Georg K. Behlmer, 'Introduction', in George K. Behlmer and Fred M. Leventhal, eds., *Singular Continuities: Tradition, Nostalgia and Identity in Modern British Culture* (Stanford, Calif.: Stanford University Press, 2000), 1–10 (p. 1).
22. Jeremy Crump, 'The Identity of English Music: The Reception of Elgar 1898–1935', in Robert Colls and Philip Dodd, eds., *Englishness: Politics and Culture 1880–1940* (Beckenham: Croom Helm, 1986), 164–90 (p. 185).
23. Archie Miles, *The Malvern Hills: Travels Through Elgar Country* (London: Pavilion, 1992).
24. Stuart Cosgrove and Paul Reas, *Flogging a Dead Horse: Heritage Culture and its Role in Post-Industrial Britain* (Manchester: Cornerhouse, 1993).
25. David Cannadine, 'Sir Edward Elgar', in *The Pleasures of the Past*, 121–30 (p. 127).
26. Lasch, 'Politics of Nostalgia', 65.
27. Lasch has subsequently extended his account of nostalgia, which he calls the 'ideological twin' of the idea of progress. Lasch, *The True and Only Heaven*, chapter 3 ('Nostalgia: The Abdication of Memory'), 82–119. This book claims to move beyond the politics of Right and Left – not an unusual position for

the early 1990s – but advocates a return to what Lasch sees as the values of petit bourgeois America.

28. Stuart Tannock, 'Nostalgia Critique', *Cultural Studies* 9/3 (1995), 453–64 (p. 453).
29. Frederic Jameson, *Marxism and Form: Twentieth-Century Dialectical Theories of Literature* (Princeton: Princeton University Press, 1971), 82.
30. Wright, *On Living in an Old Country*, 22.
31. Raphael Samuel, *Theatres of Memory*, 2 vols. (London: Verso, 1994–98), I (*Past and Present in Contemporary Culture*), 288, 290–1. See also Lowenthal, 'Nostalgia Tells it Like it Wasn't'. Lowenthal's essay is a contribution to a book arising from a conference in the 'History Workshop' series, with which Samuel was closely associated. The editors admit that the contributors revealed dimensions to nostalgia that they had not anticipated before the event. Chase and Shaw, 'Dimensions of Nostalgia', 1.
32. Tannock, 'Nostalgia Critique', 455.
33. Ibid., 456.
34. Boym, *The Future of Nostalgia*, p. xvi.
35. Tannock, 'Nostalgia Critique', 454.
36. See Dames, *Amnesiac Selves*; Stephen Cheeke, *Byron and Place: History, Translation, Nostalgia* (Basingstoke: Palgrave Macmillan, 2003); Ann C. Colley, *Nostalgia and Recollection in Victorian Culture* (Basingstoke: Macmillan, 1998); Helen Groth, *Victorian Photography and Literary Nostalgia* (Oxford and New York: Oxford University Press, 2003); Tamara S. Wagner, *Narratives of Nostalgia in the British Novel, 1740–1890* (Lewisburg, Pa.: Bucknell University Press, 2004). For studies of nostalgia and immigrant identity, see Boym, *The Future of Nostalgia*; and Andreea Deciu Ritivoi, *Yesterday's Self: Nostalgia and the Immigrant Identity* (Lanham, Md., and Oxford: Rowman & Littlefield, 2002). See also *Iowa Journal of Cultural Studies* 4 (2004), especially the Introduction by Sean Scanlan.
37. There are already some fine studies of Elgar that take a 'firm but fair' approach. See Michael De-la-Noy, *Elgar: The Man* (London: Allen Lane, 1983); Brian Trowell, 'Elgar's Use of Literature', in Monk, *Edward Elgar: Music and Literature*, 182–326; Christopher Grogan 'Foreword', in *Dream Children* and *The Wand of Youth* (Suites Nos. 1 and 2): *Elgar Complete Edition*, vol. 25, ed. Christopher Grogan (London: Elgar Society Edition in association with Novello, 2001).
38. Michael Kennedy, *Portrait of Elgar*, 3rd edn (London: Oxford University Press, 1987), 163. Kennedy is pointing out that whereas some people in the later twentieth century are fascinated by the supposed idyll of the Edwardian period, that was precisely the present from which the adult Elgar periodically longed to escape.

2: MEMORY

1. Michael Allis, 'Elgar and the Art of Retrospective Narrative', *Journal of Musicological Research* 19 (2000), 289–328 (p. 321). Allis's account of Elgar's

'retrospective aesthetic' is an important contribution, and analyses many of the passages discussed here. Still, this chapter takes an alternative approach from that implicit in his retrospective typology ('incorporation of previously-composed material'; 'programmatically-motivated recall'; 'structural recall'). On the link Allis makes with Elgar's interest in childhood, see Chapter 5, n. 6.

2. For instance, the Piano Sonatas, Op. 27 No. 2 and Op. 101, the Fifth and Ninth Symphonies, and the Cello Sonata, Op. 102 No. 1. But for an argument that the practice began earlier see James Webster, *Haydn's 'Farewell' Symphony and the Idea of Classical Style: Through-Composition and Cyclic Integration in his Instrumental Music* (Cambridge: Cambridge University Press, 1991).

3. Charles Rosen, *The Romantic Generation* (Cambridge, Mass.: Harvard University Press, 1995), chapter 3 ('Mountains and Song Cycles').

4. Carl Dahlhaus, 'Sonata Form in Schubert: The First Movement of the G-Major String Quartet, Op. 161 (D. 887)', in Walther Frisch, ed., *Schubert: Critical and Analytical Studies* (Lincoln and London: University of Nebraska Press, 1996), 1–12. On Schubert see also six contributions to *Musical Quarterly* 84/4 (2000): Leon Botstein, 'Memory and Nostalgia as Music-Historical Categories', 531–5; Walter Frisch, ' "You Must Remember This": Memory and Structure in Schubert's String Quartet in G Major, D. 887', 582–603; John M. Gingerich, 'Remembrance and Consciousness in Schubert's C-Major String Quintet, D. 956', 619–34; Charles Fisk, 'Schubert Recollects Himself: The Piano Sonata in C Minor, D. 958', 635–654; and Scott Burnham, 'Schubert and the Sound of Memory', 655–63. Karol Berger argues persuasively that certain sudden shifts and interpolations in Beethoven's early and late piano music point to a mind forgetful of the present and absorbed in inward thoughts. Karol Berger, 'Beethoven and the Aesthetic State', in Mark Evan Bonds, ed., *Beethoven Forum 7*, (Lincoln and London: University of Nebraska Press, 1999), 17–44.

5. Some further possibilities have been explored in Allis, 'Retrospective Narrative', and Aidan J. Thomson, 'Unmaking *The Music Makers*', in J. P. E. Harper-Scott and Julian Rushton, eds., *Elgar Studies* (Cambridge: Cambridge University Press, forthcoming).

6. Allis, 'Retrospective Narrative', 304. Allis's use of the term 'narrative' recalls the ideas of Carolyn Abbate, *Unsung Voices: Opera and Musical Narrative in the Nineteenth Century* (Princeton: Princeton University Press, 1991), which likewise anticipate the approach taken here in important ways. Allis also speaks of a 'nostalgic haze' in the Violin Concerto cadenza (p. 316). That phrase seems intuitively right, but he does not explain why a hazy texture should contribute to a sense of nostalgia. This chapter tries to address the question.

7. On music, see Berthold Hoeckner, 'Schumann and Romantic Distance', *Journal of the American Musicological Society* 50/1 (1997), 55–132 (pp. 60–71). On literature, see the collection of quotations assembled by James Hepokoski, 'Gaudery, Romance, and the "Welsh" Tune: *Introduction and Allegro*, Op. 47', in Harper-Scott and Rushton, *Elgar Studies*. In several respects, as these contexts imply, the Welsh tune already sounds like a memory when it is heard in the Introduction. Hepokoski characterises the tune with terms such

as memory, nostalgia, longing, loss, mirage and, most tellingly, Friedrich Schiller's concepts of the 'naive', the 'sentimental' and the 'elegiac'. He hears the *Introduction and Allegro* as a series of vain attempts by a subject to bring the tune to completeness and closure, and thus to recapture what has been 'lost'. This is a fruitful interpretation, and could be extended to many other Elgar composi- tions. It makes an interesting contrast with the approach taken in this chapter, however, which tends to emphasise a contrary process. As will become clear, memories in Elgar can be regarded as themselves active, welling up to conscious- ness unbidden, and pushing through at the 'weak points' in a form. From this perspective the experience of memory may be discomforting rather than elegiac.

8. In the words of Julian Rushton, 'Elgar's fugue begins as if a chasm has opened in the musical structure, like a crack in the ground which reveals something previously hidden, and decidedly sinister.' Julian Rushton, 'A Devil of a Fugue: Berlioz, Elgar, and *Introduction and Allegro*', *Elgar Society Journal* 11/ 5 (2000), 276–87 (p. 285).

9. Hepokoski points out that the final return of the tune carries aspects of both recapitulation and coda functions. He stresses the lack of full closure even here, however. The tune is never brought to a perfect cadence, and what he calls the 'weak' version – associated with dissolution and decay – has the last word. His reading of the final bars of the piece as a return to public duty and 'official' music resonates with the interpretation of Elgar's later orchestral works to be advanced here. In those works, though, the coda- or recapitulation- functionality of thematic returns is significantly diminished, and the effect of the contrast thereby heightened. Hepokoski, 'Gaudery, Romance, and the "Welsh" Tune'.

10. J. P. E. Harper-Scott, reflecting on the final C major chord in *Falstaff*, takes a similar view. 'Elgar was almost alone amongst early modernist composers in insisting on a return to a work's opening tonic *regardless of the cost*.' 'His music does not *earn* its return home, but simply *retreats* there, away from challenges.' 'Elgar's Invention of the Human: *Falstaff*, Op. 68', *19th-Century Music* 28/3 (2005), 230–53 (pp. 250–1).

11. One bar after fig. 143 there are chromatically descending tritones on muted horns and divided violas playing *tremolando*, with the accompaniment of a long shake on a tambourine. At 145 cellos play descending tritones *pp sul ponticello*.

12. On this chord see Harper-Scott, 'Elgar's Invention of the Human', 250–2. Daniel Grimley has also analysed the final pages of the score. ' "*Falstaff* *(Tragedy)*": Narrative and Retrospection in Elgar's Symphonic Study', paper delivered at the Elgar Conference, University of Surrey, 13–14 April 2002. It is tempting to attribute to the close of *Falstaff* a foresight similar to that which Paul Fussell finds in Thomas Hardy's *Satires of Circumstance*, published in November 1914 but composed before the Great War. Hardy's tone of desola- tion and grim irony precisely anticipated the later British understanding of the war. Paul Fussell, *The Great War and Modern Memory* (London: Oxford University Press, 1975), 3–7.

13. See for instance, Kennedy, *Portrait of Elgar*, 282.

14. This discussion has been restricted to instrumental works, but it should be noted in connection with *Falstaff* and the Cello Concerto that the closing pages of *The Music Makers* (1912) present a comparable degree of rupture. The mysterious recollection of the 'Novissima hora est' motif from *The Dream of Gerontius* is located in the penultimate position, setting the words 'A singer who sings no more'. The opening frame of the piece is then reasserted with 'We are the Music Makers' after a sudden harmonic wrench from E minor to F minor (fig. 103). However, this moment arguably represents only the final stage of the gradual unravelling of the structure on the work; see Thomson, 'Unmaking The Music Makers'.

15. Burnham, 'Schubert and the Sound of Memory', 661.

16. The quintet is the only parallel to the First Symphony in its location of thematic reminiscence at this point in the form; there are similarities too in the absolute contrasts between these introductions and the openings of the succeeding Allegros.

17. The burying of the reminiscences and the total change of mood may be among the factors contributing to the puzzlement or displeasure that some listeners have expressed in relation to the Piano Quintet. For a review of these reactions see Michael Allis, 'Elgar, Lytton and the Piano Quintet, Op. 84', *Music & Letters* 85/2 (2004), 198–238 (pp. 199–200).

18. See Hoeckner, 'Schumann and Romantic Distance', 62–71.

19. They are No. 2 ('The Serious Doll'; the solo violin adds a counter-melody), No. 6 ('The Merry Doll'), and No. 7, where the solo violin takes over the melody.

20. For an excellent account of a similar effect in Beethoven, see Berger, 'Beethoven and the Aesthetic State'.

21. Sigmund Freud, *The Uncanny*, trans. David McLintock (London: Penguin, 2003).

22. Fred Botting, *Gothic* (London and New York: Routledge, 1996), 1.

23. Julian Wolfreys, *Victorian Haunting: Spectrality, Gothic, the Uncanny and Literature* (Houndsmill, Basingstoke: Palgrave, 2002), 2. For introductory discussions of gothic, see also Botting, *Gothic*; and David Punter, 'Introduction: Of Apparitions', in Glennis Byron and David Punter, eds., *Spectral Reading: Towards a Gothic Geography* (Houndsmill: Macmillan, 1999), 1–8.

24. Terry Castle, 'The Spectralization of the Other in *The Mysteries of Udolpho*', in Laura Brown and Felicity Nussbaum, eds., *The New Eighteenth Century* (London: Methuen, 1987), 231–53 (p. 237).

25. Kennedy, *Portrait of Elgar*, 334.

26. Letters to Alice Stuart Wortley, 29 January 1911, in Jerrold Northrop Moore, *Edward Elgar: The Windflower Letters* (Oxford: Clarendon Press, 1989), 75; to Ernest Newman, 29 January 1911, in Jerrold Northrop Moore, *Edward Elgar: Letters of a Lifetime* (Oxford: Clarendon Press, 1990), 229; to Alfred Littleton, 13 April 1911, in Jerrold Northrop Moore, *Elgar and his Publishers: Letters of a Creative Life*, 2 vols. (Oxford: Clarendon Press, 1987), II, 742.

27. Jerrold Northrop Moore, *Edward Elgar: A Creative Life* (Oxford: Clarendon Press, 1984), 594–608, esp. 608; Peter J. Pirie, 'World's End: A Study of Edward

Elgar', *Music Review* 18 (1957), 89–100 (p. 94); James Hepokoski, 'Elgar', in D. Kern Holoman, ed., *The Nineteenth-Century Symphony* (New York: Schirmer, 1997), 329.

28. Letter to Ernest Newman, 5 January 1919, in Moore, *Letters of a Lifetime*, 321.

29. Allis, 'Piano Quintet'.

30. Moore, *Creative Life*, 725–8, 737; Diana McVeagh, *Edward Elgar: His Life and Music* (London: J. M. Dent & Sons, 1955), 177; Ivor Keys, ' "Ghostly Stuff": The Brinkwells Music', in Monk, *Edward Elgar: Music and Literature*, 108–20 (pp. 108 and 120); Daniel M. Grimley, 'A Smiling with a Sigh: The Chamber Music and Works for Strings', in Daniel M. Grimley and Julian Rushton, eds., *The Cambridge Companion to Elgar* (Cambridge: Cambridge University Press, 2004), 120–38 (p. 136).

31. David Pownall, *Elgar's Rondo*, in *The Composer Plays* (London: Oberon Books, 1994), 107–60; James Hamilton-Paterson, *Gerontius: A Novel about Sir Edward Elgar* (London: Granta Books, 2002; 1st pub. Macmillan, 1989), 14, 203; David Rudkin, *Penda's Fen* (London: Davis-Poynter, 1995), 53–7; Alick Rowe, *The Dorabella Variation*, directed by Celia de Wolff, Radio 4 Saturday Play, 28 June 2003.

32. Cited in Ashton Nichols, *The Poetics of Epiphany: Nineteenth-Century Origins of the Modern Literary Moment* (Tuscaloosa and London: The University of Alabama Press, 1987), 5; and in Abrams, *Natural Supernaturalism*, 419.

33. Abrams, *Natural Supernaturalism*, 419; Robert Langbaum, 'The Epiphanic Mode in Wordsworth and Modern Literature', *New Literary History* 14/2 (1983), 335–58 (pp. 336, 339); Nichols, *Poetics of Epiphany*, 4. Among the large and growing literature on literary epiphanies, see also Morris Beja, *Epiphany in the Modern Novel* (London: Owen, 1971); and Martin Bidney, *Patterns of Epiphany: From Wordsworth to Tolstoy, Pater and Barrett Browning* (Carbondale: Southern Illinois University Press, 1997).

34. Percy Bysshe Shelley, *The Poems of Shelley*, ed. Kelvin Everest and Geoffrey Matthews, 2 vols. (London and New York: Longman, 1989–2000), I, 528.

35. Percy Bysshe Shelley, *Selected Poetry and Prose*, ed. Alasdair D. F. Macrae (London: Routledge, 1991), 228, 229.

36. In terms of contemporary musicology's theory of 'sonata deformation' this is an example of the 'breakthrough' deformation, so called by James Hepokoski, developing an idea of Theodor W. Adorno's. See Hepokoski, 'Fiery-Pulsed Libertine or Domestic Hero? Strauss's Don Juan Reinvestigated', in Bryan Gilliam, ed., *Richard Strauss: New Perspectives on the Composer and his Work* (Durham, N.C.: Duke University Press, 1992), 135–75 (pp. 149–52); and, for a discussion in relation to Elgar, Harper-Scott, 'Elgar's Invention of the Human', 247–50.

37. The antitheses were never absolute, however. Chapter 3 explores a little of the dialectics of real/ideal and noble/melancholy in the work, finding these aspects in tension already in the motto.

38. Diana McVeagh remarks that, in his development sections, Elgar often 'reveals relationships between apparently unconnected themes'. She adds that 'with

recognition comes astonishment and then illumination' – the vocabulary of epiphany. *Life and Music*, 204.

39. Elgar's surviving comments on the finale are a little ambiguous, and it is debatable whether they support the present reading. See the letters to Ernest Newman of 2 and 6 November 1908 (Moore, *Letters of a Lifetime*, 200, 201) and a much later remark to Neville Cardus (*Manchester Guardian Weekly*, 2 March 1934, quoted in Moore, *Creative Life*, 539).

40. Northrop Frye, *Anatomy of Criticism* (Princeton: Princeton University Press, 1957), 223.

41. J. P. E. Harper-Scott comments that 'the episode seems almost spliced into the general scheme of the work'. 'Elgar's Deconstruction of the *belle époque*', in Harper-Scott and Rushton, *Elgar Studies*. Harper-Scott usefully reviews the confused reactions of commentators to the seemingly casual resumption of the Rondo material.

42. J. B. Priestley, *Festival at Farbridge* (London: Heinemann, 1957), 552.

43. Ibid., 553.

44. Elgar's friends Rosa Burley and W. H. Reed both referred to the Welsh tune as the 'second subject', despite the fact that it does not appear in the conventional position for a second subject in the Allegro; see Hepokoski, 'Gaudery, Romance, and the "Welsh" tune'. Priestley may be echoing these writers.

45. Priestley, *Festival at Farbridge*, 553.

46. Letter to Alfred Littleton, 13 April 1911, in Moore, *Letters of a Creative Life*, II, 741–2.

47. *The Poems of Shelley*, ed. Everest and Matthews, I, 531.

48. William Wordsworth, *Lyrical Ballads*, ed. Michael Mason (London and New York: Longman, 1992), 212.

49. The suggestion that the symphony finds a sort of 'third way' resonates in some respects with the more fully developed interpretation of the work by J. P. E. Harper-Scott. See 'Elgar's Deconstruction of the *belle époque*'.

3: NOBILITY

1. For instance, *The Black Knight*, *King Olaf*, *Froissart*, *Falstaff*, *King Arthur*, and the projected 'Gordon' Symphony.

2. See especially Meirion Hughes, ' "The Duc d'Elgar": Making a Composer Gentleman', in Christopher Norris, ed., *Music and the Politics of Culture* (London: Lawrence & Wishart, 1989), 41–68; Robert Anderson, *Elgar and Chivalry* (Rickmansworth: Elgar Editions, 2002); and Aidan J. Thomson, 'Elgar and Chivalry', *19th-Century Music* 28/3 (2005), 254–75. Hughes offers a robust and welcome appraisal of Elgar's social pretensions, but neglects the negative aspects of Elgarian nobility – an imbalance that this chapter aims to correct. Anderson casts his net wide and uncovers much fascinating information, although the book is unfocused and digressive in the extreme – a leisurely stroll through literary byways. Discussion of the music is avoided completely,

and there is little attempt to challenge or stretch the target audience of enthusiasts. Thomson offers a sophisticated reading of Elgar's attitude to chivalry in the context of post-Wagnerian German music and philosophy. His argument strongly resonates with that of this chapter in several ways. On the Victorian revival of chivalry and the idea of the gentleman, see Mark Girouard, *The Return to Camelot: Chivalry and the English Gentleman* (New Haven and London: Yale University Press, 1981); Philip Mason, *The English Gentleman: The Rise and Fall of an Ideal* (London: Deutsch, 1982); and David Castronovo, *The English Gentleman: Images and Ideals in Literature and Society* (New York: Ungar, 1987).

3. For an influential example of this line of defence, see Kennedy, *Portrait of Elgar*, chapter 9, 'Nobilmente', 163–87.

4. Martin J. Wiener, *English Culture and the Decline of the Industrial Spirit 1850–1980* (Harmondsworth: Penguin, 1992; 1st edn. 1981), esp. 3–18.

5. For a summary of the contrary arguments, see W. D. Rubinstein, *Capitalism, Culture and Decline in Britain 1750–1990* (London and New York: Routledge, 1993), 21–4.

6. Osbert Sitwell, *Laughter in the Next Room* (London: Macmillan, 1949), 196–7; cited in Moore, *Creative Life*, 775.

7. Siegfried Sassoon, *Diaries 1920–1922*, ed. Rupert Hart-Davies (London: Faber, 1981), 124; cited in Hughes, ' "Duc d'Elgar" ', 41.

8. Constant Lambert, *Music Ho!: A Study of Music in Decline* (London: Pelican, 1948), 205.

9. Cecil Gray, *Survey of Contemporary Music* (London: Humphrey Milford, 1924), 92–3.

10. Ibid., 93–4.

11. Edward J. Dent, ' "Engländer" (Die Moderne)', in *Handbuch der Musikgeschichte*, 2nd edn, ed. Guido Adler (Berlin and Wilmersdorf: Heinrich Keller, 1930), 1044–57 (p. 1047).

12. Philip Radcliffe, *E. J. Dent: A Centenary Memoir* (Cambridge: Cambridge University Press, 1976), 17–19; Trowell, 'Elgar's Use of Literature', 182–6.

13. Cited and translated in Basil Maine, *Elgar, His Life and Works*, 2 vols. (London: G. Bell & Sons, 1933), II, 279. See Guido M. Gatti et al., eds., *La musica contemporanea in europa: saggi critici* (Milan: Bottega di poesia, 1925).

14. Radcliffe, *Dent*, 18.

15. See Robert Anderson, *Elgar in Manuscript* (London: The British Library, 1990), 119; Edward Elgar, 'Falstaff', *Musical Times* 53 (1 September 1913), 575–9 (p. 576).

16. Ernest Newman, 'Elgar: Some Aspects of the Man and his Music', in Redwood, *An Elgar Companion*, 154–7 (p. 155). Repr. from the *Sunday Times*, 25 February 1934.

17. See especially Rosa Burley and Frank C. Carruthers, *Edward Elgar: The Record of a Friendship* (London: Barrie & Jenkins, 1972), 55–72; see also Mrs Richard Powell, [Dora Penny], *Edward Elgar: Memories of a Variation*, rev. and ed. Claude Powell (Aldershot: Scolar Press, 1994).

18. Percy M. Young, *Alice Elgar: Enigma of a Victorian Lady* (London: Dobson, 1978), 15.

19. The manuscript is held by the Elgar Birthplace Museum. The first ten pages and the final, unnumbered page are in the hand of Alice Elgar. The rest of the essay (the paragraphs on music), exist in pencil draft in Alice's hand, but have been copied out in a later version by a different hand. Quotations here follow the latter. Extracts from the manuscript have been quoted in Young, *Alice Elgar*, 145–8; and Anderson, *Elgar and Chivalry*, 232–41.

20. Alice Elgar, 'The Ideal in the Present', 2.

21. Ibid., 2–3.

22. Ibid., 3.

23. Burley and Carruthers, *Edward Elgar*, 65. In 'The Ideal in the Present', Alice's comparison between exhibitions in Munich and at the Royal Academy heavily favour the former.

24. Friedrich Schiller, *On the Aesthetic Education of Man in a Series of Letters*, ed. and trans. Elizabeth M. Wilkinson and L. A. Willoughby (Oxford: Clarendon Press, 1967), 7.

25. Constantin Behler, *Nostalgic Teleology: Friedrich Schiller and the Schemata of Aesthetic Humanism* (Bern: Peter Lang, 1995), 2.

26. See Schiller, *Aesthetic Education*, glossary, 316–17.

27. Despite the German influences, Alice's remarks on Watts (see text below) suggests a moralising, Victorian attitude to the 'ideal': '[There is] scarcely a picture of his which does not elevate our thoughts and point to some great lesson, some teaching clothed in the most exquisite of forms and colour, lessons which we should do well to take seriously to heart.' 'The Ideal in the Present', 8.

28. Ibid., 4–5.

29. Ibid., 5.

30. Ibid. See Anderson, *Elgar and Chivalry*, 234–6 for the full poem; see also Young, *Alice Elgar*, 65.

31. Alice Elgar, 'The Ideal in the Present', 6.

32. See Robert E. Norton, *The Beautiful Soul: Aesthetic Morality in the Eighteenth Century* (Ithaca, N. Y., and London: Cornell University Press, 1995).

33. Ibid., 9.

34. Ibid., 8.

35. Purgatorio XIV, 148–50. 'Chiamavi 'l cielo e 'ntorno vi si gira, / mostrandovi le sue bellezze etterne, / e l'occhio vostro pur a terra mira'. Alice Elgar quotes the Italian. Translation from Dante, *The Divine Comedy: 2 Purgatory*, trans. Dorothy L. Sayers (London: Penguin, 1955).

36. See, for instance, Parry's articles 'Beethoven' and 'Symphony', in George Grove, ed., *A Dictionary of Music and Musicians*, 4 vols. (London: Macmillan, 1879–89), I, 162–209; IV, 10–43; also his later book *Studies of the Great Composers*, 8th edn (London: George Routledge & Sons, 1904), 156–94 (the chapter on Beethoven), 361, 365, 376.

37. Alice Elgar, 'The Ideal in the Present', 20.

38. Ibid., 21.

39. See Carl Dahlhaus, *The Idea of Absolute Music*, trans. Roger Lustig (Chicago: University Press of Chicago, 1989).

40. 'Looking back then on the last decades of the 19th century, we may fairly conclude that, amidst a never surpassed struggle for luxury and wealth, amidst appliances, comforts and inventions which make the fact of existence a fine art amidst the ghastly Realism which dissects the morbid aberrations of the abandoned human soul and lights dark recesses of human sin with lurid gleams; amidst the gross stupidity of taste which characterizes the larger class, the historian, inspired by the lofty scenes and the sublime conceptions of our great Idealists, will yet exclaim, "truly 'there were giants in those days.' "
    May others, yet greater, arise in the ages to come to purify and inspire the generations still to be born.'
41. Edward Elgar, *A Future for English Music and Other Lectures*, ed. Percy M. Young (London: Dobson, 1968), 61. According to Young, the lines are cited from E. T. A. Hoffmann, *The Serapion Brethren*, trans. A. Ewing, 2 vols. (London: Bell, 1886–92).
42. Alice Elgar, Diary, 25 September 1908. University of Birmingham Special Collections, EE 1/2/20.
43. Letter to Ernest Newman, 4 November 1908, in Moore, *Letters of a Lifetime*, 200. Elgar's emphasis.
44. Letter to Walford Davies, 13 November 1908. Moore, *Letters of a Lifetime*, 205.
45. Alice Elgar, Diary, 21 February 1911. University of Birmingham Special Collections, EE 1/2/23.
46. Burley and Carruthers, *Edward Elgar*, 190.
47. W. B. Yeats, letter to Elgar, 23 March 1902, in *The Collected Letters of W. B. Yeats*, ed. John Kelly, 3 vols. (Oxford; Oxford University Press, 1986–1997), III, 163; Anthony Payne, 'A New Look at Elgar', *The Listener* 72 (29 October 1964), 694; Ernest Newman, 'Stately Sorrow', in *Essays on Music: An Anthology from 'The Listener'*, ed. Felix Aprahamian (London: Cassell, 1967), 101–6; Peter J. Pirie, 'Crippled Splendour: Elgar and Mahler', *Musical Times* 97/2 (1956); 70–1. See also David Cairns, 'Heroic Melancholy: Elgar Revalued', in *Responses: Musical Essays and Reviews* (London: Secker & Warburg, 1973), 219–23.
48. See Kennedy, *Portrait of Elgar*, 172, 186; Michael Kennedy, 'Elgar the Edwardian', in Monk, *Elgar Studies*, 107–17 (p. 114); and Newman, 'Stately Sorrow', 101–6 (p. 105). For the views of J. B. Priestley, see Chapters 5 and 6.
49. Payne, 'A New Look at Elgar'.
50. For a lengthier explanation and examples see Matthew Riley, 'Heroic Melancholy: Elgar's Inflected Diatonicism', in Harper-Scott and Rushton, *Elgar Studies*.
51. 'I was allowed to come down today for the first time for a month and I spent some happy quarter Hours over your Adagio in the Symphony ... My dear friend, that is not only one of the very greatest slow movements since Beethoven, but I consider it *worthy of that master*. How original!, how PURE, noble, elevating, soothing, &c &c. I can't find the words ... It's the greatest thing you have done ... I detected one or two places, where the great adagio of the Choral Symphony was recalled to my memory. Nothing in the way of a reminiscence (the Satz is *quite* your own), but just the feeling of

nobility of sentiment.' A. J. Jaeger, letter to Elgar, 26 November 1908, in Moore, *Letters of a Creative Life*, II, 715. According to Elgar's friend W. H. Reed, Richter told the orchestra before the London premiere 'Ah! this is a *real* Adagio – such an Adagio as Beethove' would 'ave writ'. On attitudes to adagio movements at this time, see Margaret Notley, 'Late-Nineteenth-Century Chamber Music and the Cult of the Classical Adagio', in *19th-Century Music* 23/1 (1999), 33–61.

52. On the first, see Riley, 'Heroic Melancholy'.

53. Ibid.

54. Thomson likewise mentions this passage in a discussion of nobility and idealism in the symphony, although his wider focus encompasses tonality and the symphony's relationship in this regard with Wagner's *Parsifal*. The present analysis in terms of the transformation of certain gestures resonates with Thomson's remarks about 'transfiguration' in a Wagnerian sense. 'Elgar and Chivalry', 259–67. Jaeger's verdict on this music was: 'At 104 we are brought near heaven. That is a lofty and inspired thought.' Moore, *Letters of a Creative Life*, II, 715.

55. James Hepokoski, 'Elgar', in D. Kern Holoman, ed., *The Nineteenth-Century Symphony* (New York: Schirmer, 1997), 327–44 (p. 329).

56. Thomson grasps the wrong end of the stick with regard to *Falstaff*. He compares the work unfavourably with Strauss's *Don Quixote*, viewing the one as a conservative, the other as a critical response to Wagnerian idealism. Falstaff is a rogue who is punished for his misdemeanours; the work 'reinforces the validity of the chivalric value-system'. 'Elgar and Chivalry', 267–74. Harper-Scott's reading of *Falstaff* as bleak and 'cynical' is more convincing. 'Elgar's Invention of the Human' (published in the same journal issue as Thomson's article).

57. Quoted in Elgar, 'Falstaff', 575. See also Maine, *Elgar*, I, 194.

58. Maine, *Elgar*, I, 194, 195.

59. Quoted in Elgar, 'Falstaff', 575. See also Maine, *Elgar*, I, 194–5.

60. Maine, *Elgar*, I, 194. For a discussion of Elgar's reading of the secondary literature on *Falstaff*, see Harper-Scott, 'Elgar's Invention of the Human', 233–7.

61. Elgar', 'Falstaff', 578.

62. Ibid., 578.

63. Thomson, 'Elgar and Chivalry', 269.

64. Elgar, 'Falstaff', 579.

65. Maine, *Elgar*, I, 197. Harper-Scott interprets the closing stages of *Falstaff* in terms of what he calls Elgar's 'cynicism', a reading in many ways in agreement with that offered here. 'Elgar's Invention of the Human', 250–2.

66. Sassoon, *Diaries 1920–22*, 80.

67. Ibid., 169.

68. Siegfried Sassoon, *Diaries 1923–1925*, ed. Rupert Hart-Davies (London: Faber, 1985), 44.

69. Ibid., 152.

70. Siegfried Sassoon, *Diaries 1915–1918*, ed. Rupert Hart-Davies (London: Faber, 1983), 124.

71. Ibid. Hart-Davies's edition states that the entry begins with '[a few bars of Elgar's Violin Concerto]'. This passage and the poem that follows it have been cited in Anderson, *Elgar and Chivalry*, 255–6, who maintains that Sassoon 'pinpoints cue 94'. Certainly the music at that point agrees with the description. Sassoon mentions hearing a work by Ravel at the concert, but it seems likely that his ensuing reflections on 'the noblest passages' refer only to the Elgar. See *Siegfried Sassoon: Poet's Pilgrimage*, assembled by Felicitas Corrigan (London: Gollancz, 1973), 83.

72. Sassoon, *Diaries 1915–1918*, 124.

73. Ibid.

4: NATURE

1. Nicholas Usherwood, *The Brotherhood of Ruralists: Ann Arnold, Graham Arnold, Peter Blake, Jann Haworth, David Inshaw, Annie Ovenden, Graham Ovenden* (London: Lund Humphries in association with the London Borough of Camden, 1981); Christopher Martin, *The Ruralists* (London: Academy, 1991); Jerrold Northrop Moore, Peter Nahum and Laurie Lee, *The Brotherhood of Ruralists: A Celebration* (Bodmin: Ruralist Fine Art, 2003).

2. See Wiener, *English Culture*.

3. Crump, 'The Identity of English Music', 184.

4. See for instance, Arthur Bliss, 'Aspects of English Music', *Musical Times* 75 (1934), 401–5 (p. 404). On musical discourse at the time of Elgar's death see Arnold Whittall, 'British Music Thirty Years Ago', *Musical Times* 105 (1964), 186–7. Whittall softens his negative judgements in 'Thirty (More) Years On: Arnold Whittall Looks Back on Thirty Years of British Music', *Musical Times* 135 (1994), 143–7.

5. Stanley Baldwin, speech to the Annual Dinner of the Royal Society of St George, 6 May 1924, cited in Judy Giles and Tim Middleton, eds., *Writing Englishness 1900–1950: An Introductory Sourcebook on National Identity* (London and New York: Routledge, 1995), 101. See David Cannadine, 'Emollience: Stanley Baldwin and Francis Brett Young', in *In Churchill's Shadow: Confronting the Past in Modern Britain* (London: Allen Lane, 2002), 159–85.

6. David Matless, *Landscape and Englishness* (London: Reaktion Books, 1998), 30–2, 90–5, 118–23.

7. See for instance, R. J. Buckley, *Sir Edward Elgar*, 2nd edn (London: John Lane, 1912), chapter 4 ('Elgar at Home'), 29–36, which draws on an interview conducted in 1896; reprinted as 'Elgar at "Forli" ' in Redwood, *An Elgar Companion*, 111–14. See also, Rudolph de Cordova, 'Elgar at "Craeg Lea" ', *Strand Magazine*, May 1904, reprinted in Redwood, *An Elgar Companion*, 115–124.

8. Elgar, *A Future for English Music*, 57.

9. Buckley, *Sir Edward Elgar*, 32; reproduced in Redwood, *An Elgar Companion*, 112.

10. 11 July 1900, in Moore, *Letters of a Creative Life*, I, 212.

11. W. H. Reed, *Elgar* (London: J. M. Dent, 1939), 112–13.

12. McVeagh, *Edward Elgar*, 166.

13. Michael Kennedy, *Elgar Orchestral Music* (London: BBC Music Guides, 1970), 16–17.

14. Michael Grundy, *Elgar's Beloved Country*, 4th edn (Worcester: Worcester City Council, 1988), 1.

15. Jerrold Northrop Moore, *Elgar: Child of Dreams* (London: Faber & Faber, 2004), dust jacket text and pp. vii–viii.

16. On Elgar's efforts at image-making, see Meirion Hughes, *The English Musical Renaissance and the Press: Watchmen of Music* (Aldershot: Ashgate: 2002), chapter 7 (pp. 161–84), especially the section on Elgar as a local musician (pp. 162–7). The literary games in Elgar's correspondence are noted by Brian Trowell, who refers to 'the love of literary allusions that characterises his letters to like-minded friends' and remarks that as Elgar 'started to move amongst upper middle-class people and to encounter fashionable opinion, [he discovered] the delights of allusion-swapping, and certain literary shibboleths'. 'Elgar's Uses of Literature', 190, 191. Diana McVeagh has compared specific passages from Elgar's prose with extracts from the writings of Gerard Manley Hopkins, Tennyson and James Thomson. 'A Man's Attitude to Life', in Monk, *Edward Elgar: Music and Literature*, 1–9.

17. Letter to Sidney Colvin, 13 December 1921, in Moore, *Letters of a Lifetime*, 359. The context for the letter was an attack on Bernard Shaw by Colvin; Elgar defended Shaw, pointing out that he was kind to young people.

18. McVeagh, 'A Man's Attitude to Life', 1.

19. Kennedy, *Portrait of Elgar*, 15; Robert Anderson, *Elgar* (London: J. M. Dent, 1993), p. xv; Grundy, *Elgar's Beloved Country*, frontispiece; Moore, *Child of Dreams*, p. ii; Daniel M. Grimley and Julian Rushton, 'Introduction', in Daniel M. Grimley and Julian Rushton, eds., *The Cambridge Companion to Elgar* (Cambridge: Cambridge University Press, 2004), 1–14. The Ovenden sketch is weirdly disproportioned; Elgar is given extremely long, skinny calves but dangles a grotesquely thick foot into the water, which at first sight appears to have six toes.

20. Pownall, *The Composer Plays*, 121. See also Kennedy, *Elgar Orchestral Music*, 5; and the discussions of the contributions of Jerrold Northrop Moore (Chapter 5), Norman Perryman, and James Hamilton-Paterson (both Chapter 7). For another image of Severn reedbeds, see John Burke, *Musical Landscapes* (Exeter: Webb & Bower, 1983), 39.

21. Kennedy, *Portrait of Elgar*, 15. See also Moore, *Creative Life*, 32.

22. The Romantic poets had long before explored the theme of childhood memories of being beside a river. See William Lisle Bowles's 'To the River Itchin' (1789), Coleridge's 'To the River Otter' (1796) – both quoted in William K. Wimsatt, 'The Structure of Romantic Nature Imagery', in M. H. Abrams, ed., *English Romantic Poets* (New York: Oxford University Press, 1960), 27, 29 – and the episode in Wordsworth's *The Prelude* recalling the river Derwent (1805 edn, bk. 1, lines 271–304).

23. An influential version of the legend is that given by Ovid. See *Metamorphoses*, I, lines 689–718.

24. Diodorus Siculus is cited by Athanasius Kircher, *Prodromus Coptus sive Aegypticus* (Rome: Typis S. cong. de Propag. fide, 1636), 131, 139. See also Lucretius, *De rerum natura*, bk. 5, lines 1376–84.

25. For Kircher see n. 24. Also Sir John Hawkins, *A General History of the Science and Practice of Music*, 2 vols. (London: Novello, [1776] 1853), I, 2, col. 2; Jean-Jacques Rousseau, *Dictionnaire de musique* (Hildesheim: Georg Olms (facs.), [1768] 1969), 306 (art. 'Musique'); see also Downing A. Thomas, *Music and the Origins of Language: Theories from the French Enlightenment* (Cambridge: Cambridge University Press, 1995), 50; and Matthew Head, 'Birdsong and the Origins of Music', *Journal of the Royal Musical Association* 122/1 (1997), 1–23 (pp. 11–16).

26. Thomas Woodrow, *Reeds Shaken with the Wind* (London: Woodrow & Co., 1893); Katherine Tynan, *The Wind in the Trees: A Book of Country Verse* (London: G. Richards, 1898). See also Bliss Carmen, *The Pipes of Pan* (London: John Murray, 1903); and Nora Hopper, *Ballads in Prose* (London: John Lane, 1894).

27. See Alison Prince, *Kenneth Grahame: An Innocent in the Wild Wood* (London: Allison & Busby, 1994), 83. To an extent though, it seems that every generation in modern English history has looked over its shoulder and seen a rural golden age in the recently vanished past. Williams, *The Country and the City*, 35–45.

28. See Jonathan Rose, *The Edwardian Temperament, 1885–1919* (Athens: Ohio University Press, 1986), 30, 64; Jackie Wullschläger, *Inventing Wonderland: The Lives and Fantasies of Lewis Carroll, Edward Lear, J. M. Barrie, Kenneth Grahame and A. A. Milne* (London: Methuen, 1995), 111–12; Prince, *Kenneth Grahame*, 91–5.

29. See Robert Dingley, 'Meaning Everything: The Image of Pan at the Turn of the Century', in Kath Filmer, ed., *Twentieth-Century Fantasists: Essays on Culture, Society and Belief in Twentieth-Century Mythopoeic Literature* (New York and Basingstoke: Macmillan and St Martin's Press, 1992), 47–57. Dingley argues that the prevalence of Pan in Edwardian literature reflects ambivalence towards the countryside, which was viewed alternately as idyllic and as alien and fearful.

30. Aubrey Beardsley, *Under the Hill, and Other Essays in Prose and Verse* (London: Paddington Press, 1977), 55–7; Arthur Machen, *The Great God Pan; and The Inmost Light* (London: J. Lane, 1894); Saki, *Short Stories and the Unbearable Bassington* (Oxford and New York: Oxford University Press, 1994) 63–8; E. M. Forster, *The New Collected Short Stories* (London: Sidgwick and Jackson, 1985), 18–39.

31. Kenneth Grahame, 'The Rural Pan' and 'The Lost Centaur', in *Pagan Papers*, 5th edn (London and New York: John Lane and The Bodley Head, 1898); 65–71 and 175–81 respectively; *The Wind in the Willows*, 101st edn (London: Methuen, 1951).

32. See James Hillman, *The Essential James Hillman: A Blue Fire*, ed. Thomas Moore (London: Routledge, 1989), 97–8.

33. Oscar Wilde, *The Complete Works of Oscar Wilde*, vol. I, *Poems and Poems in Prose*, ed. Karl Beckson and Bobby Fong (Oxford: Oxford University Press, 2000), 140–1. Robert Frost's poem 'Pan with Us' (1913) voices a comparable sentiment. See also Ivor Gurney, 'What Was Dear', *Collected Poems of Ivor Gurney*, ed. Patrick J. Kavanagh (Oxford: Oxford University Press, 1982), 214. A less famous (but earlier) example is Edmund Clarence Steadman's 'Pan in Wall Street' (1867). Also relevant is D. H. Lawrence's essay 'Pan in America', in *Phoenix*, ed. Edward D. McDonald (London: Heinemann, 1966), 22–31.

34. Robert Louis Stevenson, 'Pan's Pipes', in *Virginibus puerisque* (London and New York: Dent Dutton, 1963), 106–9 (pp. 106–7).

35. Grahame, 'The Rural Pan', 68, 67, 65.

36. Grahame, *The Wind in the Willows*, 162–3.

37. Ibid., 173.

38. Maine, *Elgar*, I, 269.

39. Cited in Young, *Alice Elgar*, 94.

40. For the scenario of *The Sanguine Fan*, see BL Add. MS 69637 and 69838; Moore, *Creative Life*, 701–3; and Anderson, *Elgar*, 269–70.

41. See Grogan, Foreword, p. xiii. The relation of Elgar's music to the 'children's play' is discussed in Chapter 5.

42. Quoted in Moore, *Creative Life*, 518.

43. W. H. Reed, *Elgar as I Knew Him* (London: Victor Gollancz, 1936), 140–1.

44. Letter to Frances Colvin, 14 March 1912, cited in Moore, *Letters of a Lifetime*, 244. This episode in the First Symphony is pivotal in Moore's account of the pastoral Elgar; he hangs an elaborate argument on it, expressed through much lyrical prose. *Child of Dreams*, 122–3.

45. A search for the darker side of Pan in Elgar's music would prove less fruitful. Unlike contemporaries such as Mahler (Symphony No. 3) and Ravel (*Daphnis et Chloë*), Elgar never allowed the god to stamp his hoof, as it were, in one of his compositions. (On Mahler, see Peter Franklin, *Mahler; Symphony No. 3* (Cambridge; Cambridge University Press, 1991), 59, 65.) Only in the late chamber music – especially the 'ghostly' moments in the Piano Quintet – and in a few shorter pieces, such as the part-song *Owls (An Epitaph)*, Op. 53 No. 4, did he explore nature in its more sinister aspects.

46. John Henry Newman, *Collected Poems and the Dream of Gerontius* (Sevenoaks: Fisher, 1992), 160.

47. Undated note to Alice Stuart-Wortley, probably from 1920. Cited in Moore, *The Windflower Letters*, 247.

48. Moore, *Creative Life*, 40–1.

49. Ibid., 41.

50. Ibid., 89.

51. Ibid., 690; see also pp. 6, 35, 95, 698–9, 323.

52. Anderson, *Elgar*, 276.

53. Miles, *Malvern Hills*, 52. Alice Elgar may have started the entire trend. See her letter to Alice Kilburn, 3 August 1900, cited in Moore, *Creative Life*, 323.

54. Translation in Kathryn J. Gutzwiller, *Theocritus's Pastoral Analogies: The Formation of a Genre* (Madison and London: University of Wisconsin Press, 1991), 84.
55. Ibid., 84–5, 236 n. 4.
56. See, for instance, James Thomson's *The Seasons* (1730), 'Summer', line 452.
57. In one of Blackwood's novels, the main character is entranced by the sound of the wind in the upper branches of a pine forest; later, in a dream-like 'wind vision', he 'sees' the wind itself in a forest, in the shape of grey, wispy threads nestling in the branches. Algernon Blackwood, *The Education of Uncle Paul* (London: Macmillan, 1909), 43–5, 127–40.
58. M. H. Abrams, 'The Correspondent Breeze: A Romantic Metaphor', in Abrams, *English Romantic Poets*, 37–54 (pp. 44–6).
59. Ibid., 37–8.
60. William Wordsworth, *The Prelude: The Four Texts (1798, 1799, 1805, 1850)*, ed. Jonathan Wordsworth (London: Penguin, 1995), 37; 1850 version, bk. I, lines 1–3. Wordsworth's revised version of 1850 is (regretfully) cited here and below instead of the more vigorous 1805 version since the latter was unknown to the Victorians.
61. Ibid., 29; bk. I, lines 33–6. See also lines 94–6. The 1805 version fits Abrams's interpretation even better: the breeze is 'creative', and there is no moralising reference to 'virtue'.
62. Ibid., 285–6; bk. XII, lines 328–35. Jonathan Wordsworth notes, however, that in this passage from the 1850 version, 'the claims for inspiration and imaginative strength' of 1805 are significantly diminished (p. xlvii).
63. The labelling of motifs here and in later chapters follows A. J. Jaeger, *The Dream of Gerontius: Analytical and Descriptive Notes*, 2nd edn (Sevenoaks: Novello, 1974).
64. On the instrument's history, see Stephen Bonner, *The History and Organology of the Aeolian Harp* (Duxford: Bois de Boulogne, 1970). The most substantial work on the instrument remains Georges Kastner, *La harpe d'Eole et la musique cosmique* (Paris: G. Brandus, Dufour et Cie., 1856).
65. See Andrew Brown, *The Aeolian Harp in European Literature 1591–1892* (Duxford: Bois de Boulogne, 1970); Geoffrey Grigson, 'The Harp of Aeolus', in *The Harp of Aeolus and other Essays on Art, Literature and Nature* (London: Routledge, 1947), 24–46; Abrams, 'The Correspondent Breeze', 38–43.
66. Quoted in Brown, *The Aeolian Harp*, 16.
67. Shelley, *Selected Poetry and Prose*, 205.
68. Wordsworth, *The Prelude* 1850 version, bk. I, lines 94–6.
69. The image of the Aeolian harp on occasion merged with other varieties of natural and even supernatural music, including reeds, rustling branches and angelic choirs. See Grigson, 'The Harp of Aeolus', 27–8; also a passage from the outlandish story by J. F. H. Dalberg – the most vivid account of the harp's music providing an escape to a spiritual other world – as quoted in Brown, *The Aeolian Harp*, 28. For the connection with trees, see Brown, *The Aeolian Harp*, 27 and 73. The image of the celestial choir appears in the writings of

Thomson, Tobias Smollet, Robert Bloomfield and Dalberg; see Brown, *The Aeolian Harp*, 18, 27, 117. The angelic choir in Part II of Goethe's *Faust* was intended by the author to be accompanied by several Aeolian harps.

70. Kastner, *La harpe d'Eole*, 138–46.
71. Powell, *Memories of a Variation*, 84–5.
72. Reed, *Elgar as I Knew Him*, 147–8.
73. Ibid., 148–9. *Gerontius* and *Sea Pictures* were composed before Elgar acquired Troyte Griffith's harp.
74. 18 September 1910. Moore, *Letters of a Creative Life*, 224. See also Ernest Newman, 'Elgar's Violin Concerto', *Musical Times* 51 (1910), 631–4 (p. 633).
75. Newman, 'Elgar's Violin Concerto', 634.
76. Other possible instances of Aeolian harp imitations in Elgar have been detected in the *Introduction and Allegro* (bar 10) and 'Enigma' Variation XIII (from fig. 56: 2) by, respectively, James Hepokoski ('Gaudery, Romance, and the "Welsh" Tune') and Kevin Jones ('The Aeolian Harp, the "Dark Saying" and the Subject of Elgar's 13th Enigma Variation', paper read to the University of Birmingham Elgar Conference 1 July 2005). Moore (*Child of Dreams*), in his search for Elgar the 'pastoral visionary', tends to hear Aeolian harp sounds everywhere.
77. David Pownall, *Elgar's Third*, in *The Composer Plays*, 197–8 (scene 35). (The reference to the dead sheep is discomfortingly prescient, given the 'foot and mouth' crisis that occurred in the UK in the spring of 2001, seven years after the play's first broadcast. At that time the carcasses of destroyed livestock littered the countryside in their thousands.) In his earlier play *Elgar's Rondo* Pownall has Elgar listening intently to an Aeolian harp, which stands for the composer's faltering creative imagination. He thinks the harp is mocking him by continually sounding an E♭ major triad, the key of the Second Symphony – the work which, in the play, he cannot move beyond. Later, one of Elgar's old acquaintances from Worcester, who is the worse for wear, suggests that Elgar should pay attention to a different kind of wind, which he produces himself. Pownall, *The Composer Plays*, 149–50.
78. Jones, 'Elgar's 13th Enigma Variation'.
79. Letter to Alfred Littleton, 13 April 1911, in Moore, *Letters of a Creative Life*, II, 742.
80. Abrams, *Natural Supernaturalism*, 330.
81. On the notion of breakthrough, see Chapter 2, n. 36. There are two occasions in his religious choral music when Elgar might be said to use sounds of nature at a moment of breakthrough: in 'Praise to the Holiest' (discussed above) and at the descent of the Holy Spirit in Part III of *The Kingdom*. In the instrumental music, however, it is much more difficult to find examples. An argument could also be made for the E♭ minor episode in the finale of the First Symphony. As indicated in Chapter 2, it is certainly a kind of breakthrough. However, although the prominent harp arpeggios have been cited as Aeolian harp music (Moore, *Child of Dreams*, 130), they entirely lack the wayward, unpredictable qualities usually associated with those sounds.

5: CHILDHOOD

1. On Ken Russell's *Elgar*, see John Gardiner, 'Variations on a Theme of Elgar: Ken Russell, the Great War, and the Television "Life" of a Composer', *Historical Journal of Film, Radio and Television* 23/3 (2003), 195–209.
2. Grogan, 'Foreword', p. xii.
3. Grogan, 'Foreword'.
4. Ibid., p. xiv.
5. A point made by Jerrold Northrop Moore in a review of the *Wand of Youth* volume in the *Elgar Society Journal* 12/5 (2002), 215–18. 'Mr. Grogan seems occasionally to fall into a pit digged [*sic*] especially for young scholars . . . It is to assume that because no MS survives, therefore no MS ever existed.' He adds, 'Would it not be more seemly to think that the creator of the music being edited knew what he was talking about?' Moore is far from impartial in this matter, however: his writings on the composer invest heavily in the idea that childhood and retrospection shaped Elgar's approach to his art. See the text below for further discussion of Moore's views.
6. Allis, 'Retrospective Narrative'; J. P. E. Harper-Scott, 'Henry and the *Gräfin/ Grinder*: Elgar and *The Starlight Express*', *Elgar Society Journal* 13/4 (2004), 15–23. Harper-Scott also addresses the issue of childhood in 'Elgar's Invention of the Human', 245; and 'Elgar's Unwumbling: The Theatre Music', in Grimley and Rushton, *The Cambridge Companion to Elgar*, 171–83 (pp. 178–82). Allis is correct to seek the context for Elgar's attitude to childhood in Romantic and Victorian ideas, although the approach taken here differs in several respects. His article weaves together certain concepts (childhood, memory, nostalgia) which this book, by its nature, seeks to differentiate. Furthermore, Allis's choice of *Dream Children* (1902) as a pivotal work is debatable for several reasons. Elgar had already explored the theme of retrospection in the *Serenade* for strings (1890; see Chapter 2) and *Caractacus* (1898), and that of haunting in *King Olaf* (1896; on both works, see Chapter 6). The music is not Elgar's best – to call it 'deceptively modest' (p. 290) is generous – and, like *The Wand of Youth*, represents a revision of music composed many years before, rendering detailed technical discussion of its relation to the epigraph by Charles Lamb problematic. Harper-Scott questions Allis's contextualisation, arguing that Elgar's view of childhood was darker than the 'comfortable Victorian idealization' of Carroll or Barrie ('Elgar's Invention of the Human', 245). Yet this distinction may be illusory: there are deeply discomforting aspects to the *Alice* books and *Peter Pan*.
7. In fact the main focus here will be on what Judith Plotz calls the 'Quintessential Child' as opposed to alternative versions of childhood that can be detected in Romantic literature. *Romanticism and the Vocation of Childhood* (New York and Houndsmills, Basingstoke: Palgrave, 2001).
8. Catherine Robson, *Men in Wonderland: The Lost Girlhood of the Victorian Gentleman* (Princeton and Oxford: Princeton University Press, 2001), 8.

9. E. A. Allen, 'Rock me to Sleep' (1869), cited in James R. Kincaid, *Child-Loving: The Erotic Child in Victorian Culture* (New York and London: Routledge, 1992), 67; diary entry by Lewis Carroll, cited in Robson, *Men in Wonderland*, 140.

10. Cited in Plotz, *Vocation*, 46. A well-known example of the redemptive child is found in George Eliot's *Silas Marner* (1861).

11. Peter Coveney, *The Image of Childhood: The Individual and Society: A Study of the Theme in English Literature* (Harmondsworth: Penguin, 1967), 240.

12. For a summary of these currents, see Robson, *Men in Wonderland*, 5–8. See also Kincaid, *Child-Loving*; Hugh Cunningham, *Children and Childhood in Western Society since 1500* (London and New York: Longman, 1995); James Holt McGovran, ed., *Literature and the Child: Romantic Continuities, Postmodern Contestations* (Iowa City: University of Iowa Press, 1999); Plotz, *Vocation*. The text that first opened up new directions was Philippe Ariès, *Centuries of Childhood: A Social History of Family Life*, trans. Robert Baldick (New York: Knopf, 1962).

13. Thomas De Quincy, *The Collected Writings of Thomas De Quincy*, ed. David Masson, 14 vols. (Edinburgh: Adam & Charles Black, 1889–90), I, 122, cited in Plotz, *Vocation*, 13.

14. LuAnn Walther, 'The Invention of Childhood in Victorian Autobiography', in George P. Landow, ed., *Approaches to Victorian Autobiography* (Athens: Ohio University Press, 1979), 64–83 (p. 69).

15. See for instance Michael Grundy, *Elgar's Birthplace at Broadheath* (booklet published by the Elgar Foundation).

16. Moore, *Creative Life*, III, 823.

17. Lucy Pipe, 'Reflections' (MS held by the Elgar Birthplace Museum), cited in Moore, *Creative Life*, 8. See Virgil's fourth *Eclogue* for the most famous auspicious birth in literature. The National Meteorological Archive does not hold information on the weather in Worcester on 2 June 1857. The nearest record is from Trelleck Vicarage in Monmouthshire. The observer's report for 2 June 1857 states 'cloudy, fresh breeze, showers'. The maximum temperature was approximately 16 °C and the minimum approximately 9 °C.

18. Moore, *Creative Life*, 11.

19. Ibid., 7.

20. Ibid., 11.

21. Ibid., 12.

22. Ibid.

23. Ibid., 26.

24. Ibid., 32.

25. BL Add. MS 63154: fo. 57v.

26. Moore, *Creative Life*, 33.

27. Moore, *Creative Life*, 34.

28. Ibid., 35. Moore hears the 'ghost' of the tune from Broadheath in the melody from *Falstaff* (1913) that Elgar referred to as 'the undercurrent of our failings & sorrows' (pp. 643–4) – a tenuous connection to say the least. On a separate point, the change from F♯ minor (as indicated in 1901) to F♯ major (as composed in 1907) tends to support Grogan's contention that the *Wand of*

Youth suites represent at the very least a revision of Elgar's earlier ideas (although one could always argue that the 1901 indication is a mistake or a lapse of memory that was later corrected).

29. Moore, *Creative Life*, 34.
30. Ibid., 47.
31. Ibid., 48.
32. Ibid., 512–16. See also, for instance, Kennedy, *Portrait of Elgar*, 222–3; *Elgar Orchestral Music*, 53.
33. Cannadine, 'Sir Edward Elgar', 128. Cannadine's devastating review, though rhetorically flamboyant and outrageously rude and unkind, hits the mark in many ways and should be better known by Elgarians.
34. On *The Starlight Express* see K. E. L. Simmons, 'Elgar and the Wonderful Stranger: Music for *The Starlight Express*', in Monk, *Elgar Studies*, 142–213; and Harper-Scott, 'Elgar and *The Starlight Express*'. On Blackwood himself see Michael Ashley, *The Starlight Man: The Extraordinary Life of Algernon Blackwood* (London: Constable, 2001).
35. Algernon Blackwood, *A Prisoner in Fairyland* (London: Macmillan, 1913), 108, 173–5. On Blackwood's affiliation to Theosophical societies and to the Golden Dawn, see Ashley, *Starlight Man*, 109–19.
36. Blackwood, *Prisoner*, 19.
37. Plato, *Phaedo*, 73c–75e.
38. The connection is pointed out by James Beswick Whitehead (see www.btinternet.com/~j.b.w/elg2.htm#18: A Visitor from the Golden D; accessed 5 January 2003). For relevant background to the topic, see Geo Widengren, *Mani and Manichaeism*, trans. Charles Kessler (London: Weidenfeld & Nicholson, 1965), 43–58; Samuel N. C. Lieu, *Manichaeism in the Later Roman Empire and Medieval China: A Historical Survey* (Manchester: Manchester University Press, 1985), 5–24.
39. The sexual symbolism of the Star Cave is unclear and unsatisfactory. The regressive interpretation may be the best – that is, entry denotes a return to the womb and children accomplish it most easily. That would imply a grotesque reworking of the *Immortality* Ode.
40. The argument that follows has points of contact with that of Harper-Scott ('Elgar and *The Starlight Express*'), who likewise searches for a perspective that might mitigate the apparent comfort of the work. However, his view of the Organ Grinder as a 'manipulator' of Uncle Henry seems far-fetched, and the existentialist argument that flows from it is therefore unconvincing.
41. The Ruralist artist Graham Ovenden alters the second line for his painting *Let Your Hair Fall over Your Eyes* (reproduced in Moore, Nahum and Lee, *Ruralists*, 103). Ovenden has created numerous images of pre-pubescent girls and is a published author on Victorian photography, in particular Lewis Carroll. See, for instance, Graham Ovenden, *Victorian Children* (London and New York: Academic Editions and St Martin's Press, 1972; Graham Ovenden and Peter Mendes, *Victorian Erotic Photography* (London: Academy Editions, 1973). In his title the words appear to be attributed to a child, who reaches out of darkness

towards the head of Elgar – portrayed gazing into the distance at the age when he composed *The Starlight Express* – as though to draw his white hair across his face. As with many of Ovenden's children, her pose and expression do not suggest innocence. Jerrold Northrop Moore's accompanying text, by contrast, identifies childhood as a fragile site of innocence in a hostile world. He complains that children have been made 'a target for state protection' and that modern society aims for 'the elimination of innocence' and thus 'the possibility of total control'. Moore, Nahum and Lee, *Ruralists*, 12.

42. Pointed out by Simmons, 'Wonderful Stranger', 167; but see also n. 39.
43. Cited in William Wordsworth, *Jacqueline du Pré: Impressions* (London: Granada, 1983), unnumbered front page.
44. Hilary and Piers du Pré, *A Genius in the Family* (London: Chatto & Windus, 1997), 133; *Daily Mail*, 22 March 1962, cited in du Pré, *Genius*, 134; Christopher Nupen, 'A Film called "Jacqueline"', in Wordsworth, *Impressions*, 110–16 (p. 115).
45. *Daily Telegraph*; cited in Elizabeth Wilson, *Jacqueline du Pré* (London: Weidenfeld & Nicholson, 1998), 80.
46. Neville Cardus in *The Guardian*, February 1973, cited in Wilson, *du Pré*, 397.
47. J. B. Priestley, *The Plays of J. B. Priestley*, 3 vols. (London: Heinemann, 1948–50), I: 472.
48. Ibid., 451.
49. Ibid. 1.
50. Ibid., 472.
51. Ibid., 476.
52. *Elgar's Tenth Muse*, dir. Paul Yule (NVC Arts, 1996).

6: IDENTITY

1. Gray, *Survey*, 78; Bernard Shaw, *Back to Methuselah* (*The Works of Bernard Shaw*, vol. XVI) (London: Constable, 1930), 167. These oppositions have since become clichés in Tennyson and Kipling criticism which later contributions either refine or oppose. See for instance Harold Nicolson, *Tennyson: Aspects of his Life, Character and Poetry* (London: Constable, 1923), 5–10; Elton Edward Smith, *The Two Voices: A Tennyson Study* (Lincoln: University of Nebraska Press, 1964), 11–21; James R. Kincaid, *Tennyson's Major Poems: The Comic and Ironic Patterns* (New York and London: Yale University Press, 1975), 4.
2. Gray, *Survey*, 81.
3. Frank Howes, 'The Two Elgars', *Music & Letters* 16/1 (1935), 26–9; repr. in Redwood, *An Elgar Companion*, 258–62 (p. 259); Harold Nicolson, *Curzon: The Last Phase 1919–1925: A Study in Post-War Diplomacy* (London: Constable, 1934).
4. Howes, 'The Two Elgars', 261.
5. Anthony Payne, 'A New Look at Elgar', 694.
6. Kennedy, *Portrait of Elgar*, 186.
7. Kennedy, *Elgar Orchestral Music*, 20; Ralph Vaughan Williams, 'What Have We Learned from Elgar?', *Music & Letters* 16/1 (1935), 13–19, p. 16; repr. in Redwood, *An Elgar Companion*, 263–9 (p. 266).

8. A. E. Sheldon, *Edward Elgar* (London: Musical Opinion, 1932), 16; Newman, 'Stately Sorrow', 104.

9. Michael Kennedy, 'Elgar the Edwardian', 117; and Kennedy, *Elgar Orchestral Music*, 37.

10. Moore, *Child of Dreams*, 130, 131. He continues: 'Thus Elgar sees clearly at last the earthly paradise around him, touching the Eden of innocence kept within him as his inheritance from his mother's faith.' The motivation for Moore's argument is not necessarily embarrassment about militarism, as it is for Kennedy. Elsewhere he uses the same private/public dichotomy in a way that echoes contemporary Right/Left politics. Moore, Nahum and Lee, *Ruralists*, 12–14.

11. For this reason Jeffrey Richards's trenchant attack on the Elgarian 'orthodoxies' of the 1960s goes too far. Jeffrey Richards, *Imperialism and Music: Britain 1876–1953* (Manchester and New York: Manchester University Press, 2001), chapter 3, 'Elgar's Empire', 44–87. Though the essay is an important contribution to the literature (see text below), Richards's musical judgement is awry: he does not take account of the compositional techniques mentioned here, and considerably overestimates the quality and importance of the music Elgar wrote after 1920.

12. For a possible exception, see n. 10 above.

13. John Baxendale, ' "I Had Seen a Lot of Englands": J. B. Priestley, Englishness and the People', *History Workshop Journal* 51 (2001), 87–111 (p. 87).

14. See the discussions of *Festival at Farbridge* (1951) and *The Linden Tree* (1948) in Chapters 2 and 5 respectively; also the play *Music at Night* (1937), in Priestley, *Plays*, I, 368; and *Three Men in New Suits* (1945), (London: Allison & Busby, 1984), 27, 29.

15. J. B. Priestley, *English Journey* (London: Heinemann, 1934), 397–406.

16. J. B. Priestley, *English Humour* (London: Longman, Green, 1929), 8; cited in Baxendale, 'Priestley', 96.

17. J. B. Priestley, *The English* (London: Heinemann, 1973).

18. *Wonder Hero* (1933) and *They Walk in the City* (1936). See Chris Waters, 'J. B. Priestley 1894–1984: Englishness and the Politics of Nostalgia', in Susan Petersen and Peter Mandler, eds., *After the Victorians: Private Conscience and Public Duty in Modern Britain* (London and New York: Routledge, 1994), 209–26 (pp. 210–13).

19. Priestley, *The English*, 243; cited in Waters, 'Priestley', 210.

20. See Waters, 'Priestley', 213–16.

21. J. B. Priestley, *Margin Released: A Writer's Reminiscences and Reflections* (London: Mercury Books, 1966), 66–7; cited in Waters, 'Priestley', 214.

22. See Baxendale, 'Priestley', 102–3.

23. Priestley, *The English*, 13.

24. J. B. Priestley, *Rain upon Godshill: A Further Chapter of Autobiography* (London: Heinemann, 1939), 206; cited in Baxendale, 'Priestley', 96.

25. Priestley, *English Journey*, 416.

26. Priestley, *The English*, 12.

27. J. B. Priestley, *The Edwardians* (London: Heinemann, 1970), 138; *The English*, 165; *Particular Pleasures* (London: Heinemann, 1975), 80.
28. Priestley, *The English*, 165.
29. Ibid., 154.
30. Ibid., 165.
31. See for instance Wright, *Old Country*; Angus Calder, *The Myth of the Blitz*, 2nd edn (London: Pimlico, 1992), 180–208.
32. Priestley, *Particular Pleasures*, 81.
33. Ibid., 82.
34. Priestley, *The Edwardians*, 138.
35. See David Cannadine, 'The Context, Performance and Meaning of Ritual: The British Monarchy and the "Invention of Tradition", c. 1820–1977', in Hobsbawm and Ranger, *The Invention of Tradition* 101–64 (pp. 134–6).
36. On these and other defensive strategies, see Richards, *Imperialism and Music*, 48; and Bernard Porter, 'Elgar and Empire: Music, Nationalism and the War', in Lewis Foreman, ed., *Oh, My Horses!: Elgar and the Great War* (Rickmansworth: Elgar Editions, 2001), 133–73 (pp. 133–5).
37. Kennedy, 'Elgar the Edwardian', 107.
38. This is the case with Porter, 'Elgar and Empire', Richards, *Imperialism and Music*, and Corissa Gould, 'Edward Elgar, *The Crown of India* and the Image of Empire', *Elgar Society Journal* 13/1 (2003), 25–35. Charles McGuire brings the historicisation of the reception of Elgar and imperialism up to date, viewing critical reactions of the 1980s and 1990s in their political context. 'Functional Music: Imperialism, the Great War, and Elgar as Popular Composer', in Grimley and Rushton, *The Cambridge Companion to Elgar*, 214–24 (p. 215). As McGuire implies, there currently seems little consensus on the extent to which Elgar was an imperialist. Gould takes the post-colonialist party line, interpreting *The Crown of India* in terms of Edward Said's notion of 'orientalism'. Unfortunately, though, *The Crown of India* is of limited musical interest, and its ideology is almost childishly overt. The application of Saidian concepts to the choral and symphonic works is a trickier proposition. Porter argues that Elgar's imperialism was belated and superficial. His arguments are endorsed by J. P. E. Harper-Scott, 'Elgar's Deconstruction of the *belle époque*'. A similar position is taken by David Cannadine, who maintains that Elgar was in turn a local, national and European figure, and that his interest in empire was superficial in comparison with contemporary artists such as Kipling and Lutyens. 'Sir Edward Elgar as a Historical Personality', paper given at the Music in Britain Social History Seminar, Institute of Historical Research, 10 February 2003. These attempts to distance Elgar from empire are not without their own drawbacks, however. The conversion scenes in *King Olaf* and *The Kingdom*, and to an extent *Caractacus*, in which military might or charismatic rhetoric prompts a vanquished community to abandon its ancient heritage and spontaneously to embrace an entirely alien culture seem to justify the ways of the Victorians to themselves. The discussion of those works in this chapter, however, highlights some unexpected complexities.

39. Peter Gay, *The Cultivation of Hatred* (*The Bourgeois Experience: Victorian to Freud*, vol. III) (New York: Norton, 1993), 35.
40. Richards, *Imperialism and Music*, 83, 84.
41. Renato Rosaldo, 'Imperialist Nostalgia', *Representations* 26 (1989), 107–22.
42. Ibid., 108.
43. Samuel Laing, 'Preliminary Dissertation', in *The Heimskringla; or, Chronicle of the Kings of Norway*, 3 vols. (London: Longman, 1844); discussed in Andrew Wawn, *The Vikings and the Victorians: Inventing the Old North in Nineteenth-Century Britain* (Cambridge: D. S. Brewer, 2000), 97–100.
44. *Charles Kingsley: His Letters, and Memories of his Life*, ed. Fanny Kingsley, 2 vols. (London: H. S. King & Co., 1891), I, 201; cited in Wawn, *Vikings and Victorians*, 136.
45. William Howitt and Mary Howitt, *The Literature and Romance of Northern Europe*, 2 vols. (London: Colburn, 1852), I, 1–13; see Wawn, *Vikings and Victorians*, 108.
46. Thomas Carlyle, *Critical and Miscellaneous Essays*, vol. V. *The Works of Thomas Carlyle*, 30 vols. (London: Chapman & Hall, 1896–1899), XXX, 247; cited in Wawn, *Vikings and Victorians*, 110; Robert Leighton, *Olaf the Glorious* (London: Blackie & Son, 1895).
47. Ernest Newman, *Elgar* (London: J. Lane, 1906), 33, 27.
48. Letter to Troyte Griffith, 25 April 1924. Moore, *Letters of a Lifetime*, 385.
49. The refrain comes from a Danish ballad about a ghostly huntsman of the night. There seems no specific connection with Odin in the original, although, since one of his personae was the 'wild huntsman', Longfellow's appropriation is not arbitrary. See Howitt and Howitt, *Literature and Romance*, I, 307–9.
50. Letters to A. J. Jaeger, 21 June and 12 July 1898, in Moore, *Letters of a Creative Life*, I, 76, 79.
51. Newman, *Elgar*, 44.
52. Sam Smiles, *The Image of Antiquity: Ancient Britain and the Romantic Imagination* (New Haven and London: Yale University Press, 1994), 1–7
53. Ibid., 129–33, 51–61.
54. Ibid., 153–8.
55. Norman Vance, *The Victorians and Ancient Rome* (Oxford: Blackwell, 1997), 222–3.
56. Ibid., 236. See also pp. 223–34.
57. G. A. Henty, *Beric the Briton: A Story of the Roman Invasion* (London: Blackie & Son, 1893), 12.
58. See especially Stuart Weaver, 'The Pro-Boers: War, Empire and the Uses of Nostalgia in Turn-of-the-Century England', in Behlmer and Leventhal, *Singular Continuities*, 43–57; also Stephen Koss, ed., *The Pro-Boers: The Anatomy of an Anti-War Movement* (Chicago and London: University of Chicago Press, 1973); Arthur Davey, *The British Pro-Boers 1877–1902* (Cape Town: Tafelberg, 1978); Bernard Porter, 'The Pro-Boers in Britain', in Peter Warwick and S. B. Spices, eds., *The South African War: The Anglo-Boer War 1899–1902* (London: Longman, 1980), 239–57; Preben Kaarsholm, 'Pro-Boers', in *Patriotism: The Making and*

Unmaking of British National Identity, vol. 1: *History and Politics*, ed. Raphael Samuel (London and New York: Routledge, 1989), 110–26.

59. Hansard, 15 August 1878, col. 2068; cited in Davey, *Pro-Boers*, 16.

60. Sir William Butler, *An Autobiography* 2nd edn (London: Constable, 1913), 415; cited in Koss, *Pro-Boers* 24–5. There was a strain of anti-Semitism in some of these attitudes.

61. Keir Hardie, 'A Capitalist's War', *The Labour Leader*, 6 Jan. 1900; cited in Koss, *Pro-Boers*, 54.

62. Edward Carpenter, New Year's Day Pamphlet 1900; cited in Koss, *Pro-Boers*, 55.

63. Weaver, *Pro-Boers*, 57.

64. Letters of 11 July 1900 and 21 August 1898, quoted in Moore, *Letters of a Creative Life*, I, 212 and 86.

65. David Ian Rabey, *David Rudkin: Sacred Disobedience* (Amsterdam: Harwood Academic Publishers, 1997), 13–14. The published script omits the original technical instructions and tries to convey their effects instead.

66. Rudkin, *Penda's Fen*, 1.

67. In this example and in Ex. 6.7 the vocal score reduction is given, since this is the reduction from which Stephen reads and plays – and which is even shown on camera.

68. Rudkin, *Penda's Fen*, 5.

69. Ibid., 15.

70. Ibid., 31.

71. Julian Rushton compares this fugue with the chorus of demons in *Gerontius* and with other musical representations of devilry. He too uses the term 'angular' to describe the kind of melodic motif typical of this tradition. 'A Devil of a Fugue', 281.

72. Rudkin, *Penda's Fen*, 37.

73. Ibid., 54. Rudkin's Elgar means the 'Sanctus, fortis' melody. In reality it was the 'prayer' motif that had originally appeared in G. R. Sinclair's visitors' book as one of the 'moods of Dan'.

74. Ibid., 47.

75. Ibid., 70.

76. Ibid., 75.

77. Ibid., 81.

78. www.pinvin.org.uk, accessed 15 April 2003.

79. Byron Adams, 'Elgar's Later Oratorios: Roman Catholicism, Decadence, and the Wagnerian Dialectic of Shame and Grace', in Grimley and Rushton, *The Cambridge Companion to Elgar*, 81–105; see also 'The "Dark Saying" of the Enigma: Homoeroticism and the Elgarian Paradox', *19th-Century Music* 23/3 (2000), 218–35 (pp. 232–3).

7: WATERS

1. Percy Scholes, 'Elgar at "Severn House" – II', in Redwood, *An Elgar Companion*, 140–6 (p. 141). First published in *The Music Student*, August 1916.

2. *Musical Standard*, 27 May 1911, cited in Moore, *Creative Life*, 616.
3. Kennedy, 'Elgar the Edwardian', 117; Kennedy, *Portrait of Elgar*, 334.
4. Grimley and Rushton, 'Introduction', 14.
5. On the mythic status of rivers see Wyman H. Herendeen, *From Landscape to Literature: The River and the Myth of Geography* (Pittsburgh: Duquesne University Press, 1986), esp. 3–12; and Simon Schama, *Landscape and Memory* (London: Fontana, 1996), 245–306.
6. Herendeen, *Landscape to Literature*, 9.
7. See Arthur Dwight Culler, *Imaginative Reason: The Poetry of Matthew Arnold* (New Haven and London: Yale University Press, 1966), 3–16.
8. C. Day Lewis, *The Complete Poems of C. Day Lewis* (London: Sinclair-Stevenson, 1992), 573–5.
9. See Albert Gelpi, *Living in Time: The Poetry of C. Day Lewis* (New York and Oxford; Oxford University Press, 1998), 82–92; and Sean Day-Lewis, *C. Day-Lewis: An English Literary Life* (London: Weidenfeld & Nicolson, 1980), 5–7.
10. C. Day Lewis, *The Lyric Impulse* (London: Chatto & Windus, 1965), 146, 152.
11. Day Lewis, *Complete Poems*, 657–8.
12. Day Lewis, *Lyric Impulse*, 153.
13. Gelpi, *Living in Time*, 174.
14. Ibid.
15. Joseph N. Riddel, *C. Day Lewis* (New York: Twayne Publishers, 1971), 145.
16. As regards the mood, it is possible that Day Lewis is not responding directly to the symphony but is alluding to the Romantic poetic tone discussed in connection with the work in Chapter 2.
17. www.normanperryman.com/performers.htm (accessed 1 March 2005).
18. Ibid.
19. Perryman's later acrylic painting *Enigma* (2000), commissioned by and displayed at the Elgar Birthplace Centre at Broadheath, does not match its predecessor: it lacks the thematic complexity of the triptych while repeating too many of its themes.
20. Norman Perryman, 'Elgar's Dream', notes to the painting, revised. Electronic file provided by the artist (2000).
21. Ibid.
22. A point made by Roger Boylan, 'Writing in Exile', *Boston Review* 27/1 (2002), 31–4 (p. 32). On occasion Hamilton-Paterson appears to attribute his own views to Elgar, as for instance the speculation that all the arts have the same 'raw material' (see below). The journal has to find a way around Elgar's well-known objection to this opinion. See Hamilton-Paterson, *Gerontius*, 69.
23. Ibid., 54–5, 93, 239–45.
24. Ibid., 126.
25. Ibid., 129.
26. Ibid., 14.
27. Ibid., 146.
28. Ibid., 203.
29. Ibid., 67.

30. Ibid., 156.
31. Ibid., 147.
32. Ibid., 117.
33. Ibid., 114.
34. Ibid., 116.
35. Ibid., 9.
36. Ibid., 158.
37. Ibid., 11.
38. Ibid., 156.
39. Ibid., 39.
40. Ibid., 67.
41. Ibid., 240.
42. Ibid., 241.
43. Ibid., 242.

Bibliography

ELGAR

Adams, Byron. 'The "Dark Saying" of the Enigma: Homoeroticism and the Elgarian Paradox'. *19th-Century Music* 23/3 (2000), 218–35.

'Elgar's Later Oratorios: Roman Catholicism, Decadence, and the Wagnerian Dialectic of Shame and Grace'. In Daniel M. Grimley and Julian Rushton (eds.). *The Cambridge Companion to Elgar*. Cambridge: Cambridge University Press, 2004, 81–105.

Alldritt, Keith. *Elgar on the Journey to Hanley*. London: Deutsch, 1979.

Allen, Kevin. *Elgar The Cyclist in Worcester and Hereford: A Creative Odyssey*. Malvern Wells: Kevin Allen, 1997.

Allis, Michael. 'Elgar and the Art of Retrospective Narrative'. *Journal of Musicological Research* 19 (2000), 289–328.

'Elgar, Lytton and the Piano Quintet, Op. 84'. *Music & Letters* 85/2 (2004), 198–238.

Anderson, Robert. *Elgar in Manuscript*. London: The British Library, 1990.

Elgar (The Master Musicians). London: J. M. Dent, 1993.

Elgar and Chivalry. Rickmansworth: Elgar Editions, 2002.

Atkins, E. Wulstan. *The Elgar–Atkins Friendship*. London: David & Charles, 1984.

Banfield, Stephen. 'Elgar's Counterpoint: Three of a Kind'. *Musical Times* 140 (1999), 9–37.

'The Dream of Gerontius at 100: Elgar's Other Opera?' *Musical Times* 141 (2000), 23–31.

Buckley, R. J. *Sir Edward Elgar*. 2nd edn. London: John Lane, 1912.

Burke, John. *Musical Landscapes*. Exeter: Webb & Bower, 1983.

Burley, Rosa, and Carruthers, Frank C. *Edward Elgar: The Record of a Friendship*. London: Barrie & Jenkins, 1972.

Cairns, David. 'Heroic Melancholy: Elgar Revalued'. In *Responses: Musical Essays and Reviews*. London: Secker & Warburg, 1973, 219–23.

Cannadine, David. 'Sir Edward Elgar'. In *The Pleasure of the Past*. London: Collins, 1989, 121–30.

Colls, Robert, and Dodd, Philip (eds.). *Englishness: Politics and Culture 1880–1940*. Beckenham: Croom Helm, 1986.

Craggs, Stewart R. *Edward Elgar: A Source Book*. Aldershot: Scolar Press, 1995.

Crump, Jeremy. 'The Identity of English Music: The Reception of Elgar 1898–1935'. In Robert Colls and Philip Dodd (eds.). *Englishness: Politics and Culture 1880–1940*. Beckenham: Croom Helm, 1986, 164–90.

De Cordova, Rudolph. 'Elgar at "Craeg Lea"'. *Strand Magazine*, May 1904. Reprinted in Christopher Redwood (ed.). *An Elgar Companion*. Ashbourne: Sequoia, 1982.

De-la-Noy, Michael. *Elgar: The Man*. London: Allen Lane, 1983.

Dent, Edward J. ' "Engländer" (Die Moderne)'. In *Handbuch der Musikgeschichte*, 2nd edn, ed. Guido Adler. Berlin and Wilmersdorf: Heinrich Keller, 1930, 1044–57.

Dibble, Jeremy. 'Hubert Parry and English Diatonic Dissonance'. *Journal of the British Musical Society* 5 (1983), 58–71.

'Parry and Elgar: A New Perspective', *Musical Times* 125 (1984), 639–43.

'Parry, Stanford and Vaughan Williams: The Creation of Tradition'. In Lewis Foreman (ed.). *Vaughan Williams in Perspective: Studies of an English Composer*. Ilminster: Albion Music, 1998, 25–47.

Doctor, Jenny. 'Broadcasting's Ally: Elgar and the BBC'. In Daniel M. Grimley and Julian Rushton (eds.). *The Cambridge Companion to Elgar*. Cambridge: Cambridge University Press, 2004, 195–203.

Elgar, Alice. *Diaries of Lady Caroline Alice Elgar 1899–1920*. University of Birmingham Special Collections. EE 1/2.

Elgar, Edward. 'Falstaff'. *Musical Times* 53 (1913), 575–79.

A Future for English Music and Other Lectures, ed. Percy M. Young. London: Dobson, 1968.

Foreman, Lewis (ed.). *Oh, My Horses!: Elgar and the Great War*. Rickmansworth: Elgar Editions, 2001.

Gardiner, John. 'The Reception of Sir Edward Elgar 1918–c. 1934: A Reassessment'. *Twentieth-Century British History* 9/3 (1998), 370–95.

'Variations on a Theme of Elgar: Ken Russell, the Great War, and the Television "Life" of a Composer'. *Historical Journal of Film, Radio and Television* 23/3 (2003), 195–209.

Gassmann, Michael. *Edward Elgar und die deutsche symphonische Tradition: Studien zu Einfluß und Eigenständigkeit*. Hildesheim: Olms, 2002.

Gatti, Guido M. (ed.). *La musica contemporanea in europa: saggi critici*. Milan: Bottega di poesia, 1925.

Gould, Corissa. 'Edward Elgar, *The Crown of India* and the Image of Empire'. *Elgar Society Journal* 13/1 (2003), 25–35.

Gray, Cecil. *Survey of Contemporary Music*. London: Humphrey Milford, 1924.

Grimley, Daniel M. 'A Smiling with a Sigh: The Chamber Music and Works for Strings'. In Daniel M. Grimley and Julian Rushton (eds.). *The Cambridge Companion to Elgar*. Cambridge: Cambridge University Press, 2004, 120–38.

Grimley, Daniel M., and Rushton, Julian. 'Introduction'. In Daniel M. Grimley and Julian Rushton (eds.). *The Cambridge Companion to Elgar*. Cambridge: Cambridge University Press, 2004, 1–14.

Grimley, Daniel M., and Rushton, Julian (eds.). *The Cambridge Companion to Elgar*. Cambridge: Cambridge University Press, 2004.

Grogan, Christopher. 'Foreword'. In *Dream Children and The Wand of Youth* (Suites Nos. 1 and 2): *Elgar Complete Edition*. Vol. 25, ed. Christopher Grogan. London: Elgar Society Edition in association with Novello, 2001.

Grundy, Michael. *Elgar's Beloved Country*. 4th edn. Worcester: Worcester City Council, 1988.

Elgar's Birthplace at Broadheath. Booklet published by the Elgar Foundation. N.d.

Hamilton-Paterson, James. *Gerontius: A Novel about Sir Edward Elgar*. London: Granta Books, 2002; original Macmillan, 1989.

Harper-Scott, J. P. E. 'Elgar's Unwumbling: The Theatre Music'. In Daniel Grimley and Julian Rushton (eds.). *The Cambridge Companion to Elgar*. Cambridge: Cambridge University Press, 2004, 171–83.

'Henry and the *Gräfin*/Grinder: Elgar and *The Starlight Express*'. *Elgar Society Journal* 13/4 (2004), 15–23.

'Elgar's Invention of the Human: *Falstaff*, Op. 68'. *19th-Century Music* 28/3 (2005), 230–53.

'Elgar's Deconstruction of the *belle époque*'. In J. P. E. Harper-Scott and Julian Rushton (eds.). *Elgar Studies*. Cambridge: Cambridge University Press, forthcoming.

Hepokoski, James. 'Elgar'. In D. Kern Holoman (ed.). *The Nineteenth-Century Symphony*. New York: Schirmer, 1997, 327–44.

'Gaudery, Romance, and the "Welsh" Tune: *Introduction and Allegro*, Op. 47'. In J. P. E. Harper-Scott and Julian Rushton (eds.). *Elgar Studies*. Cambridge: Cambridge University Press, forthcoming.

Hodgkins, Geoffrey (ed.). 'Elgar: A Bibliography'. *Music Review* 54/1 (1993): 24–62.

The Best of Me: A Gerontius Centenary Companion. Rickmansworth: Elgar Editions, 1999.

Howes, Frank. 'The Two Elgars', *Music & Letters* 16/1 (1935), 26–9. Repr. in Christopher Redwood (ed.). *An Elgar Companion*. Ashbourne: Sequoia, 1982, 258–62.

Hughes, Meirion. ' "The Duc d'Elgar": Making a Composer Gentleman'. In Christopher Norris (ed.). *Music and the Politics of Culture*. London: Lawrence & Wishart, 1989, 41–68.

The English Musical Renaissance and the Press: Watchmen of Music. Aldershot: Ashgate: 2002.

Jaeger, A. J. *The Dream of Gerontius: Analytical and Descriptive Notes*. 2nd edn. Sevenoaks: Novello, 1974.

Kennedy, Michael. *Elgar Orchestral Music*. London: BBC Music Guides, 1970.

Portrait of Elgar. 3rd edn. London: Oxford University Press, 1987.

'Elgar the Edwardian'. In Raymond Monk (ed.). *Elgar Studies*. Aldershot: Scolar Press, 1990, 107–17.

'The Soul Enshrined: Elgar and his Violin Concerto'. In Raymond Monk (ed.). *Edward Elgar: Music and Literature*. Aldershot: Scolar Press, 1993, 72–82.

Kent, Christopher. *Elgar: A Guide to Research*. New York: Garland, 1993.

Keys, Ivor. ' "Ghostly Stuff": The Brinkwells Music'. In Raymond Monk (ed.). *Edward Elgar: Music and Literature*. Aldershot: Scolar Press 1993, 108–20.

Lambert, Constant. *Music Ho!: A Study of Music in Decline*. London: Pelican, 1948.

McGuire, Charles Edward. 'Elgar, Judas, and the Theology of Betrayal'. *19th-Century Music* 13/3 (2000), 236–72.

Elgar's Oratorios: The Creation of an Epic Narrative. Aldershot: Ashgate, 2002.

'Functional Music: Imperialism, the Great War, and Elgar as Popular Composer'. In Daniel M. Grimley and Julian Rushton (eds.). *The Cambridge Companion to Elgar*. Cambridge: Cambridge University Press, 2004, 214–24.

McVeagh, Diana. *Edward Elgar: His Life and Music*. London: J. M. Dent & Sons, 1955.

'A Man's Attitude to Life', in Raymond Monk (ed.). *Edward Elgar: Music and Literature*. Aldershot: Scolar Press, 1993, 1–9.

'Elgar'. In Stanley Sadie (ed.). *The New Grove Dictionary of Music and Musicians*. 2nd edn. Vol. VIII. London: Macmillan, 2001, 115–37.

Maine, Basil. *Elgar, His Life and Works*. 2 vols. London: G. Bell & Sons, 1933.

Mark, Christopher. 'The Later Orchestral Music (1910–34)'. In Daniel Grimley and Julian Rushton (eds.). *The Cambridge Companion to Elgar*. Cambridge: Cambridge University Press, 2004, 154–70.

Monk, Raymond (ed.). *Elgar Studies*. Aldershot: Scolar Press, 1990.

Edward Elgar: Music and Literature. Aldershot: Scolar Press, 1993.

Moore, Jerrold Northrop. *Edward Elgar: A Creative Life*. Oxford: Clarendon Press, 1984.

Spirit of England: Edward Elgar in his World. London: Heinemann, 1984.

Elgar and his Publishers: Letters of a Creative Life. 2 vols. Oxford: Clarendon Press, 1987.

Edward Elgar: The Windflower Letters. Oxford: Clarendon Press, 1989.

Edward Elgar: Letters of a Lifetime. Oxford: Clarendon Press, 1990.

Review of *Elgar Complete Edition* vol. 25. *Elgar Society Journal* 12/5 (2002), 215–18.

Elgar: Child of Dreams. London: Faber & Faber, 2004.

Newman, Ernest. *Elgar*. London: J. Lane, 1906.

'Elgar's Violin Concerto'. *Musical Times* 51 (1910), 631–4.

'Stately Sorrow'. In Felix Aprahamian (ed.). *Essays on Music: An Anthology from 'The Listener'*. London: Cassell, 1967, 101–6.

'Elgar: Some Aspects of the Man and his Music'. In Christopher Redwood (ed.). *An Elgar Companion*. Ashbourne: Sequoia, 1982, 154–7.

Parrott, Ian. *Elgar* (The Master Musicians). London: J. M. Dent, 1971.

Payne, Anthony. 'A New Look at Elgar'. *The Listener* 72 (1964), 694.

Elgar's Third Symphony: The Story of the Reconstruction. London: Faber, 1998.

Pirie, Peter J. 'Crippled Splendour: Elgar and Mahler'. *Musical Times* 97/2 (1956), 70–1.

'World's End: A Study of Edward Elgar'. *Music Review* 18 (1957), 89–100.

Porter, Bernard. 'Elgar and Empire: Music, Nationalism and the War'. In Lewis Foreman (ed.). *Oh, My Horses!: Elgar and the Great War*. Rickmansworth: Elgar Editions, 2001, 133–73.

Powell, Mrs Richard [Dora Penny]. *Edward Elgar: Memories of a Variation*. Rev. and ed. Claude Powell. Aldershot: Scolar Press, 1994.

Pownall, David. *The Composer Plays*. London: Oberon Books, 1994.

Radcliffe, Philip. *E. J. Dent: A Centenary Memoir*. Cambridge: Cambridge University Press, 1976.

Redwood, Christopher (ed.). *An Elgar Companion*. Ashbourne: Sequoia, 1982.

Reed, W. H. *Elgar as I Knew Him*. London: Victor Gollancz, 1936.

    Elgar (The Master Musicians). London: J. M. Dent, 1939.

Richards, Jeffrey. *Imperialism and Music: Britain 1876–1953*. Manchester: Manchester University Press, 2001.

Riley, Matthew. 'Rustling Reeds and Lofty Pines: Elgar and the Music of Nature'. *19th-Century Music* 26/2 (2002), 155–77.

    Review of Edward Elgar, *Dream Children* and *The Wand of Youth* (Suites Nos. 1 and 2): *Elgar Complete Edition* vol. 25. *Nineteenth-Century Music Review* 2/1 (2005), 214–20.

    'Heroic Melancholy: Elgar's Inflected Diatonicism'. In J. P. E. Harper-Scott and Julian Rushton (eds.). *Elgar Studies*. Cambridge: Cambridge University Press, forthcoming.

Rowe, Alick. *The Dorabella Variation*. Directed by Celia de Wolff. Radio 4 Saturday Play, 28 June 2003. Unpublished.

Rudkin, David. *Penda's Fen*. London: Davis-Poynter, 1995.

Rushton, Julian. *Elgar: Enigma Variations*. Cambridge: Cambridge University Press, 1999.

    'A Devil of a Fugue: Berlioz, Elgar, and *Introduction and Allegro*'. *Elgar Society Journal* 11/5 (2000), 276–87.

Sassoon, Siegfried. *Diaries 1920–1922*, ed. Rupert Hart-Davies. London: Faber, 1981.

    Diaries 1915–1918, ed. Rupert Hart-Davies. London: Faber, 1983.

    Diaries 1923–1925, ed. Rupert Hart-Davies. London: Faber, 1985.

Scholes, Percy. 'Elgar at "Severn House" – II'. In Christopher Redwood (ed.). *An Elgar Companion*. Ashbourne: Sequoia, 1982, 140–6.

Sheldon, A. E. *Edward Elgar*. London: Musical Opinion, 1932.

Simmons, K. E. L. 'Elgar and the Wonderful Stranger: Music for *The Starlight Express*'. In Raymond Monk (ed.). *Elgar Studies*. Aldershot: Scolar Press, 1990, 142–213.

Sitwell, Osbert. *Laughter in the Next Room*. London: Macmillan, 1949.

Thomson, Aidan J. 'Elgar and Chivalry'. *19th-Century Music* 28/3 (2005), 254–75.

    'Unmaking *The Music Makers*'. In J. P. E. Harper-Scott and Julian Rushton (eds.). *Elgar Studies*. Cambridge: Cambridge University Press, forthcoming.

Trowell, Brian. 'Elgar's Use of Literature'. In Raymond Monk (ed.). *Edward Elgar: Music and Literature*. Aldershot: Scolar Press, 1993, 182–326.

Vaughan Williams, Ralph. 'What Have We Learned from Elgar?' *Music & Letters* 16/1 (1935), 13–19. Repr. in Christopher Redwood (ed.). *An Elgar Companion*. Ashbourne: Sequoia, 1982, 263–9.

Witts, Richard. 'Remastering the Past: 'Renewal' in Recent British Music'. *Musical Times* 142 (2001), 7–10.

Young, Percy. *Elgar OM: A Study of a Musician*. London: Collins, 1955.

 Alice Elgar: Enigma of a Victorian Lady. London: Dobson, 1978.

Yule, Paul. *Elgar's Tenth Muse*. NVC Arts, 1996. Videocassette.

CONTEXTS

Abbate, Carolyn. *Unsung Voices: Opera and Musical Narrative in the Nineteenth Century*. Princeton: Princeton University Press, 1991.

Abrams, M. H. 'The Correspondent Breeze: A Romantic Metaphor'. In M. H. Abrams (ed.). *English Romantic Poets*. New York: Oxford University Press, 1960, 37–54.

 Natural Supernaturalism: Tradition and Revolution in Romantic Literature. New York and London: Norton, 1973.

Adorno, Theodor W. *Mahler: A Musical Physiognomy*, trans. Edmund Jephcott. London and Chicago: Univeristy of Chicago Press, 1992.

 Beethoven: The Philosophy of Music. Oxford: Polity, 1998.

 'Schubert (1928)'. *19th-Century Music* 29/1 (2005), 3–14.

Ariès, Philippe. *Centuries of Childhood: A Social History of Family Life*, trans. Robert Baldick. New York: Knopf, 1962.

Ashley, Michael. *The Starlight Man: The Extraordinary Life of Algernon Blackwood*. London: Constable, 2001.

Baudrillard, Jean. *Simulacra and Simulation*, trans. Sheila Faria Glaser. Ann Arbor: University of Michigan Press, 1994.

Baxendale, John. ' "I Had Seen a Lot of Englands": J. B. Priestley, Englishness and the People'. *History Workshop Journal* 51 (2001), 87–111.

Beardsley, Aubrey. *Under the Hill, and Other Essays in Prose and Verse*. London: Paddington Press, 1977.

Behler, Constantin. *Nostalgic Teleology: Friedrich Schiller and the Schemata of Aesthetic Humanism*. Bern: Peter Lang, 1995.

Behlmer, Georg K. 'Introduction'. In George K. Behlmer and Fred M. Leventhal (eds.). *Singular Continuities: Tradition, Nostalgia and Identity in Modern British Culture*. Stanford, Calif.: Stanford University Press, 2000, 1–10.

Behlmer, Georg K., and Leventhal, Fred M. (eds.). *Singular Continuities: Tradition, Nostalgia and Identity in Modern British Culture*. Stanford, Calif.: Stanford University Press, 2000.

Beja, Morris. *Epiphany in the Modern Novel*. London: Owen, 1971.

Berger, Karol. 'Beethoven and the Aesthetic State'. In Mark Evan Bonds (ed.). *Beethoven Forum 7*. Lincoln and London: University of Nebraska Press, 1999, 17–44.

Bidney, Martin. *Patterns of Epiphany: From Wordsworth to Tolstoy, Pater and Barrett Browning.* Carbondale: Southern Illinois University Press, 1997.

Blackwood, Algernon. *The Education of Uncle Paul.* London: Macmillan, 1909.

A Prisoner in Fairyland. London: Macmillan, 1913.

Bliss, Arthur. 'Aspects of English Music'. *Musical Times* 75 (1934), 401–5.

Bonner, Stephen. *The History and Organology of the Aeolian Harp.* Duxford: Bois de Boulogne, 1970.

Botstein, Leon. 'Memory and Nostalgia as Music-Historical Categories'. *Musical Quarterly* 84/4 (2000), 531–5.

Botting, Fred. *Gothic.* London and New York: Routledge, 1996.

Boylan, Roger. 'Writing in Exile', *Boston Review* 27/1 (2002), 31–4.

Boym, Svetlana *The Future of Nostalgia.* New York: Basic Books, 2001.

Brendon, Vyvyen. *The Edwardian Age: 1901–14.* London: Hodder & Stoughton, 1996.

Brown, Andrew. *The Aeolian Harp in European Literature 1591–1892.* Duxford: Bois de Boulogne, 1970.

Burnham, Scott. 'Schubert and the Sound of Memory'. *Musical Quarterly* 84/4 (2000), 655–63.

Butler, Sir William. *An Autobiography.* 2nd edn. London: Constable, 1913.

Calder, Angus. *The Myth of the Blitz.* 2nd edn. London: Pimlico, 1992.

Cannadine, David. 'The Context, Performance and Meaning of Ritual: The British Monarchy and the "Invention of Tradition", c. 1820–1977'. In Eric Hobsbawm and Terence Ranger (eds.). *The Invention of Tradition.* Cambridge: Cambridge University Press, 1983, 101–64.

The Pleasures of the Past. London: Collins, 1989.

'Emollience: Stanley Baldwin and Francis Brett Young'. In *In Churchill's Shadow: Confronting the Past in Modern Britain.* London: Allen Lane, 2002, 159–85.

Carlyle, Thomas. *Critical and Miscellaneous Essays.* Vol. v, *The Works of Thomas Carlyle.* 30 vols. London: Chapman & Hall, 1896–9.

Carmen, Bliss. *The Pipes of Pan.* London: John Murray, 1903.

Carpenter, Edward. New Year's Day Pamphlet 1900.

Castle, Terry. 'The Spectralization of the Other in *The Mysteries of Udolpho*'. In Laura Brown and Felicity Nussbaum (eds.). *The New Eighteenth Century.* London: Methuen, 1987, 231–53.

Castronovo, David. *The English Gentleman: Images and Ideals in Literature and Society.* New York: Ungar, 1987.

Chase, Malcolm, and Shaw, Christopher. 'The Dimensions of Nostalgia'. Malcolm Chase and Christopher Shaw (eds.). In *The Imagined Past: History and Nostalgia.* Manchester and New York: Manchester University Press, 1989, 1–17.

Cheeke, Stephen. *Byron and Place: History, Translation, Nostalgia.* Basingstoke: Palgrave Macmillan, 2003.

Colley, Ann C. *Nostalgia and Recollection in Victorian Culture.* Basingstoke: Macmillan, 1998.

Colwell, Frederic. *Rivermen: A Romantic Iconography of the River and its Source.* Kingston and London: McGill-Queen's University Press, 1989.

Coombs, James. *The Reagan Range: The Nostalgia Myth in American Politics.* Bowling Green: Bowling Green State University Popular Press, 1993.

Cosgrove, Stuart and Reas, Paul. *Flogging a Dead Horse: Heritage Culture and its Role in Post-Industrial Britain.* Manchester: Cornerhouse, 1993.

Coveney, Peter. *The Image of Childhood: The Individual and Society: A Study of the Theme in English Literature.* Harmondsworth: Penguin, 1967.

Culler, Arthur Dwight. *Imaginative Reason: The Poetry of Matthew Arnold.* New Haven and London: Yale University Press, 1966.

Cunningham, Hugh. *Children and Childhood in Western Society since 1500.* London and New York: Longman, 1995.

Dahlhaus, Carl. *The Idea of Absolute Music,* trans. Roger Lustig. Chicago: University Press of Chicago, 1989.

  'Sonata Form in Schubert: The First Movement of the G-Major String Quartet, Op. 161 (D. 887)'. In Walther Frisch (ed.). *Schubert: Critical and Analytical Studies.* Lincoln and London: University of Nebraska Press, 1996, 1–12.

Dames, Nicholas. *Amnesiac Selves: Nostalgia, Forgetting and British Fiction, 1810–1870.* Oxford and New York: Oxford University Press, 2001.

Dante. *The Divine Comedy: 2 Purgatory,* trans. Dorothy L. Sayers. London: Penguin, 1955.

Davey, Arthur. *The British Pro-Boers 1877–1902.* Cape Town: Tafelberg, 1978.

Davis, Fred. *Yearning for Yesterday: A Sociology of Nostalgia.* London and New York: Macmillan, 1979.

Day Lewis, C. *The Lyric Impulse.* London: Chatto & Windus, 1965.
  The Complete Poems of C. Day Lewis. London: Sinclair-Stevenson, 1992.

Day-Lewis, Sean. *C. Day-Lewis: An English Literary Life.* London: Weidenfeld & Nicolson, 1980.

De Quincy, Thomas. *The Collected Writings of Thomas De Quincy,* ed. David Masson. 14 vols. Edinburgh: Adam & Charles Black, 1889–90.

Dingley, Robert. 'Meaning Everything: The Image of Pan at the Turn of the Century'. In Kath Filmer (ed.). *Twentieth-Century Fantasists: Essays on Culture, Society and Belief in Twentieth-Century Mythopoeic Literature.* New York and Basingstoke: Macmillan and St Martin's Press, 1992, 47–57.

Doane, Janice, and Hodges, Devon. 'Introduction'. In Janice Doane and Devon Hodges (eds.). *Nostalgia and Sexual Difference: The Resistance to Contemporary Feminism.* New York: Methuen, 1987, 3–14.

Du Pré, Hilary, and Du Pré, Piers. *A Genius in the Family.* London: Chatto & Windus, 1997.

Fisk, Charles. 'Schubert Recollects Himself: The Piano Sonata in C Minor, D. 958'. *Musical Quarterly* 84/4 (2000), 635–54.

Forster, E. M. *The New Collected Short Stories.* London: Sidgwick & Jackson, 1985.

Franklin, Peter. *Mahler; Symphony No. 3.* Cambridge; Cambridge University Press, 1991.

Freud, Sigmund. *The Uncanny,* trans. David McLintock. London: Penguin, 2003.

Frisch, Walter. ' "You Must Remember This": Memory and Structure in Schubert's String Quartet in G Major, D. 887'. *Musical Quarterly* 84/4 (2000), 582–603.

Frye, Northrop. *Anatomy of Criticism*. Princeton: Princeton University Press, 1957.

Fussell, Paul. *The Great War and Modern Memory*. London: Oxford University Press, 1975.

Gardiner, John. *The Victorians: An Age in Retrospect*. London and New York: Hambledon and London, 2002.

Gay, Peter. *The Cultivation of Hatred*. *The Bourgeois Experience: Victorian to Freud*. Vol. III. New York: Norton, 1993.

Gelpi, Albert *Living in Time: The Poetry of C. Day Lewis*. New York and Oxford: Oxford University Press, 1998.

Giles, Judy, and Middleton, Tim (eds.). *Writing Englishness 1900–1950: An Introductory Sourcebook on National Identity*. London and New York: Routledge, 1995.

Gingerich, John M. 'Remembrance and Consciousness in Schubert's C-Major String Quintet, D. 956'. *Musical Quarterly* 84/4 (2000), 619–34.

Girouard, Mark. *The Return to Camelot: Chivalry and the English Gentleman*. New Haven and London: Yale University Press, 1981.

Grahame, Kenneth. *Pagan Papers*. 5th edn. London and New York: John Lane and The Bodley Head, 1898.

  The Wind in the Willows. 101st edn. London: Methuen, 1951.

Grigson, Geoffrey. *The Harp of Aeolus and other Essays on Art, Literature and Nature*. London: Routledge, 1947.

Groth, Helen. *Victorian Photography and Literary Nostalgia*. Oxford and New York: Oxford University Press, 2003.

Grove, George (ed.). *A Dictionary of Music and Musicians*. 4 vols. London: Macmillan, 1879–89.

Gurney, Ivor. 'What Was Dear'. *Collected Poems of Ivor Gurney*, ed. Patrick J. Kavanagh. Oxford: Oxford University Press, 1982.

Gutzwiller, Kathryn J. *Theocritus's Pastoral Analogies: The Formation of a Genre*. Madison and London: University of Wisconsin Press, 1991.

Hardie, Keir. 'A Capitalist's War'. *The Labour Leader*. 6 Jan. 1900.

Harrison, J. F. C. *Late Victorian Britain*. London: Routledge, 1991.

Hawkins, Sir John. *A General History of the Science and Practice of Music*. 2 vols. London: Novello, 1853.

Head, Matthew. 'Birdsong and the Origins of Music'. *Journal of the Royal Musical Association* 122/1 (1997), 1–23.

Henty, G. A. *Beric the Briton: A Story of the Roman Invasion*. London: Blackie & Son, 1893.

Hepokoski, James. 'Fiery-Pulsed Libertine or Domestic Hero? Strauss's Don Juan Reinvestigated'. In Bryan Gilliam (ed.). *Richard Strauss: New Perspectives on the Composer and his Work*. Durham, N.C.: Duke University Press, 1992, 135–75.

  Sibelius: Symphony No. 5. Cambridge: Cambridge University Press, 1993.

Herendeen, Wyman H. *From Landscape to Literature: The River and the Myth of Geography*. Pittsburgh: Duquesne University Press, 1986.

Hewison, Robert. *The Heritage Industry: Britain in a Climate of Decline*. London: Methuen, 1987.

Hillman, James. *The Essential James Hillman: A Blue Fire*, ed. Thomas Moore. London: Routledge, 1989.

Hirsch, Marjorie. 'The Spiral Journey Back Home: Brahms's "Heimweh" Lieder'. *Journal of Musicology* 22/3 (2005), 454–489.

Hobsbawm, Eric, and Ranger, Terrence (eds.), *The Invention of Tradition*. Cambridge: Cambridge University Press, 1983.

Hoeckner, Berthold. 'Schumann and Romantic Distance'. *Journal of the American Musicological Society* 50/1 (1997), 55–132.

Hoffmann, E. T. A. *The Serapion Brethren*, trans. A. Ewing. 2 vols. London: Bell, 1886–92.

Hopper, Nora. *Ballads in Prose*. London: John Lane, 1894.

Howitt, William, and Howitt, Mary. *The Literature and Romance of Northern Europe*. 2 vols. London: Colburn, 1852.

Hutchinson, Frances. *The Political Economy of Social Credit and Guild Socialism*. London: Routledge, 1997.

Jameson, Frederic. *Marxism and Form: Twentieth-Century Dialectical Theories of Literature*. Princeton: Princeton University Press, 1971.

   Postmodernism, Or, The Cultural Logic of Late Capitalism. London and New York: Verso, 1991.

Kaarsholm, Preben. 'Pro-Boers'. In *Patriotism: The Making and Unmaking of British National Identity*. Vol. I, *History and Politics*, ed. Raphael Samuel. London and New York: Routledge, 1989, 110–26.

Kastner, Georges. *La harpe d'Eole et la musique cosmique*. Paris: G. Brandus, Dufour & Cie., 1856.

Kincaid, James R. *Tennyson's Major Poems: The Comic and Ironic Patterns*. New York and London: Yale University Press, 1975.

   Child-Loving: The Erotic Child in Victorian Culture. New York and London: Routledge, 1992.

Kingsley, Charles. *Charles Kingsley: His Letters, and Memories of his Life*, ed. Fanny Kingsley. 2 vols. London: H. S. King & Co., 1891.

Kircher, Athanasius. *Prodromus Coptus sive Aegypticus*. Rome: Typis S. cong. de Propag. fide, 1636.

Koss, Stephen (ed.). *The Pro-Boers: The Anatomy of an Anti-War Movement*. Chicago and London: University of Chicago Press, 1973.

Laing, Samuel. 'Preliminary Dissertation'. In *The Heimskringla; or, Chronicle of the Kings of Norway*. 3 vols. London: Longman, 1844.

Langbaum, Robert. 'The Epiphanic Mode in Wordsworth and Modern Literature'. *New Literary History* 14/2 (1983), 335–58.

Lasch, Christopher. 'The Politics of Nostalgia', *Harper's* 269 (1984), 65–70.

   The True and Only Heaven: Progress and its Critics. London and New York: Norton, 1991.

Lawrence D. H. *Phoenix*, ed. Edward D. McDonald. London: Heinemann, 1966, 22–31.

Leighton, Robert. *Olaf the Glorious*. London: Blackie & Son, 1895.

Lieu, Samuel N. C. *Manichaeism in the Later Roman Empire and Medieval China: A Historical Survey*. Manchester: Manchester University Press, 1985.

Lowenthal, David. *The Past is a Foreign Country*. Cambridge: Cambridge University Press, 1985.

'Nostalgia Tells it Like it Wasn't'. In Christopher Shaw and Malcolm Chase (eds.). *The Imagined Past: History and Nostalgia*. Manchester and New York: Manchester University Press, 1989.

McGovran, James Holt (ed). *Literature and the Child: Romantic Continuities, Postmodern Contestations*. Iowa City: University of Iowa Press, 1999.

Machen, Arthur. *The Great God Pan; and The Inmost Light*. London: J. Lane, 1894.

McKellar, Ian B. *The Edwardian Age: Complacency and Concern*. Glasgow: Blackie, 1980.

Martin, Christopher. *The Ruralists*. London: Academy, 1991.

Mason, Philip. *The English Gentleman: The Rise and Fall of an Ideal*. London: Deutsch, 1982.

Matless, David. *Landscape and Englishness*. London: Reaktion Books, 1998.

Miles, Archie. *The Malvern Hills: Travels through Elgar Country*. London: Pavilion, 1992.

Moore, Jerrold Northrop, Nahum, Peter, and Lee, Laurie. *The Brotherhood of Ruralists: A Celebration*. Bodmin: Ruralist Fine Art, 2003.

Newman, John Henry. *Collected Poems and the Dream of Gerontius*. Sevenoaks: Fisher, 1992.

Nichols, Ashton. *The Poetics of Epiphany: Nineteenth-Century Origins of the Modern Literary Moment*. Tuscaloosa and London: University of Alabama Press, 1987.

Nicolson, Harold. *Tennyson: Aspects of his Life, Character and Poetry*. London: Constable, 1923.

Curzon: The Last Phase 1919–1925: A Study in Post-War Diplomacy. London: Constable, 1934.

Norton, Robert E. *The Beautiful Soul: Aesthetic Morality in the Eighteenth Century*. Ithaca, N.Y., and London: Cornell University Press, 1995.

Notley, Margaret. 'Late-Nineteenth-Century Chamber Music and the Cult of the Classical Adagio'. *19th-Century Music* 23/1 (1999), 33–61.

Novalis, *Briefe und Werke*. 3 vols. Berlin: L. Schneider, 1943.

Nupen, Christopher. 'A Film called "Jacqueline" '. In William Wordsworth (ed.). *Jacqueline du Pré: Impressions*. London: Granada, 1983, 110–16.

Ovenden, Graham. *Victorian Children*. London and New York: Academic Editions and St Martin's Press, 1972.

Ovenden, Graham, and Mendes, Peter. *Victorian Erotic Photography*. London: Academy Editions, 1973.

Parry, Hubert. *Studies of the Great Composers*. 8th edn. London: George Routledge & Sons, 1904.

Plotz, Judith. *Romanticism and the Vocation of Childhood*. New York and Houndsmills, Basingstoke: Palgrave, 2001.

Porter, Bernard. 'The Pro-Boers in Britain'. In Peter Warwick and S. B. Spices (eds.). *The South African War: The Anglo-Boer War 1899–1900*. London: Longman, 1980, 239–57.

Powell, David. *The Edwardian Crisis: Britain 1901–14*. Basingstoke: Macmillan, 1996.

Priestley, J. B. *English Humour*. London: Longman, Green, 1929.

English Journey. London: Heinemann, 1934.

Rain upon Godshill: A Further Chapter of Autobiography. London: Heinemann, 1939.

The Plays of J. B. Priestley. 3 vols. London: Heinemann, 1948–50.

Festival at Farbridge. London: Heinemann, 1957.

Margin Released: A Writer's Reminiscences and Reflections. London: Mercury Books, 1966.

The Edwardians. London: Heinemann, 1970.

The English. London: Heinemann, 1973.

Particular Pleasures. London: Heinemann, 1975.

Three Men in New Suits. London: Allison & Busby, 1984.

Prince, Alison. *Kenneth Grahame: An Innocent in the Wild Wood*. London: Allison & Busby, 1994.

Punter, David. 'Introduction: Of Apparitions'. In Glennis Byron and David Punter (eds.). *Spectral Reading: Towards a Gothic Geography*. Houndsmill: Macmillan, 1999, 1–8.

Rabey, David Ian. *David Rudkin: Sacred Disobedience*. Amsterdam: Harwood Academic Publishers, 1997.

Riddel, Joseph N. *C. Day Lewis*. New York: Twayne Publishers, 1971.

Ritivoi, Andreea Deciu. *Yesterday's Self: Nostalgia and the Immigrant Identity*. Lanham, Md., and Oxford: Rowman & Littlefield, 2002.

Robson, Catherine. *Men in Wonderland: The Lost Girlhood of the Victorian Gentleman*. Princeton and Oxford: Princeton University Press, 2001.

Rosaldo, Renato. 'Imperialist Nostalgia'. *Representations* 26 (1989), 107–22.

Rose, Jonathan. *The Edwardian Temperament, 1885–1919*. Athens: Ohio University Press, 1986.

Rosen, Charles. *The Romantic Generation*. Cambridge, Mass.: Harvard University Press, 1995.

Rosen, George. 'Nostalgia: A "Forgotten" Psychological Disorder'. *Clio Medica* 10/1 (1975), 29–51.

Rousseau, Jean-Jacques. *Dictionnaire de musique*. Hildesheim: Olms (facs.), [1768] 1969.

Rubinstein, W. D. *Capitalism, Culture and Decline in Britain 1750–1990*. London and New York: Routledge, 1993.

Saki. *Short Stories and the Unbearable Bassington*. Oxford and New York: Oxford University Press, 1994.

Samuel, Raphael. *Theatres of Memory*. 2 vols. London: Verso, 1994–8.

Sassoon, Siegfried. *Siegfried Sassoon: Poet's Pilgrimage*, assembled by Felicitas Corrigan. London: Gollancz, 1973.

Schama, Simon. *Landscape and Memory*. London: Fontana, 1996.

Schiller, Friedrich. *On the Aesthetic Education of Man in a Series of Letters*, ed. and trans. Elizabeth M. Wilkinson and L. A. Willoughby. Oxford: Clarendon Press, 1967.

Shaw, Bernard. *Back to Methuselah. The Works of Bernard Shaw*. Vol. XVI. London: Constable, 1930.

Shaw, Christopher, and Chase, Malcolm (eds.). *The Imagined Past: History and Nostalgia*. Manchester and New York: Manchester University Press, 1989.

Shelley, Percy Bysshe. *The Poems of Shelley*, ed. Kelvin Everest and Geoffrey Matthews. 2 vols. London and New York: Longman, 1989–2000.

Selected Poetry and Prose, ed. Alasdair D. F. Macrae. London: Routledge, 1991.

Smiles, Sam. *The Image of Antiquity: Ancient Britain and the Romantic Imagination*. New Haven and London: Yale University Press, 1994.

Smith, Elton Edward. *The Two Voices: A Tennyson Study*. Lincoln: University of Nebraska Press, 1964.

Starobinski, Jean. 'The Idea of Nostalgia'. *Diogenes* 54 (1966), 81–103.

Stevenson, Robert Louis. *Virginibus puerisque*. London and New York: Dent Dutton, 1963.

Stewart, Susan *On Longing: Narratives of the Miniature, the Gigantic, the Souvenir, the Collection*. Durham, N.C., and London: Duke University Press, 1993.

Tannock, Stuart. 'Nostalgia Critique'. *Cultural Studies* 9/3 (1995), 453–64.

Thomas, Downing A. *Music and the Origins of Language: Theories from the French Enlightenment*. Cambridge: Cambridge University Press, 1995.

Turner, Bryan S. 'A Note on Nostalgia'. *Theory, Culture and Society* 4/1 (1987), 147–56.

(ed.). *Theories of Modernity and Postmodernity*. London, Newbury Park and New Dehli: SAGE Publications, 1990.

Tynan, Katherine. *The Wind in the Trees: A Book of Country Verse*. London: G. Richards, 1898.

Usherwood, Nicholas. *The Brotherhood of Ruralists: Ann Arnold, Graham Arnold, Peter Blake, Jann Haworth, David Inshaw, Annie Ovenden, Graham Ovenden*. London: Lund Humphries in association with the London Borough of Camden, 1981.

Vance, Norman. *The Victorians and Ancient Rome*. Oxford: Blackwell, 1997.

Wagner, Tamara S. *Narratives of Nostalgia in the British Novel, 1740–1890*. Lewisburg, Pa.: Bucknell University Press, 2004.

Walther, LuAnn. 'The Invention of Childhood in Victorian Autobiography'. In George P. Landow (ed.). *Approaches to Victorian Autobiography*. Athens: Ohio University Press, 1979, 64–83.

Waters, Chris. 'J. B. Priestley 1894–1984: Englishness and the Politics of Nostalgia'. In Susan Peterson and Peter Mandler (eds.). *After the Victorians: Private Conscience and Public Duty in Modern Britain*. London and New York: Routledge, 1994, 209–26.

Wawn, Andrew. *The Vikings and the Victorians: Inventing the Old North in Nineteenth-Century Britain*. Cambridge: D. S. Brewer, 2000.

Weaver, Stuart. 'The Pro-Boers: War, Empire and the Uses of Nostalgia in Turn-of-the-Century England'. In George K. Behlmer and Fred M. Leventhal (eds.). *Singular Continuities: Tradition, Nostalgia and Identity in Modern British Culture*. Stanford, Calif.: Stanford University Press, 2000, 43–57.

Webster, James. *Haydn's 'Farewell' Symphony and the Idea of Classical Style: Through-Composition and Cyclic Integration in his Instrumental Music*. Cambridge: Cambridge University Press, 1991.

Whittall, Arnold. 'British Music Thirty Years Ago'. *Musical Times* 105 (1964), 186–7.

'Thirty (More) Years On: Arnold Whittall Looks Back on Thirty Years of British Music'. *Musical Times* 135 (1994), 143–7.

Widengren, Geo. *Mani and Manichaeism*, trans. Charles Kessler. London: Weidenfeld & Nicholson, 1965.

Wiener, Martin J. *English Culture and the Decline of the Industrial Spirit 1850–1980*. Harmondsworth: Penguin, 1992; 1st edn. 1981.

Wilde, Oscar. *The Complete Works of Oscar Wilde*. Vol. I, *Poems and Poems in Prose*, ed. Karl Beckson and Bobby Fong. Oxford: Oxford University Press, 2000, 140–1.

Williams, Raymond. *The Country and the City*. 2nd edn. London: Hogarth Press, 1985.

Wilson, Elizabeth. *Jacqueline du Pré*. London: Weidenfeld & Nicholson, 1998.

Wimsatt, William K. 'The Structure of Romantic Nature Imagery'. In M. H. Abrams (ed.). *English Romantic Poets*. New York: Oxford University Press, 1960.

Wolfreys, Julian. *Victorian Haunting: Spectrality, Gothic, the Uncanny and Literature*. Houndsmill, Basingstoke: Palgrave, 2002.

Woodrow, Thomas. *Reeds Shaken with the Wind*. London: Woodrow & Co., 1893.

Wordsworth, William. *Lyrical Ballads*, ed. Michael Mason. London and New York: Longman, 1992.

The Prelude: The Four Texts (1798, 1799, 1805, 1850), ed. Jonathan Wordsworth. London: Penguin, 1995.

Wordsworth, William. *Jacqueline du Pré: Impressions*. London: Granada, 1983.

Wright, Patrick. *On Living in an Old Country: The National Past in Contemporary Britain*. London: Verso, 1985.

Wullschläger, Jackie. *Inventing Wonderland: The Lives and Fantasies of Lewis Carroll, Edward Lear, J. M. Barrie, Kenneth Grahame and A. A. Milne*. London: Methuen, 1995.

Yeats, William Butler. *The Collected Letters of W. B. Yeats*, ed. John Kelly. 3 vols. Oxford; Oxford University Press, 1986–97.

Index

Printed in Great Britain by
Amazon.co.uk, Ltd.,
Marston Gate.